DOUBLE EAGLE

Written with passion and honesty, this incredible behind-the-scenes look at the life of a master spy details some of the policies, procedures, and pranks that make espionage so endlessly fascinating.

Mr. X describes the meticulous planning and delicate timing used to successfully blackmail highly placed individuals into working for the intelligence service.

He details how false identities were created for agents by stealing the passports of thousands of foreigners who visited Poland and how secret reports were sent from one agent to another on microfilm—hidden in toothpaste or shaving cream tubes.

DOUBLE EAGLE

Another riveting chapter from the fascinating world of espionage.

⊞ ESPIONAGE/INTELLIGENCE LIBRARY ⊞

DOUBLE EAGLE

The Autobiography of a Polish Spy Who Defected to the West

Mr. X with Bruce E. Henderson and C. C. Cyr

BALLANTINE BOOKS • NEW YORK

Library of Congress Catalog Card Number: 78-55651

ISBN 0-345-30192-7

Manufactured in the United States of America

First Ballantine Books Edition: January 1983

TO MY SON, JAREK

Contents

DOSSIER

NAME: Mr. X. (To reveal present cover name might subject him to retaliation by Polish agents.)

BORN: Warsaw, 1930.

PHYSICAL DESCRIPTION: Height: 5'11"; Weight: 200 lbs.; Hair: brown; Eyes: blue.

FAMILY: Upper-middle-class Catholic.

CHILDHOOD: Grew up during rise of fascism and Nazism in Europe; as youth during World War II survived German invasion and occupation of Poland, raiding German supply trains for provisions; witnessed famed uprising of the Warsaw Ghetto, and smuggled Jews out of the ghetto after revolt was crushed.

1947–49: Converted to Communism.

1949–53: Studied at University of Warsaw; major area of study: economics. Became a Communist campus activist.

1953: Recruited into the UB *(Urzad Bezpieczenstwa)*, the Polish Intelligence Service.

1953–54: Attended intelligence school, Polish Intelligence Service, Warsaw. Graduated with the rank of lieutenant.

1954–56: Assigned to Department 1, Branch 4, Polish Intelligence Service, Warsaw, coordinating intelligence agents' activities in Great Britain and Scandinavia.

1956–58: Polish embassy attaché in Stockholm; actually head of Polish Communist illegal espionage network in Sweden.

1958: Expelled from Sweden for spying.

1958–60: Posted in Department 1, Branch 1-A, Polish Intelligence Service, Warsaw, carrying out espionage support assignments.

1960: In Paris during assassination of Polish agent Wladyslaw Mroz.

1960–64: Assigned to cover position in Polish Foreign Ministry, Warsaw, as director of Department of Poles Living Abroad, engaged in propaganda and espionage. Growing disenchantment with Communism leads to decision to work against the system.

1964–66: Made Polish embassy first secretary in Oslo; in fact, head of Polish illegal net in Norway; beginning of role as double agent for CIA.

1967: Returned to Warsaw under orders, but escaped to the West. Rank at the time: lieutenant colonel.

1967–68: Debriefed by CIA; carried out recruiting assignments for CIA abroad; tried in absentia by Polish military tribunal and sentenced to death.

1969 TO PRESENT: Resided in various locales in the United States, working on his own under new identity; a man without a country.

CURRENT MISSIONS: To attain United States citizenship, get son out of Poland, contribute to the liberation of his homeland.

Prologue: Assassination in Paris

ON THE NIGHT OF OCTOBER 24, 1960, IN A SUBURB in Paris, a slender middle-aged man whose mundane mien masked his desperate state drove into a parking lot next to a subway station, planning to leave his car and take the Métro to a scheduled appointment downtown in the City of Lights. He was never to keep the engagement. Suddenly, from out of the autumnal darkness, a second car—a black Mercedes-Benz with diplomatic license plates—screeched up alongside him. A group of men piled out and hauled the lone man into the back seat of their vehicle. After making doubly certain that they were not being followed, the abductors took their quarry to a city dump in the northeastern section of Paris. There, in spite of his pleas for mercy, he was beaten, kicked, and—after the reading of a one-paragraph execution order—shot to death. As he lay dying, his face was smashed with rocks to make him less recognizable. Then his corpse was heaved into an empty well.

The victim was Wladyslaw Mroz, chief of the Polish illegal intelligence network for Western Europe. Caught in the middle of the undercover Cold War, he was assassinated for alleged treason. In these pages the full details of his murder are being revealed for the first time. If the events of that night spelled the end for Mroz, they were to presage a new beginning for me. At the time, I also was a career officer in the Polish Intelligence Service. For almost a decade I had been a dedicated Communist spy. Yet my fanatical faith had been ebbing. The brutal elimination of Mroz—a sickening episode that still gives me nightmares—was a key factor in what was to be my decision to become a double agent for the West. Ultimately, I was forced to escape to the United States. Today, I too am under death sentence for treason against the Polish regime.

I was one of the highest ranking intelligence officers of a Communist country ever to flee to the West; my rank was lieutenant colonel in the Polish UB, or secret service, whose ranks correspond to the military. But my defection was kept secret at the time. This book is the story of my life, which has never before been publicly disclosed.

One hears a great deal about the KGB, the Soviet secret service, but perhaps less recognized in the West is the important spying role played by the intelligence services of the Eastern European Communist countries, and their intimate working relationship with the Soviet Union and its KGB. All of the Eastern European satellites operate espionage networks that are coordinated closely with—and frequently by—the KGB, and that feed intelligence information directly to Moscow. Thus these Eastern European nets are, in effect, a key arm of the worldwide Russian espionage web.

Of the Eastern European spying organizations, by far the most important is the Polish Intelligence Service. The reason is rooted in a historical phenomenon—the traditional exodus of Poles to other lands because of their own country's poverty, political instability, and unfortunate geographical position between larger, more powerful European neighbors who have repeatedly overrun Poland in their wars with each other. At least twenty-five percent of Poland's native-born population is living abroad, the vast majority emigrants.

This fact is a unique asset to the Polish Intelligence Service and, in turn, the Russian KGB. Because of the number of Poles living abroad, the Polish UB has more opportunities than the intelligence services of other Eastern European nations to recruit individuals who are already living in strategic countries in the West.

Thus Poland is deeply involved in the cloak-and-dagger Cold War being waged unremittingly, if clandestinely, between the espionage apparatuses of East and West. It was this fact that spelled the end for Wladyslaw Mroz.

I first met Mroz in 1953, when he was a part-time instructor at the Polish Intelligence School in Warsaw, which I was attending at the time. Even though he was only a little over thirty, he was already an experienced intelligence staff officer. As I was later to discover, during this period he was also the officer in charge of the illegal Polish espionage network in Scandinavia. He had been among those who, in 1947–49, had organized our net in the northern countries.

Not only for the younger officers such as myself, but for the old-timers as well Mroz was an example. Born in Eastern Poland, he had fled with his family to Russia during World War II. He had been the youngest student ever to graduate from the Polish Intelligence School organized by the Russians during the war in the city of Kujbyszew, in the Soviet Union. After the war he returned to Poland and began his working career in his native country's intelligence service.

Mroz's wife—they had two children, and at the time of his assassination his wife was pregnant with their third child—was born in France. She thus helped Mroz become familiar with the French language and French customs. He traveled abroad a great deal, always using a fictitious foreign identity and a foreign passport, even when departing from Poland. At the beginning of his career he was especially active in Scandinavia; later, his work spread to France, West Germany, Belgium, and Switzerland.

In 1953–54, Mroz was instrumental in helping organize Branch 1, which was designed to be a new, all-embracing arm of the Polish Intelligence Service in Western Europe that would function underground, or illegally. In the future, it was projected, this branch would replace the other branches of the service that worked from so-called legal positions, such as

diplomatic posts. The objective was to eliminate contact between official Polish installations abroad and our agents. I
hardly need to emphasize the importance that this reorganization had for our operations. It was carried out in almost total
secrecy, and those involved in Branch 1, with the exception
of Mroz and a few others, were completely unknown to the
rest of our staff officers.

In 1957 it became obvious that Mroz would be the leader
of the entire Branch 1 operation. It was decided, however, that
he would function from a cover position outside of Poland. In
November 1958 I replaced Mroz in headquarters, where he had
been engaged in logistical support of illegal activities, operating
under what was known as Branch 1-A. He began an intensive
training program that was to prepare him to leave Poland for
a minimum of ten years and, if necessary, forever.

In the early summer of 1959, Wladyslaw Mroz, according
to plan, "disappeared" from Poland. Only I and a few other
persons knew that he was surreptitiously posted to Paris. I can
personally confirm that the whole program was completed sat-
isfactorily. Everybody interested in it was extremely pleased.

During the summer of 1960, nevertheless, we received an
alarming report from the Russians that the French had an agent
in the Polish Intelligence Service who was supplying them with
valuable information, including details of our underground operations in the West. Everybody was suspected *except* Mroz.
At approximately the same time, Colonel Bryn, who had allegedly been kidnapped by the Americans in Hong Kong, appeared at the Polish embassy in Paris asking to return to Poland.

During the investigation of his case by the Polish authorities,
it became clear that he had been told, by someone, many
important things that he had not previously known. We were
now sure beyond a doubt that Western counterintelligence was
learning far too much about us. Yet we still did not suspect
Mroz. On the contrary, we were concerned that he was in great
danger, since the Americans or the French were quite possibly
aware of his work.

It was concluded that we would recall Mroz to Poland.
Everybody was surprised when he tried to invoke a thousand
reasons to delay his return to his homeland: his wife was sick,

pregnant, etc. In spite of the urgency of the situation, he failed to appear for several appointments at headquarters; after ignoring half a dozen calls, he didn't even show up for the last call, which was worded in the most urgent terms. We were now certain that it was none other than Wladyslaw Mroz who was supplying the information to the West.

The decision was quick and final. Mroz had to be killed before he could compromise everything and everybody, if he had not already done so. It would have been unfeasible if not impossible to take him out of France against his will. In a smaller country, such as Sweden or Holland, we might have been able to smuggle him out on a Polish boat, but such things are more difficult in France. And if we had been caught, it might have blown our entire intelligence operation in France and precipitated a diplomatic crisis between Paris and Warsaw. No, much simpler to eliminate Mroz on the scene. The assassination was organized by the resident chief of Polish intelligence in France at the time, whose cover was that of an officer in the Polish embassy in Paris. (Our planned separation of illegal operations from legal cover positions, while proceeding apace, had not yet been completed in France and several other countries.)

A group of our intelligence officers was about to return from South Viet Nam, where they had been stationed under the cover of the International Control Commission, a body set up by the 1954 Indochina Peace Conference at Geneva and made up of representatives from Poland, India and Canada. In Saigon, a special team was organized to liquidate Mroz. Simultaneously, preparations were underway in Paris. The main problem was how to get Mroz into our hands, because he was probably under French or American protection. It was concluded that we had to use his father, who was still in Poland, and one of Mroz's best friends.

Mroz was informed through the normal channel of communication that his father had been involved in a serious car accident. A few days later, by careful design, one of Mroz's old friends from Warsaw "accidentally" met him on a street in Paris. Both were interested in talking, and they drifted into a coffee shop. Mroz's friend said that he did not have time for an extended conversation just then; he suggested a place to meet two days later at 11 P.M. Wladyslaw Mroz would never arrive for this meeting, which was to have taken place on October 24, 1960.

On the evening of October 24, a functionary of the Polish embassy in Paris, W, had dinner at Restaurant B with a member of the Polish parliament, Z, who was on an official visit to France and knew nothing of the plan to assassinate Mroz. The dinner between the embassy official and the visiting Polish parliamentarian was a backstop in case something went wrong. If, after abducting Mroz, it had been discovered that those carrying out the plot were under surveillance, Mroz would have been taken to the dinner.

They knew that Mroz would travel by auto to a particular subway station. The idea was to abduct him at a parking lot adjacent to the underground station, or to cause him by some other means to stop his car long enough that he could be forced into another car. Everything went according to plan. He was successfully forced into another auto at the parking lot.

At the beginning he was told that he was to be taken to meet with one of the chief deputies of the Polish parliament in a place in Paris convenient for the Poles. The well-known name of Wladyslaw Wicha was mentioned to him. Wicha—who had nothing to do with the assassination—was at the time not only a member of the Polish parliament, but also Poland's Minister of Interior and a member of the politburo of the Polish Communist Party. Mroz's abductors then told him that he was being taken to Warsaw. He said that he would refuse to go, invoking various innocuous explanations.

Of course, both stories about where he was going were only ruses to gain time, so that the kidnappers could make certain that they were not being followed. After they were sure that everything was clear, Mroz's escorts took him to the city dump. Only then did he realize what was going to happen to him. Up to that point, he evidently had not sensed just how much evidence his former comrades had against him, and perhaps he hoped that he could still maintain his innocence.

Mroz was about forty years old, approximately five feet, ten inches tall, relatively slim, with a dark brown crew-cut.

Generally speaking, he was a good-looking fellow; one could say almost handsome. The assassination team's car was a German Mercedes belonging to the Polish embassy in Paris, with diplomatic plates. The driver of the car was M, an attaché of the Polish embassy. On one side of the back seat of the car was J, code clerk of the Polish embassy in Paris and an officer of Branch 1 of the Polish Intelligence Service. On the opposite side of the back seat was S, who was the overall leader of the group in the car. S was at the time a member of the Polish consular staff in Paris, and deputy chief resident agent of the UB. Sitting between J and S was Mroz.

They had several guns, all of them equipped with silencers. Until the last minute the guns were kept by J in a special diplomatic pouch, protected by the proper seals.

After they left the car and dragged Mroz a couple of yards away, he was beaten and kicked. Then J opened the diplomatic pouch and handed guns to two of the group. At this point M, who had remained in the car as lookout, joined the two with Mroz, after checking with the surveillance in the area to make sure that everything was okay.

S started reading the very short verdict informing Mroz that he was going to be killed because of the death sentence imposed on him by the Polish government. The accusation was treason. It was now quite obvious to Mroz what was going to happen. In spite of several blows and kicks, he went down on his knees and begged for the opportunity to have more time. He would explain, he pleaded, exactly what had been happening and why he had had no choice except to cooperate. He said that he had been blackmailed and forced, that he had been doing it in order to protect his own life and those of his pregnant wife and his children.

Of course it was too late. They were under orders; they did not have a choice. J, who was obliged to carry out the execution, told all present—as he had even before Mroz was kidnapped—that he wanted everybody in the car to participate in the execution. He felt that Mroz deserved this from all of them and that he, J, should not be the only one doing the shooting. At this point the others were nervous and angry but at the same time also felt a little sorry for J, who didn't want to take the whole blame for the killing.

At the very last second J said to Mroz: "You will die, son of a bitch, like a dog, a dirty, dirty dog. You do not deserve anything better—" Before he had finished the sentence, J shot Mroz somewhere in the forehead or between the eyes. Mroz fell down on his face, and, at this time, several other shots were fired, mainly into his chest and head, from a very close range. It is difficult to say for sure which shot or shots really killed Mroz. But there were at least two or three shots fired by each of the people surrounding his body.

A moment later, S, who was obviously very familiar with the area, yelled: "Help me!" They grabbed Mroz's legs and started dragging him to an empty well approximately twenty-five yards away. At this point J went completely berserk and started kicking Mroz's inert body. When they reached the empty well, all of them together pushed the body of Wladyslaw Mroz in. S gave orders to throw as many different objects as possible into the well to cover Mroz's corpse. So they threw pieces of brick and rocks and empty containers—more or less what you would expect to find in a garbage dump—over the body, which was lying probably sixty feet down in this empty, dry well.

After a couple of minutes, S said: "Let's get the hell out of here!" They ran to the car, and J demanded the guns, all of which were dropped into the diplomatic pouch. J was very, very busy trying to seal the pouch again. They took the same places in the car they had had before and sped away from the area, driving directly to the Polish embassy. There they were invited to the office of W, where a couple of bottles of French cognac—Martell and Hennessy—were opened, and everybody had a drink. J left immediately for the code room to send the cable to Warsaw. A few minutes later it was confirmed that the twelve to fourteen people in the four surveillance cars were safely back in the Polish embassy compound. The action was over.

Perhaps three-quarters of an hour later, I was at the hotel where I was staying. There I encountered Z, the member of the Polish parliament who had had dinner with W. Z was returning from the dinner, and was very happy about the evening with W. He didn't realize, and maybe he has never realized, that he was used as a front for the whole operation.

M, J and S were shortly afterward recalled from Paris to Warsaw—one by one, over a period of time, in order not to arouse suspicion. To the best of my knowledge, none of the three ever left Poland again. As far as I know, they completely disappeared from the Polish Intelligence Service and the Polish Foreign Service. This is significant, because it indicates that even though they were selected to carry out the Polish government's orders to assassinate Mroz, the government obviously never trusted them to station them abroad again. I am the only one who knows the story who was lucky enough to be able to leave Poland again.

Two days after the elimination of Mroz, I returned to Warsaw. In the airplane I opened a French newspaper and saw a story about the assassination of Mroz. There was a picture of him, but he was identified only as a Polish immigrant who had for some reason been murdered. I couldn't understand the article too clearly because I couldn't read French well. With the help of Z, who was leaving France with me and who was proficient in reading French, I was able to absorb the contents of the story. While assisting me in this, Z was at the same time asking me whether I knew the man and whether I knew anything behind the story, to which I replied: "No, I do not have the slightest idea about the man or the story. I am surprised. I feel that it is some kind of provocation or fabrication." And I concluded: "Well, we'll find out later on in Poland."

The French press later described the episode somewhat more accurately—that the victim had been a Polish intelligence agent, and had probably been eliminated by his own people because he had become a double agent. The intimation was that perhaps the CIA was involved, not French intelligence.

The case was handled extremely badly by the French authorities, in terms of both counteraction and propaganda potential. Investigating the assassination, the French counterintelligence service arrested more than a score of persons on espionage charges. However, none were Polish intelligence staff officers. All of our espionage staff officers from France, Belgium, West Germany and Switzerland not involved in the assassination had returned to Poland under orders at least twenty-four hours before Mroz was killed, precisely to avert any possibility of reprisals against them. Thus the Polish agents arrested by the French could say little if anything, and then only about their individual activities, because each had as a contact only a single staff officer—who was no longer in France. Because of the lack of evidence, all of our arrested agents were eventually either released from custody or given very short terms of imprisonment. And the French have never captured the killers of Mroz.

Why France did not make more of the case I still do not understand. They could have made a great scandal, but instead they said nearly nothing about it. As a result, the episode has been, up to now, one of the untold stories of the clandestine Cold War.

To me personally, the murder of Wladyslaw Mroz has been much more than that. It was instrumental in my decision to reject the Communist system. I must admit that at the time of Mroz's death, I was part and parcel of that system. But even then I was having growing doubts about Communism, and after the killing of Mroz these doubts began gnawing on me with an intensity that finally I could not bear.

He had once been my friend. I had followed his example when he was a young, enthusiastic, active Communist. I will never know for certain whether he was indeed a traitor, whether he had really changed his mind. I do know that I have changed my mind and that I was a traitor. Therefore, I don't have any reason whatsoever to condemn him. He had been exposed to more or less the same kind of life that I had. As my experiences changed me, his may have changed him. But in this kind of business, when you are a traitor you have to be aware of the danger of assassination, as Mroz knew very well.

There is a small doubt in my mind that he was a traitor at all. Whether he was or not, he was assassinated without proof of the facts. The mere suspicion was enough for him to be sentenced to death, without any formal investigation or trial, and to be killed in the most brutal, barbaric way.

Mroz's death forever forces me to think about my own life and my own experience with bitterness, pain, shame. Because somebody somewhere decided that it was proper to kill Mroz, he was killed. The decision could not be questioned, at least openly. A man was murdered, even though nobody had any real guarantee or assurance that this man had to be killed.

In the wake of that event, the thought went through my mind that this could happen to any of us in the Polish intelligence apparatus. That it had probably happened many times to many others. That it could happen to anybody, because the battle for individual rights, the war for the human spirit, does not count in a Communist system.

I could only imagine how the wife and children of Mroz were going to feel. How were they ever going to understand what had happened to their husband and father and why?

Many years earlier, when I had been very young and very enthusiastic, I was perhaps ready to kill anybody if ordered to do so. But by 1960 it wasn't the same. Mroz's liquidation was a turning point in my life. I didn't know exactly what I was going to do and when, but I did know that I was a potential follower of Wladyslaw Mroz.

So, after several more years of soul-searching, I switched sides and went to work for the West. Then, in February 1967, I found it necessary to flee to the West. The decision cost me my marriage—my wife, who remained a disciplined Communist, divorced me—and for all intents and purposes it has cost me my only child, my son, who is being held hostage by the Polish authorities. They have prohibited him from joining me.

Why have I written this book? Certainly not to make money or to provide a political or ideological polemic. I am not a theoretician. I can only give my points of view as a former intelligence officer for a Communist state. In that, I am different from Alexander Solzhenitsyn. He writes as a victim of the Communist apparatus: I write as one who was part of it.

The principal purpose of this book is to get my son out of Poland.

I had no choice when I left Poland. Earlier, I had been on assignment in Norway with my wife and my son Jarek, and perhaps I should never have gone back home. However, my wife was determined to return to Poland. We did so—then, shortly after, I had to flee, and I left them both there.

At the beginning of my new life in the United States, I supposed that if I wanted to have my son with me, it would be best if I kept quiet. But after more than ten years of trying this approach, I came to the conclusion that there is no way to solve anything amicably with a Communist regime. The Communist regime in Warsaw is not concerned about my son, but is very much concerned with hurting me. Even after he passed the entrance test for high school, he was not accepted— only because he is my son.

I know now that I face a long fight to get Jarek out. I trust that this book will, in some way, help. The Communist regime in Warsaw will never free my son unless it is forced to by world opinion. I can understand their trying to hurt me so much. But why are they hurting this innocent young man who has done nothing against them? He simply wants to see his father. If I make his tragedy—and my tragedy—public, I may possibly generate enough pressure to liberate him. Perhaps President Reagan will read this book.

There is another reason for this book. I hope that in some modest way it will be read as a kind of appeal for moral support for the Polish people. I realize that many officials in Washington will not be pleased by this. My former friends in Washington have made it only too clear to me that they do not want me rocking the boat between Poland and the United States. But in spite of all the accommodation between Eastern Europe and the United States in recent years, the basic moral issue in Poland remains the same: the systematic obliteration of basic human rights. This has been made still more evident by the dissident movements in Eastern European satellite countries, such as the Charter 77 group in Czechoslovakia, and the official repression of dissident writers, artists and others.

I should like my book to represent a different approach to the subject of political defection. The tendency among many defectors is to suggest that everything in their old country is bad, everything in their new country is good. I do not believe that this is usually true, and it is certainly not true in my case. Not everything in today's Poland is bad, and not everything in the United States is good. I have had anguishing experiences in both countries. But I want my American readers to have fresh insights into the problems of human beings living in a country such as Poland. I am not the typical immigrant from Poland or any other Communist country. I was very close to the highest echelons and decisions of a Communist government, especially in the areas of intelligence and foreign relations.

And I want my Polish-American readers, too, to be more aware. There could be quite a lobby composed of persons of Polish origin in the United States. There are at least 6,000,000 Americans of Polish extraction. I hope to bring home to them— at least to those who do not already know—how rotten Communism is.

The title of this work is based on the fact that the eagle is the national symbol of both the United States and Poland. And therein lies a certain irony.

Several European countries are the habitats of species of eagles, but the Polish eagle is unique in that it possesses a crown. The crowned eagle thus became deeply embedded in the history and lore of Poland. Even after World War I, when Poland became a republic, the crowned eagle remained the national symbol. When the Communists came to power following World War II, they realized that they could not eliminate the eagle as Poland's national symbol. To do so would have been politically unacceptable. What they did, with typical ingenuity, was to remove the crown from Poland's official bird.

Whatever the other contributions of this ideological triumph, it has served further to estrange Polish Communist bureaucracy from the rest of Polish society. For instance, in every official Polish publication the eagle will be seen without its crown. Yet no Polish emigrant who identifies with his Polish heritage will touch such a publication. At any meeting of Polish emigrants in the United States, Great Britain, or elsewhere, the Polish flags, Polish emblems, and all of the other symbols evoking the homeland depict the eagle with a crown. If the eagle does not have a crown it is not authentic, according to our moral and patriotic standards.

This book will probably join the Polish exile publication *Kultura* on the official blacklist in Poland. It will be dangerous for persons in Poland to have this book in their possession. Yet many in my homeland will be tremendously interested in reading my story. They will try to get their hands on it in one way or another. At least some parts of the book are probably going to be reproduced on typewriters, and enjoy a wide clandestine distribution. The distribution of opposition publications is an old tradition in Poland, rooted in Polish resistance to repeated foreign conquerors.

It is not easy to put down on paper many of the things that I am revealing in this book. I can prove everything that I say in these pages with names, addresses, telephone numbers and other substantiating facts. Nevertheless, one major problem that I am confronted with is how many—and which—names I should name, because many of the agents involved are still abroad, while others are still on active duty in Warsaw. To divulge all the names I know would have very serious consequences for these persons, many of whom I still consider my friends.

I think of Janusz D, one of our resident agents in Sweden. Following the assassination of Wladyslaw Mroz in Paris, D, who was among those we heard might have been compromised by Mroz, escaped with his wife, under orders, to Poland. D was married to a Norwegian woman. I know that she doesn't want to continue living in Poland. Her family back in Norway, who of course are unaware that their son-in-law is a Polish spy, cannot understand why she left everything in twenty-four hours and moved to Poland. They cannot accept the fact—and she cannot accept it either—that they are probably never going to see each other again. Although she was his wife, she did not know that D was a staff officer of the Polish Intelligence Service. Perhaps publishing D's full name here could somehow help normalize her situation. Yet revealing their names might also complicate their plight.

There is another problem. Many of the persons involved in this book have children. The children cannot be responsible for the acts of their parents, and therefore should not suffer the consequences.

Even with the guilty, the question of names is sometimes

a problem. Everyone makes errors. Often what we did ten years ago we would not do today. Sometimes it is extremely difficult to correct an error made a decade or two decades ago. We simply have to continue paying for the mistake. And this requires courage. Many of my ex-friends are quite brave, and I do not wish to add to their burdens.

PART ONE

The Cross
and the Swastika

WHY DID I BECOME A COMMUNIST? AS WITH MOST persons who are infected with this disease, there were many reasons for my case—all contributing to the implantation, in my being, of the bacteria of hostility and hatred. In my own instance, the factors included my early childhood under the repressive influence of Poland's Roman Catholic Church, the death of my father at the hands of the Germans during World War II, my struggle for survival during the war years in Warsaw, and the impotence of my country's traditional political institutions.

I was born in Warsaw on June 17, 1930. At the time, my parents had recently moved from Warsaw to Zabki, a small town some six miles from the capital.

My father's name was Tadeusz-Antoni K, and at the time of my birth he was an employee of the post office. He had wanted to be a lawyer, but that had been impossible because he came from a relatively poor family with many children. For two or three years he tried to study at the University of Warsaw while also holding down a job, but finally he had to give up his formal education. He always wanted to go back to school.

My father was quite a socially and politically oriented man. Although he never received a law degree, his studies had given him quite an extensive legal background, and he became an unofficial lawyer for the Polish trade union organization. He defended fellow post office employees before an arbitration board where the employees resolved differences with the postal authorities.

During my childhood I lived in many different sections of Poland. This was because my father was in more or less permanent conflict with his superiors in the post office, and as a result was transferred nearly every year. This was quite expensive and hardly beneficial to the well-being of the family. During my years of primary school, I was in at least six or seven schools—a new school year, a new school. It was just routine.

I had twin brothers five years younger than I. Life was difficult for us in the material sense, but we were quite happy at home. Although we had the usual family spats, we always felt a sense of togetherness. My pleasant memories of my home are very dear to me to this day.

In spite of our happy home life, my father was a rather unhappy person. Many times he would talk to me about the lack of justice in Poland. This preoccupation was the *leitmotif* of his life. As far as I know, he was never a member of any political party. But it was obvious to me, after I became old enough to be politically aware, that my father was a sympathizer of the left-wing Polish Socialist Party.

He worked hard trying to support our family. Government employees of my father's level earned just enough to eke out a living. Very often, as he was leaving home for work, he would ask my mother for a few *groszy* for lunch; that was enough in those days to buy a modest meal. But he was a heavy cigarette smoker, and he would use the coins to purchase a package or two of cigarettes instead of eating. He knew that he could not afford both. In spite of my father's modest station in life, he was always relatively well dressed and left no doubt in anyone's mind that he was a white-collar worker.

My father had an interesting circle of friends, and quite often he invited them home. My mother did not particularly like these gatherings, but I was eager to listen. The men would tolerate me if I didn't bother them. It wasn't until years later that I realized that some of my father's friends were, without a doubt, Communists. Perhaps even my father did not know, because if you were a member of the Polish Communist Party before the war, you didn't run around telling everybody.

Although these persons were Communists, what they were talking about was not the Communism that I discovered later in my life. They were talking about some kind of paradise that does not exist—not in Communist Russia or in Red China or in any other Communist country.

The religious mood in my home was a very liberal one. Although my father was from a staunchly Catholic family, he did not pay too much attention to organized religion. This was probably because he had gone to a high school run by the Marjanie Brothers, a religious order under the supervision of the Vatican, and had not enjoyed their tutelage.

If you asked him whether he was a Catholic, he would say, "Yes," but he was against the clergy, against the structure of the church. He was not a church-goer.

My mother, being from a mixed Protestant-Catholic family, considered herself a Catholic but did not really care which church she attended. And although we children were told that we should go to church on Sunday, we were not forced.

But at school I had a religious class with the priest, and he would ask me why I had not been present in church. He had a list of names, and anyone who did not give a good explanation was kicked out of class.

Thus, although I hated to go to church, I went—I couldn't afford not to. I even went to confession two or three times a week to say all my sins; confessions were organized by the priests in school.

I think it was this kind of coercion that, in the long run, created political opponents for the church. If you are forced to do something, you are not going to like it. Many persons will bow to the situation because they are forced to, but they will use the first opportunity to say no.

Because of my father's constant transfers, I had an opportunity to see a great deal of my country and its many problems. In 1940 Poland had thirty-three million inhabitants, including two million Ukrainians, two million Bialo-Russians,* and numerous Jews and Germans.

When I was six years old, our family lived for a year in a

*Who are distinct from Russians.

suburb of Ostrow-Mazowiecki, some sixty or seventy miles from Warsaw. Ostrow-Mazowiecki was a city of 30,000 inhabitants, approximately half of whom were Jewish. Our house was near the highway, and one day I recall seeing several trucks loaded with men dressed in brown shirts, with swastikas on their arms. They were singing and shouting. When they passed our house they waved to me, and I waved back. They looked like soldiers. At that age, I did not know what the swastika meant. A few minutes after the trucks passed, I heard shooting and screaming coming from the town. Half an hour later I saw the same trucks coming back along the highway. At this moment my father arrived home. I was still watching, not really knowing what was going on. My father shouted, "Get in the house!" The returning brownshirts were passing by; they waved to me again and I waved to them. My father became furious. I had never before seen him so angry. "Go home!" he shouted. "What are you doing here? Why are you waving to them?"

I said, "They're waving to me. What's wrong?"

We went into the house and my father started telling me about what had happened downtown. He said that the men had ridden into the market where the Jewish people were selling fish, bread and other wares. The men broke windows and destroyed the Jewish-owned stores. They did not kill anybody—it wasn't yet as it was in Germany. But they injured many persons.

An hour later, truckloads of police sped by, going like hell in the direction of the nearby forest. Thirty minutes later, the police returned. They hadn't caught any of the brownshirts; they didn't want to. Still later, the nationalists came again and wrought more havoc among the Jewish populace.

I could see that my father was against these assaults, but I could not understand why they happened. My father did not make any speeches to me. He simply said: "They are fascists."

At that time I didn't know what that meant either. But that, too, I was to learn.

The Quick
and the Dead

I WAS NINE YEARS OLD WHEN WORLD WAR II BE-
gan. My father was then working at the Central Post Office
in Warsaw.

I will never know how deeply my father was involved in
the underground movement against the Nazis. In any case,
early in 1941, when a large number of employees of the Warsaw
Post Office were arrested by the Gestapo and accused of underground activity, among those arrested was my father.

One of my father's former friends, S, had become an open
collaborator with the German occupiers. At the time S was a
high official of the Central Post Office in Warsaw. Before the
war, he had been accused of stealing some letters, and had
been one of my father's unofficial "legal clients." It later became evident that he had indeed stolen them for the Germans—
and that he had been an intelligence agent for the Germans for
many years before the war; but at the time S was accused, my
father did not know of his friend's pro-German activities, and
he defended him as he had other employees of the post office.
My father succeeded in getting the charges against S dropped.

After my father's arrest by the Gestapo, my mother went
to S for help. S promised to do what he could to get my father
out of jail. One morning several days later, we were informed
by our doorman that a German car had left somebody on the
street in front of our apartment house. We barely recognized

the inert form of my father. He had been beaten almost unconscious.

For several months, my father remained a convalescent. Food was scarce. I remember that my father was always very apprehensive when listening to the stories—quite common at the time—about people who were eating horsemeat. Well, I knew that my mother, for a long period of time, had been serving us horsemeat for dinner. My father, however, didn't realize it.

One day, during some kind of argument with my father, my mother said: "Don't condemn anybody for eating horsemeat if they don't have anything else to eat."

My father replied that it did not matter how hungry he was, he would never eat horsemeat.

I'm sure that my mother didn't want to do it, but in anger she announced: "Well, as a matter of fact, I'm worried about tomorrow, because for weeks now I've been serving horsemeat, but I don't have any left and I couldn't find a place to buy any today. So I'm afraid that tomorrow we aren't going to have any dinner."

My father was stunned. He couldn't say a single word. He ran to the sink and threw up. He never again ate any kind of meat at home.

I went into the streets and started stealing everything I could in order to make some money to keep my family alive. Unfortunately, my father was informed by someone that I was selling cigarettes and newspapers on the streets. He was humiliated. One evening when I came home he slapped me across the face. He had never struck me before. It was a tragic situation. We were completely without means; he was not able to work; he needed care and medical help. Yet, in spite of our plight, he was furious at me and did not speak to me for many days. Nonetheless, I kept on working in the streets; I had to.

Finally, my father couldn't take our situation any longer—it was too humiliating for him—and he went to live with his parents. A few days later he took a turn for the worse. I remember when my paternal grandparents came to our home and informed my mother that my father was dying. I literally ran to help him. Not having any other means of transportation, I hired a small horse-drawn cart, commonly used for transporting bricks. I shall never forget placing my father on this cart and hauling him to the Ujazdowski Hospital. It was a Tuesday. My father died the following Friday, on October 27, 1941.

My mother, my three younger brothers and I were now completely alone, still without any means of support. We were forced to move into a smaller apartment that consisted of one room with a kitchen. We shared a public bathroom with other occupants of the apartment building.

Since my mother was unable to support the family, I continued my *laissez-faire* enterprises on the streets. Nevertheless, I was fortunate enough to be able to continue to go to school. It was a tough life: because of my work, I would not get home until early in the evening, and I still had my homework to do.

After several months I started working for a small manufacturer of candies and other confections. I worked for him in order to learn how to make his products. When I was only twelve years old, I opened my own very small candy factory in our tiny apartment.

Gradually, thanks to my new business, I began earning more money, and our family situation became somewhat easier. But the improvements were short-lived; by 1943 there were very few persons in Warsaw who could afford to buy candies, and I slowly ran out of customers. I tried selling cigarettes and newspapers again, but after a while there weren't any cigarettes or newspapers to sell either.

I couldn't earn enough money to support my young brothers and my mother. The question of surviving the next day became our sole concern. Finally, I turned to stealing in earnest. There was absolutely nothing to eat at home. Nothing to sell, no buyers either. There was even very little to steal in wartime Warsaw. I became involved with a group of young kids my age, who worked on the streets in different kinds of activities.

We decided that the best way to make money was to steal from the German trucks and trains transporting goods to the Eastern front.

The trains—often composed of seventy or more freight cars—would have to slow down while passing through some areas of Warsaw. Although the trains usually had German guards aboard while they were traveling cross-country, the guards were removed when the trains were going through Warsaw. Instead, guards were posted at bridges and other strategic places along the tracks.

We began jumping the trains. At night, as the trains went by, ten of us would leap onto them and throw everything we could from the cars. Friends of ours were waiting at prearranged places to pick up the stuff. We employed basically the same tactics with German supply trucks passing through Warsaw. Of course, it was a dangerous business, and many of my young friends were wounded or killed.

Sometimes there was food; sometimes there were shoes. Once we threw and threw and threw shoes, only to discover the next morning—those Germans are so well organized!— that in the freight car we had ransacked there had been only left shoes. We had thousands of left shoes and not one right shoe. We couldn't sell the shoes to cobblers, because there was no leather available even to remake left shoes into right shoes. We did manage to sell many left shoes, but at ninety percent below what the price would have been had they been part of a pair.

After tossing our loot from the train, we had to jump off at just the right place. If you jumped too close to where the German guards were stationed, you could be shot or bit—these guardsmen all had big, ferocious German shepherds.

Sometimes we had to jump back onto the trains. We would leap off, happy that the operation was over, and hoping that our cohorts had been able to pick up everything. And suddenly two Germans with dogs would appear out of nowhere, shouting and unlimbering their guns. By now the train would be disappearing down the track ahead of us, but still traveling relatively slowly. We did not have any choice. We could be arrested, we could be beaten, we could be killed if the Germans got us. A shot would ring out. We would run after the train and jump onto the rear car.

I remember once when one of the youngest of our band, a fat fellow nicknamed Rura (in English, Pipe), perhaps twelve years old—I was not more than thirteen—started running with us to escape the German troops. Rura was not as fast as the rest of us were. It was eight or nine o'clock at night, but it was summer so there was still some light. The Germans opened fire. The rest of us managed to reach the last car of the train and hop on. Rura was so close, and yet so far. We were yelling at him, "Run faster damn it, Rura!" Holding each other's hands, we formed a human chain and stretched down to try to get him. He began crying in panic and desperation, and the train was going faster and faster. He could hear—and we could see— that the Nazi guards were still shooting at us and the dogs were getting closer and closer. The dogs were trained to jump at once for your throat.

We got Rura in by grabbing his hands. Just at that moment, one dog leaped and bit him on the buttocks. I will never forget Rura's scream.

As he clambered onto the accelerating train, somebody kicked the dog away. And the Germans had to stop shooting for fear of killing some of their own in the growing darkness. While we were riding on to another safe spot, Rura was screaming with pain. We were afraid that he would alert German guards along the tracks again. One of us hit him several times and told him, "Shut up!"

We jumped from the train once more a mile or two later. That night we had a great deal of difficulty finding a secure house for Rura. Wherever he may be today, he is missing one of his buttocks. As a result, his right leg does not function properly, and he limps. But he survived the war, which was a major accomplishment in Warsaw during this time.

I remember another incident in 1943, when somebody gave us a message that there were several train cars at the railroad station from one of the city's big confectionary factories. This factory, which had been closed at the beginning of the war, had resumed production of candies and chocolate; the Germans were appropriating all of its output and transporting it to Germany. There was cocoa, honey, sugar—all precious luxuries produced from the factory's prewar inventory, and all extremely expensive. We could imagine what was probably in those wagons.

We organized a group of twenty youths. The railroad station was guarded by the Germans, but the wagons were parked at a siding that was somewhat distant from the nearest guard. We managed to break into one of the cars and began to steal the most expensive items, starting with honey. Nobody in Warsaw had known the taste of honey for years. We also started taking sugar. You could buy anything in the war-starved city with sugar.

But after we had opened a second car, crowds at the station discovered the wagons too, and everybody started running like crazy to join in the looting. Women opened their purses and filled them with honey poured directly out of barrels. These human beings were desperate. If you had a chunk of sugar, you could be killed for it.

Someone screamed: "Germans! Germans!" German troops had discovered the looting, and the people started fleeing. Then, a few minutes later—such are the exquisitely brutal coincidences of war—Russian planes on an air raid arrived overhead and started bombing the entire railroad station. Everything was flying, human bodies—German and Polish—mixed with honey, sugar, candies, chocolate, and other precious sweets.

I was lucky. I jumped into a nearby ditch and survived without a scratch.

In 1943 the Germans decided to kill all of the people in the Warsaw Ghetto, the walled center of the capital's Jewish population. The area's normal population was approximately 150,000, but when the decision was made to eliminate the ghetto perhaps as many as half a million persons were packed into it. Jews from all of the smaller towns of Poland had been herded by the Germans into the Warsaw Ghetto. No Jews were allowed out of the ghetto, on pain of death.

Jews were dying on the streets of the ghetto from starvation. Although it was against Nazi occupation regulations, I, a non-Jew, slipped into the ghetto often during this period. As you walked on the pavement you literally had to make your way around rotting corpses. No one was even allowed out of the ghetto to carry the bodies to a cemetery. The wall around the ghetto was patrolled by German guards, and if you came close to the wall they would shoot. In order to prevent cholera or other disease from spreading from the ghetto, every couple of weeks the Germans would permit trucks to come in and pick up the stiff and bloated corpses. They were stacked on trucks and carried off to be dumped into mass graves.

My group organized a gang to smuggle food and other goods to the Jews through young Jews who were sent out as forced labor. They were often given money by wealthy Jews in the ghetto.

Those young Jews who were still healthy and strong were taken by streetcars to the outskirts of Warsaw every day. From the end of the streetcar line, they were forced to walk another five miles, and then spend the rest of the day building military fortifications against the Russians. At nightfall, the Jews walked the five miles back to the streetcar line and were hauled back to the ghetto.

The streetcars carrying Jews were painted blue—in contrast to Warsaw's other trolleys, which were red—and bore white Stars of David. As many Jews as possible—usually more than one hundred—were packed into the streetcars, the windows of which had been broken by slave-labor passengers seeking better ventilation. German police guards, usually of the lowest mentality, rode the steps of these trams full of Jews.

Since the ghetto was opened only to carry out the dead and to let the blue streetcars in and out, our gang's only contact with the other inhabitants of the ghetto was through the forced laborers on the trolleys. We would run alongside the trolleys with newspaper-boy sacks full of vodka, rolls and other precious items. We would offer the German guards bottles of vodka and ask whether we could jump on. More often than not they would let us, for they had already been bribed by the Jews inside the streetcars. The Jewish laborers would have money and other valuables with which to buy the guards and purchase anything and everything possible from our street gang.

Once we were aboard the trams, the scene became pandemonium. The Jews—indescribably filthy and lice-ridden, since they were not permitted even a bar of soap in the ghetto—would be fighting among themselves for the simple amenities that we were auctioning. They would offer any price. They would give us gold cigarette lighters for bottles of rubbing alcohol, valuable rings for bread rolls—my mother was baking a new sack of rolls every day. We were often forced by the guards to sell only to Jews who had made private payoffs to the guards in order to receive special consideration. We were rarely allowed more than five minutes on the streetcars. After we jumped off, the guards frequently shot at us in order to make it appear that they were doing their job. Many of our boys were killed in the process. I myself was fired upon many times; once a youth on my left was killed and a fellow on my right was wounded.

We also organized escapes from the streetcars. Certain of the young Jews would decide to try to flee, and would pay us to help them. These operations were carried out by the older, more experienced members of our gang. We knew the intersections where the trolleys would stop momentarily, and would make arrangements for the Jews to jump off there. One of our favorite escape points was in front of the Warsaw Zoo. We would have a truck waiting nearby, together with changes of clothes, and drive the escapees to the forests outside Warsaw. There they would be dropped off to fend for themselves.

This was a dangerous business indeed. The German guards on the trolleys were held responsible for any escapes, and the Jews on the streetcars were counted both on leaving and on returning to the ghetto. Moreover, the Germans posted a standing reward of 20,000 marks for the capture of a Jew—which engendered dangers from other directions. One time, two Polish ruffians out for a reward began chasing two of our Jews after they had leaped from their streetcar. Our gang leader, B, ran up to the two interlopers and asked: "What are you doing?"

"They're escaping Jews. We're going to capture them and get the reward."

I was standing only a few steps away, watching the exchange. B was tough. He would have killed his own mother if the price was right.

"So you want the reward?" B said. "Well, I'll give you your reward now."

He whipped an automatic pistol from under his coat and shot both of the bounty-hunters dead on the spot.

Later, after our two Jews had changed clothes, B returned

and put their armbands—bearing the Star of David and identifying them as Jews—on the arms of the two dead men, who
lay sprawled on the ground. This was as much an act of retribution as an effort to confuse the Germans.

Concerning my experiences during this period, I can only
say that I could never envision anything more horrible or terrible. I saw hundreds and hundreds of dead people on the
streets.

I was delivering food and medical supplies to people in the
ghetto. I was helping Jews escape. As a youth less than fourteen
years old, I was risking my life at least twice every day. Before
the Warsaw Ghetto uprising, the only way to help a Jew escape
directly from the ghetto was to meet him with a waiting truck
after he jumped over the wall. Such an attempt didn't have the
slightest chance of success if it was done by one or two individuals. These dashes for the wall had to be organized in groups
of twenty or more. Only with such large groups could there
be any hope that at least a few of the escapees would reach a
truck waiting to transport them out of the city. Usually half or
more of the escapees were killed while jumping over the wall.
But this was the only chance a Jew in the ghetto had; there
was no other way for a Jew to leave the ghetto—except at the
point of a German gun, headed for the extermination camps.

For instance, it would be planned that on a specific day a
group of Jews would attempt to jump over the wall. The wall
surrounding the ghetto was perhaps seven or eight feet high.
Stationed along the outside of the wall were German guards
and Polish police. At a prearranged time, usually in the late
afternoon to take advantage of approaching nightfall, my gang
would be waiting a block or two away from the wall with a
truck to pick up the escaping Jews.

Suddenly there would be shooting, and the Jews, who had
been provided with guns, would be leaping over the wall, firing
as they came. The nearest German guards and Polish police,
who were by no means heroes, would hit the ground, seeking
cover from the bullets that were flying all over the street. Some
of the Jews would put guns to the heads of cowering Germans
and Polish policemen, killing them immediately. The other
Jews would run down the street amid a fusillade of gunfire

from other guards. Of the twenty or so young Jews from the ghetto who had attempted the escape, perhaps only two or three would make it to our truck.

Maybe fifty or sixty other persons would be lying in the streets, killed or wounded by shots fired by everyone involved—by Germans, by Polish police, by Jews, by us. This was the price you paid for the lives of two or three—the killing or wounding of at least fifty or sixty. The crowning irony was that, more often than not, the two or three Jews who did manage to reach the truck would turn out not to have any money or other valuables. All of the escaping group's money or jewelry or gold had been in the possession of the Jews who were now lying on the pavement dead or wounded, and who would be picked up in a few moments by the Germans or the Polish police.

I remember the day in April of 1943 when the Warsaw Ghetto uprising started. The Jews in the compound were desperate. Day after day, the Germans had been hauling thousands of the Jews to the concentration camps to be killed. Finally, after approximately half of the ghetto's swollen population had been taken away, a group of the underground Jewish army decided that since they were going to die anyway, they would die fighting.

On this specific morning, the German troops entered the ghetto as usual to pick up the next few thousand Jewish people for the extermination camps. For the first time they were welcomed by the gunfire of the Jewish resistance. And the Germans had to withdraw.

The German occupation troops stationed in Warsaw might have had an even more difficult time with the uprising had it not been for the fact that just coincidentally some former members of Field Marshal Rommel's *"Afrika Korps"* were returning to Germany through Warsaw. They eventually crushed the Warsaw Ghetto uprising, but it was no easy task. The Jews fought like hell.

On the afternoon of the first day, the ghetto was completely surrounded by Germans, principally the feared SS. The German tanks destroyed the wall encircling the ghetto in several places, and then the tanks and German soldiers tried to enter the ghetto.

They were greeted by another tremendous wave of fire—shots from the windows, from the roofs, from every possible place. Outside the ghetto there were a great number of spectators watching. For a few minutes it was real hell. Everybody was shooting. I could see Jewish fighters firing at the Germans from behind the chimneys of the apartment houses. I could see some of the Jews being hit by German bullets, and rolling down and falling from the roofs. One of them was caught by his leather coat on the corner of the building. I remember that his body hung from the roof corner for several weeks before the Germans finally took him down. They deliberately left the corpse hanging from the roof—it was clearly visible from both inside and outside the ghetto—as an example of what was going to happen to all of the Jewish fighters in the ghetto.

Amazingly, however, the uprising in the ghetto continued for weeks. A small group of Jewish resisters, equipped with a very limited quantity of guns and ammunition, were fighting like lions. The Germans never expected that it would take them so long to put down the Warsaw Ghetto revolt. It was one of the most heroic episodes of armed resistance against the Germans during World War II.

After the uprising had to all intents and purposes been defeated, we began smuggling Jews from the ghetto using a small horse-drawn cart. The cart was hauling bricks from destroyed buildings in the ghetto for re-use in construction projects on the outside. Such a small cart was able to transport two or more Jews under the pile of bricks. There were still at least several hundred Jews hiding in the ruins of the ghetto.

On one particular day we got four Jews out of the ghetto by means of the cart. They were delivered to the area of the construction company that was scavenging the bricks. Under the escape plan, arranged in collaboration with the owner of the construction company, the Jews were to be picked up by a truck and taken to another location outside of Warsaw, from whence they could make their way to the forest.

Well, on this particular day things didn't happen as planned. I remember that the four Jews were sitting on the bench in the yard of the construction company, dirty, exhausted, half-alive, waiting for the truck that was supposed to take them out of the city. Fifteen minutes went by, and still the truck did not show up. This surprised us, since such life-or-death projects were usually extremely well coordinated. The employees of the construction company were uncharacteristically silent, terribly busy with their duties. The owner of the company, who was co-responsible for the whole operation, was absent.

Concluding that something was seriously wrong, we—together with these four sick and exhausted Jews—decided to leave the area immediately on foot. I don't remember exactly how many minutes later it was—maybe five, maybe seven—that suddenly we heard and then saw German cars, loaded with SS and Gestapo officers, speeding in the direction of the construction company.

It was then that we realized that our partner in this particular enterprise, the owner of the construction company, had for one reason or another decided to sell the whole operation to the Germans. If we had waited five minutes more in the yard of the construction company, we would have been arrested and probably shot. The four Jewish men certainly would not have lasted five minutes if the Gestapo and SS had found them. Fortunately, we managed to elude our pursuers. But that was the end of one of our channels of escape from the ghetto.

Of course, the Jews were not the only ones who suffered during the war. There were very few Polish families of any religion that did not lose loved ones. My own family was an example. My father's brother, Uncle Wladyslaw, who was involved in the underground movement, was killed under very mysterious circumstances in 1942, a year after my father died. Someone bound Wladyslaw's hands and feet and left him on the streetcar tracks. He was cut to pieces by a tram.

Yet there is no denying that the Jews were the prime target of persecution by the Nazis. A case in point was my Jewish uncle-in-law, Lutek, who had married my Aunt Sophia over her father's objections.

It was not long after the couple's return to Poland after living for a time in Russia that the Germans decided that the Jewish population of Poland could live only in ghettos. The Nazis ordered all of the local Jewish population into special districts—the poorest part of each town. Uncle Lutek and his

parents were taken to the Warsaw Ghetto. Since Aunt Sophia
was not Jewish, she was not required to go and, by mutual
agreement with Lutek, did not join them. She bought a small
apartment outside the ghetto and stayed there with members
of her family. Because of the name and position of his family,
Lutek was elected deputy commissioner of the Jewish police
in the ghetto. He had no choice. The Germans ordered the Jews
to create special police, and the Jews decided among themselves
who would comprise their police force.

The Germans provided the Jewish police with food, but they
used them for extremely dirty jobs—for example, to load onto
trucks the bodies of those who had died on the streets of the
ghetto or been executed by the Germans. The Germans did not
like to enter the ghetto, and would often order the Jewish police
to bring out Jews to be sent to concentration camps. There was
an archway between the two sections of the Warsaw Ghetto,
called the "Big Ghetto" and the "Small Ghetto." Jewish police
could be seen dragging other Jews across the archway to be
taken away.

But if those who made up the force did not follow German
orders, they risked endangering the lives of their relatives, in
addition to immediately losing their own lives. Even so, most
of the Jewish police were ultimately killed by the Nazis. Ironically, many of those who did survive were prosecuted after
the war on charges of collaboration with the Germans.

To save themselves, a number of Jews built an underground
network of bunkers. To acquire a hiding place in the bunkers,
which sometimes reached several floors underground, was extremely expensive. A few weeks after the uprising, the Germans
discovered the bunker where Lutek's family was hiding. Lutek,
in his capacity as a leader of the Jewish police, was obliged
to surround the area with his men while the Germans routed
everyone from the hiding place. The Germans shot all of the
inhabitants of the bunker: Lutek was obliged to witness the
shooting of his father and mother.

After nearly everyone in the ghetto had been slain following
the revolt, it became obvious to members of the Jewish police
that they too were going to be killed. Lutek and some of his
colleagues decided to run away, and for weeks hid in the

ghetto's burned-down houses and other ruins. They then decided to attempt to escape from the ghetto. At last, while changing hiding places every day and bartering expensive items such as gold, jewels and cigarettes for food, they made contact with my gang.

It was extremely difficult to get them out of the ghetto at this stage. The Jews drew lots to determine who would go first, and we picked them up one after another, with the help of the fellow who had a horse-drawn wagon in which he was hauling bricks from buildings in the ghetto. (The same man who later betrayed our mode of escape to the Nazis.) Since the wagoner did not usually want to take more than one fugitive per day, it took numerous days to get them out. Aunt Sophia covered all of the expenses, including payments to the wagon driver and to other members of my gang. I would accept nothing, because I was helping with the operation as a personal favor to Aunt Sophia.

Later, unfortunately, most of Lutek's group was discovered by the Germans in an apartment house where they had hidden. The German troops used axes to break into the apartment building. They went from floor to floor, smashing holes in the walls in search of fugitives from the ghetto. Finally, the Germans managed to reach the top floor. They broke through the rubble into the Jews' hiding place, rounded up everyone in sight, and then set about stealing all of the valuables that the Jewish policemen had with them. This group of fugitives had collected the heirlooms of hundreds of persons; they had done so as a desperate hedge against death. Only by having something of value to barter for food, safe lodging and other necessities could these hapless men even hope to survive the destruction surrounding them. The Jewish police had in their possession a staggering amount of money, expensive jewels, everything you could think of.

But it did most of them no good. My uncle was hiding behind a door with an automatic pistol. The Germans were so excited about getting their hands on the loot that they did not see him. They took all of his friends downstairs and killed them in the courtyard of the apartment house.

An hour or so later, while still hiding in the building, Lutek heard steps behind him. Peering in the direction of the sound, he saw German boots. Thinking that this was a member of the German search squad who had stayed behind to find more loot, Uncle Lutek opened fire. But in a moment, he discovered that he had wounded one of his best friends, who had not been among the group executed and who was looking for shelter. He was wearing German boots probably because he had no shoes.

The next day my gang transported my uncle out of the apartment building, preparatory to helping him get out of Warsaw. His wounded friend was left for the following day, because a fellow who was helping us did not want to take the wounded man before Uncle Lutek was out. When the next day came, Lutek's friend was no longer there. It could be that the Germans came back and discovered him. We never learned what happened to him, and we never saw him again.

Getting Uncle Lutek out of the city was a terrible business. It was impossible at the time to take him on the public transportation system, because he might have been recognized as a Jew. We had to hire a *doroszka*, a kind of horse-drawn taxicab. I followed on a bicycle, while Aunt Sophia accompanied Lutek in the carriage. A short distance from her apartment, where we had decided he should stay temporarily, she stopped the *doroszka*, got out with my uncle, and paid the driver a good tip. Of course, the latter suspected that he had been giving transportation to a Jew. He said, "Lady, I'm not stupid. I was risking my life, and you're going to pay me much more for it than this." Aunt Sophia did not have much more money, and she was certain that even if she did pay the driver more, she would not be rid of him. However, she had come prepared for such a situation. Aunt Sophia—sister of my mother and wife of my Jewish uncle—produced a pistol from her purse and told the *doroszka* driver that if he did not disappear at once, she was going to kill him. Believe me, the driver vanished very quickly.

By then Lutek was in terrible condition. He had run out of water to drink and soap for washing. There were sores all over his body, and he smelled like a pig. We spent hours scrubbing the caked dirt off of him.

Still later, we literally had to run through the city garbage dump in order to reach a second apartment that we had picked out for my Uncle Lutek. A few days later, after getting some medical treatment for him, we finally succeeded in spiriting him out of Warsaw. Aunt Sophia had rented a house in Otwock, a summer resort twenty-five miles from the city. The trick was to deliver Lutek to the railroad station in Warsaw. We did so by dressing him as an old woman. He rode alone on the train to Otwock, where he took refuge in Sophia's cottage.

However, Lutek was not comfortable in his new surroundings. He did not feel well, and his fear bordered on paranoia. A few weeks later, to our chagrin, he disguised himself again and returned to the city. Since for him to stay permanently with Aunt Sophia in Warsaw would have been too dangerous for her, he took up hiding in an apartment occupied by a group of partisans of the Polish national underground army. The apartment was situated on famed Skorupki Street in downtown Warsaw, near Marszalkowska Street. The partisans had a radio station that maintained contact with London. Uncle Lutek paid them well for letting him hide in their redoubt; he did not want to stay anywhere except in Warsaw.

The arrangement worked reasonably well until August 1944, when there was another civilian uprising in Warsaw—this one organized by the Polish underground and the Polish government-in-exile in London. Practically every civilian left in the city who could carry a weapon joined the revolt in order to have a hand in Poland's liberation. Suddenly Lutek was again in the midst of trouble. During the uprising the Germans bombed the city from the air. One evening after my uncle had left the apartment to go to another house to buy some liquor, a bomb scored a direct hit on the apartment house in which he had been hiding, and he had no place to return to.

This second Warsaw uprising lasted for sixty-two days. By then the Germans were taking virtually all of Warsaw's remaining civilians—men, women and children—to labor camps and concentration camps. A recognizable Jew would, of course, have been shot on sight. Miraculously, my uncle escaped arrest again. Hiding in the ruins of burned-out buildings, running from basement to basement, foraging for food like an animal, drinking from the little water that was left in the toilets, Lutek managed to live.

Meanwhile, my mother, three brothers and I were living in the district of Warsaw called Praga, on the east side of the Vistula River. The five of us occupied a one-room apartment with three beds, a table, four chairs and a small wall-kitchen which had a single faucet and cupboard. The apartment was on the ground floor and was regularly invaded by rats. I remember that my brothers and I had sticks that we used in a competition to see which of us could kill the most rats. But they kept coming back. During the late 1944 uprising, our side of the river experienced a relatively minor revolt, which the Germans finished in a few days. Only a small number of insurgents were involved, and they were all killed. Then, during September, Praga was "liberated" by the Russian and Polish armies.

Immediately after the Soviet occupation, we moved to Otwock, into a two-story brick apartment house separated by a garden from Aunt Sophia's cottage. Our apartment was larger and more comfortable than our one room in Praga, but we were too close to the local railroad station. The Germans would shell Russian trains passing through Otwock, and we would run to our basement. Sometimes we would spend all day huddled in the basement with our neighbors in the building and with Aunt Sophia, counting the artillery shells as they screamed in and exploded around us. They often numbered fifty or more between dawn and sundown. Many houses in Otwock were hit, and trees in our neighborhood were destroyed. But we were lucky; neither our building nor Sophia's cottage was touched.

Lutek left the city in December 1944. Facing bitterly cold weather and snow, he had finally conceded that he did not have much chance of continued survival in Warsaw. An added danger was that, as he roamed about, he was leaving tracks in the snow that alone were enough to lead to his discovery by the Germans. One day, when an SS officer stopped his car near Uncle Lutek on one of the city's otherwise-deserted streets, Lutek approached the German, drew a gun, and said simply: "You will take me out of Warsaw or I will kill you." Not having much choice, the Nazi drove Uncle Lutek out of the capital and left him on a highway near a village called Gora-Kalwaria.

Lutek scurried into an adjacent forest, where he took refuge next to several unattended horses. That night, a peasant from the village arrived to feed the horses and found my uncle. Lutek, who through it all had retained some money and valuables for bartering, made yet another deal: When the peasant came to tend his horses, he would bring my uncle food. In the meantime, Lutek contrived a makeshift dwelling. In this way he survived the rest of December.

On the seventeenth, eighteenth and nineteenth of January 1945, the Russians launched a new offensive that liberated all of Warsaw, though in the process they virtually destroyed what was left of the city. On the day after Poland's capital was occupied by the Russian army, Uncle Lutek went to our family home in Warsaw and uncovered caches of money and other objects of value that he had hidden there. He had tried to find his wife, but by then we were all in Otwock.

On days when the Germans were not shelling Otwock, I would walk to and from the city—selling bread and other food to the population, and buying items that we needed in order to survive. During these visits to the city, I often dropped in at our old apartment in Praga to rest for a couple of hours before walking home, and also to hide the money from my sales so that I would not be robbed. One day I found Uncle Lutek sitting on the staircase. He had been waiting there in the hope that one of us would come by. I took him to our temporary home in Otwock—nobody could believe it when we both arrived.

Lutek's story is not untypical of what happened to countless Jews in Europe during World War II.* Hardly any Jews survived the conflict in Poland, and especially in Warsaw, without having suffered similarly tragic and bizarre experiences.

In spite of all this, I hardly ever missed school. After school,

---

*Lutek became a very powerful man in Poland for a couple of years, but later he found himself in trouble again when he was recognized by another Jew and denounced as a former member of the Jewish police in the ghetto. Today, in ill health and retired, he lives quietly in Warsaw.

at about two or three o'clock, I would start work. Essentially it was stealing and selling—newspapers, cigarettes, cotton, sugar, honey, coal, anything I could get my hands on—in order to buy whatever my family needed to survive another day or week. In the process I was beaten up countless times by rival gangs, by youths who were older and stronger than I was, by Germans, and by various street characters. Quite often it took me days or weeks to recuperate. Most of my teeth were kicked either out or loose by one or another individual. When I arrived in the United States more than two decades later, the American dentists and doctors were amazed by the disfigured shape of my gums and teeth.

At the very end of the war, a group of us were buying guns from Germans in order to sell them to the Polish underground. This was a dangerous business because some of the Germans were not really prepared to sell the guns. They only wanted money, and were ready to kill. Another time we organized a group of young boys who would hunt for homosexuals with the purpose of gaining entry into their homes and apartments in order to steal. Still other times we broke into German-owned stores at night. When we were extremely desperate, we hid along the streets at night—in spite of the curfew, under which no civilian was allowed on the street after dark—in order to attack a single drunk German soldier, strangle him to death, and take his gun and his uniform and his boots.

Power
and Arrogance

WHEN POLAND WAS FINALLY LIBERATED IN 1945, IT was obvious that Poland's political system had to be changed. With the country in ruins and poverty, many young persons of my age felt that it was an ideal time for reform and renewal. From the very beginning we were conscious that there were only two alternatives: you were either for Communism or against.

Much of the population of Poland was against a Communist system; some would have liked to eradicate all Communists from Poland. So part of the Polish underground went into the forests again, this time to battle the Russians and their allies, the Polish Communists. Fighting between pro- and anti-Communist forces was not finally ended until 1951, when the anti-Communists assassinated the No. 2 man in the Polish army, General Swierczewski, touching off a government counterassault that finally eliminated the underground movement.

Liberation by the Reds hardly brought on the millenium as far as living conditions in the nation were concerned. In some respects life was even worse than during the German occupation: we lacked bread, food, jobs, everything.

Things became so bad that my youthful friends and I again went into the streets and began stealing food and other goods from our occupiers' transports—only this time they were Russian, and traveling from east to west instead of from west to east. We raided the Russian supply trains in the same way that we had hijacked the Germans'. We made some interesting deals with the Russian soldiers, and were even stealing and selling our loot in cooperation with them. The Russians were easy to buy because they were always interested in vodka. (German soldiers had often been equally cooperative.)

I worked the streets for many months. Finally, on one of our hijacking raids, I broke my leg jumping off a Russian supply truck and landed in a hospital. When I left the hospital, I decided that I wanted to get away from this kind of life.

I virtually had to start my life over again from point zero. It was impossible for me to find a place in a Warsaw school—the school year had started, and, besides, there were at least fifty percent more candidates than places. So I moved to Lodz, a large city with a textile industry that is sometimes called the Polish Manchester. My mother's brother, who was an officer in the Polish army, had acquired a large apartment there that had formerly been occupied by a German. Because the war was still going on, he was in Germany fighting alongside the Russians on the Western front. My uncle's parents and I took up residence in his spacious apartment. I had left my mother and three younger brothers in Warsaw, but still had to assist them financially. Ultimately I took my youngest brother in with me in Lodz. But I could not find a job. The local economy of Lodz, as was the case across Poland, had been virtually destroyed. I was too young. I had no skills.

There was only one thing to do: revert to my old lifestyle. Some friends and I organized a gang. We succeeded in getting a monopoly on the distribution of tickets to several movie theaters in Lodz, and then sold the tickets on the black market. It was impossible to purchase a ticket to a movie in any of the theaters without buying it from us. In a war-weary land hungry for entertainment, this was a lucrative business, and I was soon able to send funds to my mother and my two brothers in Warsaw, as well as help my grandparents and my youngest brother.

Even though my group's movie-ticket monopoly was bringing in a substantial profit, it wasn't enough for us. We began stealing cars and parts from cars, which we sold to professional dealers who resold the equipment in other sections of the country. One night a Russian convoy on the way to the German front stopped in one of the squares of Lodz. Supplied by us with vodka, the Russian soldiers got drunk and fell asleep. The next morning the whole convoy, numbering 200 to 250 trucks, was not able to leave because here a wheel was missing, there a battery or generator. Some of the trucks, which had been loaded with ammunition and other military equipment, were partly empty.

We organized another gang that was really very dangerous. In some operations we carried weapons, and it reached the point where we had open battles with the so-called people's militia, the name for the police in a Communist country—which Poland had become. Some of our forty or fifty members were even policemen. We had one battle with the people's militia that paralyzed the whole downtown area of Lodz. One of the gang's leaders, B, was sentenced to death and executed. Another, P, escaped from Poland in 1948 or 1949 and is today reportedly somewhere in Australia. Even though my country had been liberated from the Germans, the three years of my stay in Lodz, from 1945 to 1948, were a terrible period in the history of Poland. Our No. 1 enemy was the Russian army and its imposed Polish regime which, with the exception of slogans, couldn't offer us much at all.

During all of this I never abandoned my desire to resume my formal education. I was supported by my mother, who was able to bear a great deal but not the idea of her children's giving up school. I had managed to get into a school in Lodz, but the classroom atmosphere was more depressing than edifying, for half of my classmates were homeless street urchins whose parents were in German concentration camps, in the Polish underground, hiding somewhere in the West, or dead. Nevertheless, I stayed in school and managed to advance through three grades of junior high. I was the only member of my street gang who went to school.

My checkered life in Lodz went on for three years, encompassing the end of the war and Europe's unsettled postwar period. In the spring of 1948 I decided to run away from Lodz and return to Warsaw. I cut off all ties and connections with my cohorts in Lodz so that none of them would know what had happened to me. I am glad I did so, for I was later informed that most of my gang-friends went to prison under quite serious sentences.

I started a new life in Warsaw. By now my home city had begun to recover somewhat from the devastation of the war. I enrolled in a respectable school, and found a series of honest part-time jobs—as a messenger, as a clerk, as an accountant. I began to live a comparatively decent existence. I wanted to forget the whole past. I kept away from the streets.

At the same time, I began to develop deeper philosophical and political feelings. I decided that I wanted to give my country something, to do something that I felt would be good for Poland.

At first I wished neither to be a Communist nor to oppose the movement.

But in addition to the fact that I wanted to do something, there were other pressures at work—the pressures exerted on everyone by the Communists themselves. The Communists had already decided that whoever was not with them was against them, and I did not want to be against. Therefore perhaps mine wasn't really a decision. Perhaps I did not jump but was pushed. I still do not know exactly which forces impelled me into Communism. I do know that I was not quite sure what would come from this thing called the Communist movement. For a time I even considered joining the anti-Communist side. Part of the reason it took me a while to reach a decision was that I was a Catholic.

In any case, I joined the Communist youth organization. At the time I couldn't recognize the true features of this movement, but it offered hope. I became chairman of the Communist youth organization at my school, Roesler. In the company where I was working part-time—a construction firm—I became extremely active politically. I was studying, working, and embarking on the role of an activist both socially and politically.

In the beginning, we were not told by the Communist organization not to go to church. The party used its influence against the church, but had not yet declared religion anathema. You could participate in a Communist youth rally on Saturday and go to mass on Sunday.

By 1949 the struggle between the church and the system had become more dramatic. Things reached the point where trying to be a part of both of these conflicting camps became psychologically unbearable. The speakers at the Saturday meetings I was attending were attacking the church, and on Sunday morning my priest was attacking the government.

As a new convert to Communism, I soon found myself in ideological battle with the Roman Catholic church, and especially with the priest at my school, who was also secretary to Poland's prince of the Catholic church, Stefan Cardinal Wyszynski. The priest's name is well known in Poland—it was Alojzy N. A Jesuit from Silesia, he was at the time delivering a weekly nationwide sermon on behalf of the Catholic church. He was a spellbinding speaker.

On Father N's program over the Communist-ruled radio, he was not allowed to make outright anti-Communist statements. But in a subtle way he appealed to the ideas that made up Poland's traditional mode of life, and that were totally different from the Communist mold.

Finally he was arrested. He had been organizing graduate students across the country into small circles to study the Catholic approach to books and movies produced by the regime.

Father N's efforts eventually earned him seven years in prison. He was released only in the fall of 1956.

Prior to his arrest, knowing that I was the chairman of the Communist organization in our school, he was very nasty to me. He frequently forced me to leave the classroom. He confused me—I was still pretty much a political illiterate—by asking me political questions in public. And I, envying his expert knowledge of Communism, hated him as much as I believe that, in a certain way, he hated me.

After various disputes with Father N, I verbally attacked him in a public conference of the Warsaw Communist youth organization. I demanded that he be thrown out of the schools. He accused me of having physically beaten him up with the help of my friends, alleging that I had nearly killed him. He was going around Warsaw with his face covered with bandages, declaring that his injuries had been inflicted by me. Well, whether his injuries were real or contrived (and I'll never know), it wasn't true that I had caused them. This was the last straw, the moment when I broke off completely with the Catholic church of Poland.

I began working actively against the church. My Communist comrades and I would center our attention on a particular village—usually one that was relatively large and well-to-do. There would always be one priest who effectively ran the village. We would create a small Communist youth organization in our selected village.

In the beginning, only five or ten persons would belong. The first to attack them would be the local priest. On the first Sunday after our arrival, during the Sabbath masses, he would suddenly warn: "Danger has come to our village in the form of a Communist devil, and I cannot understand why such good Catholics as Mr. and Mrs. So-and-So would let their son or daughter join this."

We spread propaganda in favor of abortion. Today abortion is legal in Poland, but for all intents and purposes it is still illegal in a small village. If a girl in a Polish village wants to get an abortion, she has to run away from home. And if the priest learns that she has gone to the city to have an abortion, she can forget about returning to her village.

Thus it was the Roman Catholic church itself that brought about my break with Catholicism, rather than the influence of Communist propaganda. I came to detest the inordinate power that the church possessed in Poland, and the arrogance and intolerance with which the clerics wielded their power.

After my split with the church, I turned into a most difficult person for everybody around me. I lost any sense of compromise. Whoever did not follow the party and government program was my enemy.

I became such an activist that at my school—and also at the office where I worked—everybody felt obliged to ask me for political guidance. At work I was only a young clerk, and in school I was as much a student as any of my classmates, but my influence became formidable. Whether my colleagues liked or hated me, I represented the political factor, the Communist opinion. And by then the Communists, backed by Poland's Russian "liberators," were looking over everyone's shoulder.

Finally—I cannot say exactly on what day the transformation occurred—I began to feel a tremendous power in my hands. At the same moment, I now belatedly realize, that sense of power started destroying me. But there was no turning back—and at the time I did not have any desire to do so. For one thing, I felt less and less alone. Day after day we had more and more Communists in Poland, both homegrown and imported from the Soviet Union in the form of "advisors." In my new political activities I had obvious enemies, but I also had around me more and more persons with the same sympathies. It took years for me to learn that all of them were not real friends, for they were supporting me in my new-found sense of power and purpose.

The School on Dluga Street

UPON COMPLETING HIGH SCHOOL I WAS ACCEPTED into the university system without even an entrance examination. At this time it was quite difficult for others to get into the university system, but I had a special diploma, giving me free entry into any university I chose. Only one such diploma was awarded in any one high school graduating class. Needless to say, you could not get this special diploma unless you were actively involved in the Communist movement.

I selected the University of Warsaw, and enrolled in the fall of 1949. Upon my arrival I, along with other matriculating activists, was invited by the president of the university and the dean of my department—I had chosen economics as my major—to a meeting. We newcomers could sense at once that we were already marked to be leaders at the university. And we could feel that the professors and administrative heads were expected to give us personal attention and special privileges.

Soon after classes began, I found myself, as a result of my aggressiveness and the support of my fellow student activists, at the top of the leadership of the campus Communist organization. Neither the president nor the dean of the school could do much without our organization's support. By 1950 I was president of the student association, which formed an important arm of Communist influence at the university. In 1952 I was accepted as a full-fledged member of the Polish Communist party—a rare honor in a Communist country.

By then my dedication to the movement knew no bounds. At that stage I would have given my life for the cause. My life to that point had been tragic and traumatic. I was still poor— in spite of my popularity, my political activities, and my leadership role at the university, I did not have one decent suit. But I was so devoted to the Communists that I worked twenty-four hours a day without caring.

Still, as I have conceded, the taste of political power was a kind of intellectual disaster for me. I had a long way to go really to become educated. Even though I was considered a good student, I decided that academic learning was no longer the most important thing. I achieved status through political activities rather than grades.

After only one year at the university, I became a professorial assistant to Professors Skrzywan and Fedak, men of great intellect but non-party members. Around them were several other assistants, most of whom were not party members either. I was sent to the professors' department "to wake and shake up their whole team"—to make them and their assistants aware of "their obligations under socialism." Again it was my political activity that helped me get this important assignment.

In my position as professorial assistant I often acted as a lecturer. I discovered that I was capable of being a really good teacher when my lectures involved a concrete, specific professional subject. I began to enjoy my lecturing assignments. I started teaching at the university's evening school and at high schools around Warsaw, not only for the money but because I liked the experience. It gave me pleasure when my students appreciated the way I engaged their minds.

It was during this period that I married Krystyna. She was a beautiful brunette, with middle-class Roman Catholic parents. I was not so politically consumed as to be immune to matters of the heart, and I fell in love with her at first sight.

When Krystyna and I decided to be married, my old adversary, the church, again reared its head. Having renounced Catholicism, I had no intention of ever again attending mass, much less of being married in the church. But my wife-to-be was not ready yet for such a break with tradition. I finally succeeded in convincing her that the church should play no part in our wedding, but I wasn't able to persuade her parents. They simply could not accept the idea of an atheist as a son-in-law.

I at last agreed to get married in the church. I had to get permission from the Communist youth organization, however. They said, "Well, if you really feel that you have to do so, then do it." It was a time when this was still possible. Later you could not get any such permission; you could not even ask for it.

At the time, Krystyna was not a Communist. Soon after our marriage I converted her to Communism. Ironically, later on, when I changed my mind about Communism, I could not change hers.

By the time I neared the end of my career at the University of Warsaw, I was taking part in a multiplicity of political activities. Among other things, I was helping to draft a plan for the collectivization of Polish farmers, and participating in related "security" actions. We students would go to a village that was to be collectivized and remain for a week or so, talking with the inhabitants to find out which were in favor of collectivization and which were against. The security police would then base their file on the village on information that we supplied.

One Sunday in the spring of 1953, I was called to the university to meet "some persons." When I arrived at the office of the university branch of the Communist party, there were several individuals waiting for me, and I had a very strange discussion with them. I was asked scores of wide-ranging questions about my life and beliefs. Some of the questions were so complex that I could not even reply to them. I could sense that this was something important.

Good Communist that I was, I asked no questions. There was a similar session on the following Sunday. Finally I was told that the Communist party expected a special kind of service from me. Later I was advised in general terms that it was some manner of work in a foreign service. To that I replied that I did not know any foreign languages. I was told that that was "exactly" what they wanted, that they would teach me.

I was told that I should leave the university in order to enter some kind of special training school. So vague and circumspect were my recruiters that it was difficult to conjecture what they were talking about. I truly did not suspect that it was to be intelligence. What crossed my mind was that perhaps it had something to do with the Polish Foreign Service. At the time, I didn't even know that we were in the intelligence business—maybe Russia was, I thought, but not a small country such as Poland.

In any event, I rejected the proposal because I had decided that for all my Marxist dedication, I wanted to stay at the university and one day become a full professor. I rationalized this to myself by saying that I could be more politically influential on the campus than anywhere else. The truth of the matter was that I had started to love my budding profession as a teacher.

I discovered later that several other students had received similar overtures. Most acceded without protest, but only a few were ultimately accepted into the "special service."

After I said no, I did not have a moment of peace. I was invited here and there; I was asked why I would not do what the party was expecting from me. I was even promised that if I did not like the position, I could return to the university and would have no reason to be worried about my future. But those talking to me hastened to add that in all probability I would never return, because these official duties were so important for the Communist party and the government that it was unimaginable that I would turn away from the position. However, they were not in a position to tell me just then exactly what I would be doing.

There were also hints that the material rewards would be most attractive. In spite of my activity at the university, I was still living at a marginal level. My wife and I were sharing a four-bedroom apartment with three other young couples. In five months Krystyna was to give birth to our first and only child—our son Jarek—and this loomed large in my thoughts. I discussed the situation with my mother, with my wife. Not knowing all the details of the offer, they advised me not to accept it. They pointed out that my friends on the campus were certain that I could some day be a successful professor at the University of Warsaw.

In the end, nevertheless, I decided to take the job, whatever it would be. One reason by now was sheer curiosity—what with all the enigmatic overtones, I had become anxious to see what this was all about. I signed a document stating that I was going to join this certain organization. By then I knew that it was a secret service of some sort, but I had no specifics.

In October 1953, three months before I was to be graduated from the university, I was ordered by my recruiters to report to a special school in Warsaw. I left the university, but was worried that I might not receive my degree. Although I had completed my examinations, I still had a special paper to write. One day, not long after I left the campus, I was called in by the university, ostensibly to face a board of professors who were to question me as to my qualifications to receive a degree. But there were no questions. The board merely congratulated me and advised me that I had won my degree, which I received. Later, I saw in my secret service file a note: "Comrade Janusz should receive his diploma without writing his final paper because he is performing a special service for the party and for the government."

The institution to which I reported was completely off-limits to the public and bore a forbidding cover name: Central Committee School of the Polish Communist Party. It was on Dluga Street, near the Warsaw arsenal.

I began attending this school full-time. I met only one person there from my university. I discovered later that, of more than thirty students from the University of Warsaw who had been interviewed as possible candidates for the school, only two of us had been accepted. The other—it was good to see at least one familiar face—was Roman Kwiatkowski, a friend of mine who would be killed in 1960 in Yugoslavia. Strange as it may seem, it took several months to comprehend exactly what kind of institution we were attending and what kind of activity we were going to be involved in. A group of veterans of the intelligence service were undergoing retraining in a building next door, and we neophytes, encountering the veterans every now and then, would ask them what was going on. The usual answer was: "If you don't know, we're not going to tell you." Finally one of the older fellows divulged to one of our classmates that we were in intelligence, and the latter brought the report back to us. We asked our school leaders about this and were told that they did not want to hear any more such rumors. But very gradually our instructors confirmed our suspicions. It was sometime in December or January when we were told exactly what kind of academy this was and what we would be doing later on. It was a special intelligence school, to prepare us to be officers in the Polish Intelligence Service.

We started classes on October 12, 1953. There were sixty-five students representing all of the universities in Poland, usually one or two from each university. All were male.

At the very beginning we were given an extremely thorough political brainwashing. Although all of my classmates were, like me, already Marxists, our new indoctrination was clearly designed to leave no trace of ideological doubt in our minds. For two months we had ten or twelve hours per day of political and ideological lectures, discussions, meetings, Communist party activity. There were also two hours a day of language training, for which we were divided into small groups.

One cycle of lectures, to which we listened with particular interest, consisted of specialists telling us of the difficulties experienced by diplomats and other representatives of Communist governments who were living in the West. We were told of the provocation and blackmail levied by the capitalist camp against comrades abroad. Hundreds of stories were recited about the provocations, dirty methods, and types of blackmail likely to be used against us whenever we traveled to the Western countries.

Our indoctrination underlined how nasty and barbaric the FBI and CIA were; how tense, how guarded we would have to be every minute that we were in the West. It was, in sum, a crash course in Communist paranoia. And finally, of course, we were assured that Communist officials abroad were doing nothing wrong in those Western nations, but were simply striving to develop a peaceful cultural relationship with their people.

We were also lectured on the history, the structure and the methods of the French, British, West German, American, Italian, and even Yugoslavian intelligence and counterintelligence services. (Tito, because of his independence from Moscow, was at this time classified as an enemy.) There was no Western secret service that we were not briefed about. Above all, we were warned how much the capitalists hated us Communists— how every capitalist country was doing everything possible to destroy us.

This initial curriculum was a perfect preparation for the second phase of our indoctrination course, in which we learned how much we should despise capitalists and why, how we were justified in using our own dirty methods to win this ideological battle, and how we were expected to employ such methods aggressively and cold-bloodedly, without any qualms. We studied intensively the experiences of the Polish intelligence and counterintelligence services working in Great Britain, the United States, France, Italy, Scandinavia, West Germany, Berlin, Yugoslavia, Canada, Latin America, and even the Vatican.

In the school on Dluga Street we lived under great pressure. There was a six-day study week, and we were obliged to be in class at eight o'clock every morning. Only the few of us who were married were permitted to spend nights at home, and this only after great difficulty in persuading our superiors.

Let me describe one comparatively easy day. First we had two hours of lectures, principally on political subjects such as the class struggle. The next two hours were devoted to lectures on professional subjects such as intelligence and counterintelligence. Between twelve and two o'clock we had our language classes. Then we had a thirty-minute lunch break. After our quick lunch, we were permitted to participate in various kinds of sports, including volleyball and basketball.

Usually this play period was over by approximately four P.M. Between four and six o'clock we had a collective discussion about problems that we had studied during the previous day. These discussions were actually a regular check on whether we had been doing our homework. At six o'clock we had one hour for supper, and then we were obliged to study from seven o'clock until ten. We studied alone or in groups of two or three, depending upon the subject. Small groups were permitted, for instance, in the case of languages. Somebody a little more advanced could help a friend or friends. Two- or three-person groups were also permitted when we had problems to be prepared for the next day's collective discussion.

The bedrooms accommodated five to seven students. Roommates were assigned on the basis of the language that they were studying and their proficiency in that language. If a room held six persons, all of them studying English, two would be from the advanced English level, two from the medium level, and two from the group of beginners.

Administratively, the school was arranged into two classes. Each had its own leader, a highly experienced counterintelligence officer. He was with us, in body or in spirit, twenty-four hours a day. Our class leaders were T. Kozera and L. Pawelec.

The school day ended around 10 P.M. and those few who had permission to go home hurried off in order to spend as much time as possible with their wives before returning to class the next morning. Students who lived at school were permitted to go out as long as they were back by midnight. However, that permission could be revoked any time that a student began lagging in his studies. Single students were not allowed to visit their families more than once a month. We had our own security guards—not outside but inside. We had to show our identification cards to the guards in order to be allowed outside.

During Christmas break, we were given several days' vacation, and every student was allowed to go home. Immediately after our return, we had our first meeting with a person who was to exert a major influence on all of our lives: Witold Sienkiewicz, chief of the Polish Intelligence Service.

A blond, slightly balding, good-looking man with intense blue eyes, he stood about five feet, eleven inches tall and weighed about 200 pounds. Sienkiewicz had been Poland's master spy since 1951. In that year he had replaced his predecessor, General Komar, after Komar fell into party disfavor and was arrested. Sienkiewicz had been secretary of the Communist party in Lodz, a relatively minor post. His background was obscure; rumor had it that he might have been of Lithuanian origin, and may at one time have been leader of the Communist youth movement in Lithuania. A Lithuanian-born Polish author, Henry Sienkiewicz, was awarded the Nobel Prize in 1929. Whether they were related or not I do not know, but even in Communist countries it is sometimes a big help to have such a prestigious family name.

Witold Sienkiewicz was, as you would say in the States, the epitome of cool. He could have two drinks or twenty drinks and never get drunk. He never said anything that he would regret. When he looked at you with his cold blue eyes, you felt that he was able to read your mind. And you knew that whatever you were discussing had to be his way. Tough as he was, you respected him. And he was capable at times of a dry sense of humor.

Sienkiewicz was both a pragmatist and a moralist. When one of our agents got caught in a bar during an altercation, Sienkiewicz explained that he was punishing the man not because he had been in the bar, but because he had failed to get out before the police arrived. In another case, two of our operatives, by mutual agreement, were screwing each other's wives. Sienkiewicz called the agents in and penalized them not because of their wife-swapping, but because they had failed to keep the scandal to themselves. Similarly, Sienkiewicz did not have any problem with a married agent's having a mistress as long as the situation was kept quiet. On the other hand, he became furious when he discovered that one of our single agents was sleeping surreptitiously with the wife of one of our officers. Sienkiewicz's reaction was that there are so many single girls available that a single man has no cause to seduce another man's wife.

Once we had a New Year's Eve party. Sienkiewicz was at the head of the top officers' table with his wife. A slightly drunk guest started going around the leaders' table asking each of the wives in turn to dance. Sienkiewicz told the fellow to bug off. The fellow said no. Sienkiewicz hit the fellow so hard he could not get up.

Years later, when I was stationed in Sweden, the UB had a two-day conference in Warsaw on how to improve our results. In his opening address to the meeting, Sienkiewicz said that we were not doing our job. Our intelligence-gathering was down; our recruiting was down. Stalin or no Stalin, he declared, our intelligence business would go on.

I rose and asked why the Foreign Ministry wasn't cooperating with us more. (Poland's foreign minister at the time was Adam Rapacki.) I cited examples of non-cooperation and nepotism in the Polish embassy in Sweden. As I spoke, Sienkiewicz had a smile on his face.

At the close of the conference, Sienkiewicz delivered a two-hour speech. Toward the end of his remarks, although he did not mention my name, he reminded us that we had both young persons and older persons in the party and the government. "The old guard," he said, "was fighting for this country—paying with their blood—while the younger people were in school. I respect both groups. But I'll never let it be said that the egg is wiser than the chicken. The chicken is wiser."

Sienkiewicz went on—and by then I had no doubt that he was alluding to my criticism. "I know what's wrong with the Foreign Ministry. But it is not up to us to correct it. And remember that when you are criticizing the Foreign Ministry you are criticizing Comrade Rapacki. He is also aware of the situation in the Foreign Ministry. And he is working to change it. But I don't want you young fellows to consider us older fellows fools. We shall listen to each other, but we shall never let the egg be wiser than the chicken."

Afterward, a friend in the audience said to me: "Be careful with this man. He never forgets anything. Make peace with him, or this will be the beginning of the end for you."

Getting back to the first time I saw Sienkiewicz, for us students, meeting him face-to-face was electrifying. Our excitement was heightened by the fact that Sienkiewicz's identity was not publicly known outside the UB. I remember that years later, when I was posted in a clandestine position in the Foreign Ministry, there was a restricted distribution list for secret cables from overseas that had been decoded. (The cables, identified by the color of the paper they were reproduced on, were distributed in a locked briefcase.) There was always one name on the list that, to the vast majority of those involved in the ministry, was a mystery: "W. Sienkiewicz." As part of my cover act, I would from time to time demand to know from my Foreign Ministry superiors the identity of Sienkiewicz. They could never tell me. Some were convinced that no W. Sienkiewicz existed, that the name was a code name for the UB.

Sienkiewicz's lecture to us neophyte spies was a model of simplicity. He explained that we were candidates for the special kind of work involved in the Polish Intelligence Service. He told us quite openly, and with the necessary explanations, what kind of jobs we were preparing for, how difficult our continued training was to be.

Sienkiewicz seemed to be trying to be very frank. At the end of the meeting, he declared that any of us who were afraid or who did not like the mission or who did not feel suited for intelligence work had every right to quit then. No one did so right then, but a few days after Sienkiewicz's lecture and lectures by others of the UB hierarchy, the warnings began to take effect. One lecturer with a heavy Russian accent said to us: "There is no way you can make it if you have five percent or even one percent of any doubt about Communism. You must have no church burdens. This must be absolutely clear."

Even before this lecture was over, one student arose and confessed: "I am one of those who have doubts. I am still struggling with a small percentage of my feelings, struggling with my conscience. It could be that a year or two from now I would drop out of this service."

We were shocked. It was unimaginable that anyone would make such a statement. But today I must concede that the fellow had guts. Of course he was immediately dismissed from the school. And he wasn't the only one.

From time to time someone else would abruptly stand up and announce: "I have come to understand that I am not really a Communist because there is a percentage of me that I believe is still Catholic."

The rest of us, especially our supervisors, were understandably startled by such a confession because of the ideological testing that had already been imposed. The student involved would depart from the school in a matter of minutes, and his name would go somewhere on a blacklist.

Other students fell victim to the highly complicated screening process that continued even after we had been accepted into the school. I later learned that our backgrounds had been investigated to the third generation: the slightest suspicion of questionable conduct, or connection with the West, could disqualify the best candidate. It was enough, for instance, to have a relative, and not even a close relative, who was a priest. It was enough for a member of one's family to be in touch by letter with a friend from high school or primary school who was in the West, even if they hadn't seen each other for twenty years. Those ejected were literally in tears when they were forced to leave. Some were on the verge of committing suicide—a few did.

As our studies intensified, we were subjected to several bizarre experiments. For instance, we were told to prepare to go through training to be parachutists. We packed and unpacked parachutes, and we went through exercises in jumping. Finally, we were taken in cars to the military airport, ordered into a plane, given equipment, and told to be ready for takeoff. At the last minute the jump was canceled. The purpose of the whole exercise was not to make us parachutists but to test our courage. Some students broke on the way to the airport, suddenly declaring that they would not jump for any price. They were immediately dropped from the class.

Parties were organized for us at which our supervisors provoked us to drink, to see who could drink and at what point we would be drunk. Some of the experiments we were subjected to were rather nasty. For example, we were taken to resorts on two-week "vacations." Suddenly women would appear. Married students were told that they would not be condemned if they took the women to bed—but the assurance was an intentional ruse.

During one such outing, at a mountain resort, I was introduced to a divorcee about twenty-one or twenty-two years old. I became rather excited about her, and we went on a short one-day trip. We did not have sexual relations, but soon after our return our elected student leader approached me and asked why I had taken her out.

"That is none of your business," I replied curtly.

"It is my business," my student comrade retorted. "If you can cheat on your wife, how can we trust you?"

One woman—and this was a part of the program that, unfortunately, some students discovered too late—had gonorrhea. She was a veteran informant and agent of the UB. After she went to bed with one of the students, he got sick. He went to a physician, paid for his treatment, and kept quiet. Well, all of us were told one day that he had been expelled from the school, and we were told exactly why: He had failed to report his illness to his superior. We were warned that there was nothing in our lives that we could keep to ourselves. Everything, good or bad, including medical problems, had to be reported.

We had training in the use of guns and technical equipment. Our shooting exercises included target practice with automatic and small-caliber weapons, both Western-made and Eastern-made. We learned how to aim and fire tiny pistols built to look like a flashlight or fountain pen; they contained only one bullet, but it was enough to kill someone. Much of this camouflaged weaponry was made in Japan.

Our most extensive training was in the use of mini-cameras. We were required to be absolutely expert in clandestine photography. For example, we would be given a hundred-page document to photograph within a limited number of minutes under varying light conditions, and would not be permitted to miss, either through oversight or improper exposure, more than one page. We also became adept with conventional cameras, particularly in taking pictures from short and long distances with telescopic lenses. Every morning each of us would be given a roll of film. The next morning we had to hand in prints of the photographs we had taken. (We were required to develop our film and make our prints ourselves.) Our pictures were thoroughly critiqued. As a result of this process, we all became rather excellent photographers—even professional, I might say.

Our training as spies likewise taught us such arcane skills as how to make a copy of a key using a bar of soap (press the key into the soap in order to duplicate the configuration); how to use a hot egg to copy a signature (roll the egg over the original signature and it will imprint itself on the eggshell); how to steam open a letter using a coffee pot; how to use ultraviolet light to read the contents of a letter without opening the envelope; how to find and pick up fingerprints without destroying them; and how to identify forged handwriting (in order to make sure that handwritten messages from an agent are authentic).

We were also introduced to the use of incapacitating drugs and poisons. We learned to drop drugs into coffee or tea in order to make someone sick or unconscious for a few hours. The only advice given us was: "If you are told to drop one or two pills, don't drop in more or less. Do exactly as you are told." As for using lethal methods, we were told there are situations in which a traitor must be killed. The explanation was: "We don't like to do it, but if we have to we will." Years later on that October night in Paris, following Wladyslaw Mroz's last ride, I was to remember that direction.

We were also advised, quite frankly, that the moment might come when we ourselves would have to be eliminated, or when we would have to decide to kill ourselves. There could be situations in which we knew too much but had been compromised by the other side and were vulnerable, situations in which we could be broken and made to talk, situations in which we would choose suicide over spending the rest of our lives in prison. Unfortunately—and tragically—this last message may have registered all too well on the minds of many of my colleagues in the intelligence service. Years afterward, faced with disillusionment or scandal or the humiliation of having fallen into party disfavor, they committed suicide with the pills given to them.

We had memory exercises. We would be called to the office and asked by one or more persons exactly what we had been doing the previous Monday or Tuesday. Or sometimes you would be asked exactly what you were doing, for instance, between seven o'clock and eight o'clock that morning before you came to school (if you were among those permitted to go home). You would be asked the exact number of the streetcar or bus that you took, or, if you had walked, the exact route that you took.

One morning my infant son was sick, and instead of returning to school on time I had to find a doctor and go to a pharmacy to buy medicines. I arrived at school at about nine. After half an hour I was called to the office. I was confronted there by a fellow who was later to become my friend and help me in several situations—B. Baginski.

But on this day I hated him. He exuded an air of professional hostility toward me. As security officer of the intelligence school, he interrogated me as to precisely what I had been doing between five and nine in the morning. Having been without sleep nearly the whole night because of my child's sickness, I was not thinking too clearly, and I mixed up my hours and minutes. Suddenly I discovered that this fellow knew every step that I had made that morning, to the minute.

I became angry and bitter. But then I remembered the words of Sienkiewicz, who had warned us during our training: "Your name is going to stay forever in our files, and we will never let you do anything on your own as far as the interests of the secret service, the country, the government and the Communist party are concerned. You can forget about any future independent job or activity. You can forget about ever going abroad on your own. We will never let you leave this country on your own if you go through this program."

At a certain stage, our political indoctrination was reduced to a minimum. We were still under political pressure; we still had some seminars and lectures; and we were still obliged to have discussions among ourselves. But such catechisms were mainly organized by the Communist party unit and its leadership at school, and were no longer so much a part of the program of the school. By now our curriculum consisted almost entirely of only two subjects—intelligence work and language. It was, I must say, very interesting.

We were obliged to read a great deal, and often our regularly scheduled weekend activities were canceled in order to permit us to stay at school and study. Most of our reading material was top secret intelligence material in the form of printed catalogues with from ten to two hundred pages.

A large part of our training involved finding solutions to

hypothetical intelligence problems. One example: "What would be the best method by which to recruit an agent in the United States? Keep in mind that methods that might be feasible to utilize in one country may not be practical in another."

We had our final examinations in July 1954, just before Poland's national holiday, which is roughly comparable to the United States' Fourth of July. All of us were promoted to the rank of lieutenant in the Polish Intelligence Service—as students we had had no formal rank. After our "graduation" a ceremony was held, and those of us who had become friends exchanged gifts. We were then given several weeks' vacation. As much as I enjoyed it, I was filled with the tension of anticipation. I was now an officer of the Polish Intelligence Service. I was about to embark upon my career as a spy.

PART TWO

The Wages
of Loyalty

WE STARTED WORK AT THE BEGINNING OF THE following September. On the appointed day, we reported, one by one, at carefully timed intervals of ten to fifteen minutes, to the corner of Pulawska Street and Ksawerow Street in the Mokotow district of Warsaw. From there we were taken individually to the headquarters of the Polish Intelligence Service, which was situated adjacent to this intersection.

The building had an interesting cover: publicly, it was thought to be part of the central command of the Polish police, or "citizens' militia," as it is called. Even persons living or working around the building had no reason to think that it was anything else. But only the façade of the structure and the offices fronting on the sidewalk looked anything like a police headquarters. Only ten to fifteen percent of the building was occupied by police units, and they were there principally to provide a cover for us.

The building was a huge, four-story, block-type structure, built in the shape of several T's attached to one another. We used a separate entrance in an area completely apart from the false entrance. I was sent at once to Branch 4, Department 1. Branch 4, at this time, was responsible for intelligence-gathering in Great Britain, France, Italy, the Vatican, Switzerland, Belgium and The Netherlands. Department 1 was responsible for political, scientific and economic intelligence in the areas of Branch 4's responsibility. Military espionage was handled by the military intelligence service, known as Z-2, which was under the supervision of the Polish Defense Ministry.

Branch 4 was the largest and most important section of the Polish Intelligence Service. Later, after certain reorganizations, we lost the British section but gained all of the Scandinavian section—a development that was to prove important to me, since I eventually became officer in charge of the Scandinavian desk.

My new boss at Branch 4 was Colonel Z. Dybala, who was known to United States counterintelligence by the false name of Jaworski. He was a top man in the UB, and had an interesting background, including a great deal of experience in the United States. Before long he was to become a deputy to the chief of the Polish Intelligence Service. In the beginning I had a difficult time with Dybala, but later we became friends, unfortunately. I say unfortunately because after I finally began to understand this man, and to really like and admire him, he committed suicide in connection with a corruption scandal. That was in 1962.

Five years after his suicide, and after I had defected from Poland, Dybala's wife Helen committed suicide. They and others like them did not take their lives because they were primitive or stupid or sick. They had serious and pitiable reasons for doing so. They had been ready to do anything for Communism, but the Communist system had pushed them to the point where they felt they could not go on. They did not want to desert the ideology that they had believed in for so many years; yet they could not accept the form that that ideology had degenerated into in Russia, Poland or any other present-day Communist country. And they couldn't take any more. They were completely conscious of their acts and psychologically healthy when they killed themselves.

But I am getting ahead of my story. Adjusting to my new job and my new boss was not easy. At the University of Warsaw I had been treated by my superiors with consideration and respect. Suddenly I was faced with a boss who cared about nothing except succeeding in his work. We subordinates were nothing but soldiers who should be ready to die at his command.

The discipline was brutal, unremitting. We were working ten, twelve, fourteen hours a day, and we were never sure that we were going to get home any particular afternoon or evening. Everything was decided by Dybala. (Our wives were informed by briefers from the UB that we were involved in a type of secret work for the Polish Communist party, but they were warned not to tell other members of our families or outsiders or to ask any questions. However, since we intelligence officers were usually assigned to the same apartment buildings, our wives became acquainted, and not even the state apparatus could prevent them from gossiping with one another about what their husbands were doing.)

Soon after joining Branch 4, I had a very trying experience. I was sent on a mission with a veteran intelligence officer. While we were supposed to be working, my experienced companion was doing nothing but causing trouble. When we returned, we were both punished. I did not feel that I deserved it. I started to argue with Dybala, and he told me that I was a son of a bitch.

It had been years since anybody had said anything like that to me, not since the violence-ridden days of my youth. My reaction to such an insult was still the same—I became furious. I could kill a person who called me a son of a bitch. It was the law of the street.

I told Dybala: "Perhaps you're a son of a bitch and perhaps your grandmother was too, but don't say anything like that to me again, because if you do I'll break your neck."

Well, the fellow was so shocked that for a moment I was seriously afraid he would drop dead. I left the room, slamming the door so hard that I partially destroyed the wall around the door, and returned to my office.

I shared an office with a more experienced officer, Ryszard Ronda, who was then a good friend of mine but who later became possibly my worst enemy (and I his). When I told him about this situation, he said, "You're finished forever." Indeed, I found myself doing nothing for two weeks. I was coming to the office, sitting and twiddling my thumbs.

Then one day Dybala opened the door to my office and asked, "What are you doing this evening?"

"As far as I know, nothing special."

"Could you be here at seven P.M.?"

I said, "Yes, okay."

I came at seven o'clock. We had a discussion that lasted until three or four o'clock in the morning. It was an arduous session. I was not afraid to argue, and gave up nothing from my point of view. Colonel Dybala was at first ready to throw me out of the office, perhaps even through the window.

The fact that a brash young officer was trying to protest astounded Dybala. And yet I was arguing in a relatively intelligent manner. I was seriously convinced that I was right—that the methods he was using to deal with problems and the way he ran his office were impossible for me or any other honest, devoted Communist to tolerate.

That I think was his weak point. He wanted to be a good Communist, and he believed himself to be one. At the time, although I was young and still not too experienced, I too believed that I was a good Communist. I told Dybala that although I did not consider myself the best Communist, I wanted to be one of the best. I believed in every step, every action, every word of the party. I was prepared to give my life if necessary for Communism. I had given up my job at the university. I had studied zealously at intelligence school. I was earning reasonably good money now, but it was only a couple of hundred *zlotys* more than the average university graduate could expect, and I could make that much easily on my own, without being in this business. So I did not have much to lose in a material way by leaving the intelligence service. I could go the next day if necessary. Nevertheless, I wanted to stay, and I wanted to be a crystal-clear-thinking Communist. I believed Communism to be the best idea in the world, something that not only I but everybody else should work to achieve. But I was not going to be kicked around by any party bureaucrat.

I was saying only what I felt. Later, of course, I was to lose this faith, but at the time I was most devout. In the end it was, I think, an enlightening discussion for both of us, although I was not sure that night what I had really accomplished. He tried to break me mentally, but he didn't succeed.

A couple of weeks later, we had a meeting of our Branch

4 Communist party unit. There were, at this time, only a few of us newcomers stationed with Branch 4 at headquarters. Most of the staffers were highly experienced officers. Theoretically I had no chance whatever of being elected to the leadership of this party unit. There were many candidates, all veterans of the secret service.

Imagine my surprise, and everyone else's, when Colonel Dybala got up and said: "Well, I have a candidate, and I know that he is going to be the best candidate. His name is Janusz K, and I propose him for first secretary of our party unit."

The vote was secret. A few minutes later, I was the most astounded person in the world—I had actually been elected first secretary of the Communist party in this branch of the Polish Intelligence Service.

From this point my career in the secret service skyrocketed. It finally dawned on me that Dybala did consider me the most capable officer in his department. And there is little doubt in my mind that this was because I had been so persuasive and unyielding in my discussion with him. Everybody else was terribly fearful of Dybala—I had probably been the first person in a long time, or ever, to argue with him about firmly held beliefs.

Professionally as well as politically, my experiences in Branch 4 were most interesting. My immediate supervisor, K, was a senior intelligence officer in charge of the British desk. In the future K would become well known as an extremely clever Polish Press Agency "correspondent" in London, Paris and several other foreign cities. He later disappeared for a period, then turned up as the second secretary of the Polish embassy in Washington, D.C. He was a very intelligent man, but I never felt comfortable with him. He impressed me as being more a bureaucrat than an ideologue, a typical organization man who worked hard for the Communist system but who was extremely opportunistic.

An ex-employee of the Communist party organization in Lodz, K had been transferred to the UB in Warsaw and placed in charge of the British desk because he had had past connections with Witold Sienkiewicz. But K was a very insecure man who tried to make up for his sense of insecurity by manifesting an exaggerated sense of importance. He was so worried about his career and future that he made life difficult for everyone around him. I had trouble with K, but because I was being protected by Dybala, I was in a relatively good position. Especially after I became first secretary of the Branch 4 Communist party unit, K could cause me little hardship. Even though K did not really hurt me, as my first supervisor he gave me something less than an inspiring image of the intelligence service and my future in it. Finally, sometime in November or December of 1954, he was transferred to the Polish Press Agency and sent abroad as an agent posing as a foreign correspondent. He and his wife were later divorced, and she married another Polish intelligence officer who had been stationed in London at the same time as K.

The names *siodemka* and *jedynka* were used among operatives of the Polish Intelligence Service to refer to the service or branches of it; never was a full name used. It was rather like agents of the Central Intelligence Agency referring to their organization as "The Company."

Let me describe the organization and functioning of Department 1.

Department 1 was divided into twelve branches. In most cases branch chiefs were senior officers with the rank of lieutenant colonel or colonel. After any kind of trouble—for example, after someone of importance in the government defected to the West—the Polish Intelligence Service was reorganized. Some responsibilites were transferred from one branch to another, numbers of the branches and departments were changed, and so on. While I was in Department 1 there were five or six reorganizations. Thus the numbers of the various branches and departments are less important than the work that the units, whatever their changing numbers, carry out. So let me operate with the numbers that obtained when I was in Department 1, but do not pay too much attention to them.

In every intelligence service activity is divided, to a greater or lesser degree, into two parts. One is so called legal activity. An ambassador's residence in a foreign country, the embassy chancellery, or any other kind of diplomatic installation abroad is run by persons who are sent abroad as diplomats, or as representatives of various international organizations. Intelligence agents and their contacts in such positions, as well as their efforts to recruit spies, are "legal." That is, intelligence activities are being carried out from the open cover, so to speak, of the role of diplomat or some other official. Governments of all nations accept and participate in this practice on a more or less *quid pro quo* basis. Only if a diplomatic spy goes too far, and is caught in *delito flagrante,* is he expelled as a *persona non grata.*

In Poland's case, the legal intelligence ring in a foreign country is always focused around the Polish embassy, the commercial office, or the consulate. Each country has a resident agent, and probably one or two resident deputies. Intelligence and staff officers are also posted in the country under the cover of being Polish diplomats. The "diplomats" make contact with the resident agents, recruit other agents, and deliver money, instructions and materials to the residents.

This type of activity is becoming less and less useful today. With modern means of surveillance, it is too easy for diplomats to be followed and caught with their contacts. Foreign ministries of host countries are sometimes not privy to their governments' most valuable information. Thus, more important is the "illegal" spy web. Our legal resident agent was often involved in the setting up of a new or expanded illegal operation in a foreign country, but employees of the embassy were absolutely excluded from any kind of permanent contact. Illegal agents are usually citizens of the foreign countries involved.

Branch 1 of Department 1 masterminded Poland's worldwide illegal spy network. This branch, with its web of informers, ran their show without the involvement of anyone from Polish embassies or other Polish installations abroad.

If there is a problem in a legal operation, the employee or diplomat involved is simply kicked out of the country—sometimes very quietly, sometimes not so quietly. Because of the doctrine of diplomatic immunity, you cannot arrest a diplomat even for espionage. You can create a scandal and order him to leave, but he can be back in Warsaw or Moscow or Washington in forty-eight hours, free to take up another assignment.

By contrast, in an illegal business, if you are caught you are finished. An illegal agent in an illegal net has absolutely no chance of survival when discovered by the counterintelligence service of the country in which he is operating. He can be arrested at any time, and if he is, nobody is going to help him. He can expect only a statement from the government for which he was spying claiming that it has no connection with him or the case. And he then goes to prison for five, ten, twenty years, or life. In some countries, you can expect the death sentence.

Yet it is this illegal net that harvests the best intelligence. Illegal spies are in a position to discover and tap secrets that are beyond the reach of diplomats or other official envoys and their contacts. Illegal espionage is also the most demanding. And because its dangers are greater, so are its rewards. In the Polish UB, for example, we were paid double for illegal missions. Moreover, every day of such service was counted double, as far as benefits, advancement and retirement were concerned. An illegal agent of thirty-four might have twenty years of service on his record, even though he only started at twenty-four. All of this was monetary reward for risking the danger of being caught by the other side and jailed or shot.

If war broke out tomorrow and there should no longer be a Polish embassy in, for example, France, there would still be an illegal net of Polish agents in France maintaining contact with intelligence headquarters in Warsaw. They and their fellow spies elsewhere would not need the Polish embassy in Paris, Washington, London, Stockholm or anywhere else.

Naturally, therefore, the operations of Branch 1 of Department 1 were of special importance to Poland's Communist regime. Those intelligence staff members with the highest qualifications—the best education, the best knowledge of foreign languages, the broadest experience—were working in Branch 1. They even received a special supplement over and above their regular salaries.

This branch was run principally by three groups: one composed of experts on the United States, another of experts on France, and the third made up of specialists on West Germany. There was a fourth influential group that was expert on Scandinavian affairs, and another important group composed of specialists on Great Britain.

Italy was likewise very important. But in talking about the Italian section of the Branch, I should really say the Vatican section, since ninety-nine percent of its work dealt not with Italy but with the Vatican. The situations in the Vatican and the Roman Catholic church—and the relationship between Poland and the Catholic church—are a focus of major interest in the operations of the Polish Intelligence Service.

Branch 1 could not have existed without its supporting arm, which was designated as 1-A. For instance, we had a group in Branch 1-A dealing only with the problem of legalization in a foreign country. It is extremely difficult to plant a foreign agent in a country without a tremendous amount of knowledge. You have to know everything necessary for the construction of a fictitious person—you have to know where your agent is to have been "born," and everything that this person has done since his birth. You have to know how to register the birth of a child in that country, how to get a birth certificate, what kind of papers and diplomas are required, and, in the case of the United States, how to apply for and obtain a Social Security number, a driver's license, credit cards. The smallest detail cannot be overlooked. The official construction of an individual's life must be perfect from A to Z. If the slightest detail should be wrong—a date that doesn't jibe, an address that is fictitious—your agent's cover can easily be discovered by counterintelligence of the foreign country involved.

When I came to the United States and American friends were obtaining all of these papers for me, I—who had once served in Branch 1-A—could have helped them as a consultant. In fact, had I been permitted to do the job on my own, I believe that I could have done it more quickly and better than some of the employees of the United States government.

Branch 1-A was manned by brilliant and efficient people. For example, Wladyslaw Mroz was once assigned to Branch 1-A and was actually prepared and sent abroad from Branch 1-A.

Branch 1-A put special effort into researching and obtaining myriad kinds of documents. We had an employee in Washington who did nothing but collect all of the official and unofficial publications, papers and forms that he could get his hands on. Such material helped us learn how to be accepted in the United States.

In this branch we also produced foreign passports. Our production of foreign passports was on a high level, in terms of both quantity and quality. We duplicated West German, French, Canadian, United States and Scandinavian passports, among others.

In Branch 1-A of Department 1 we had experts who could forge any kind of signature, or fabricate any kind of document, to look precisely the way the original looked—at least to the untrained eye. We had to follow the developments in every country regarding the kinds of documents used. There are many countries, such as France, where passports are not issued by a central office. They are issued by the departments (provinces) of France, and a French citizen applying for a passport usually receives it from a local office. Moreover, passport offices in different countries change letters or numbers on passports from time to time. It is extremely important that you know when there is a change of signature or of the number sequence or of any other fixture on a nation's passports. It is even important that you know when there is a change of the clerk who fills out passports in handwriting, as is done in some countries. Often these clerks hold their jobs for a long time, but if one day one retires or becomes sick and a new person is giving out the passport, there is a telltale difference in the handwriting.

Forged printing, which requires special equipment, is not necessary in many countries. In France, for instance, ninety percent of the preparation of a passport is done in handwriting. Although in France the clerk is responsible for preparing and issuing the passport to the applicant, somebody else, such as the mayor or the prefect of police, is going to sign the passport. Therefore you have to be informed as to whether or not this person is still signing the passports. You have to be totally accurate, for if the border guards, who know about such changes, discover that the passport must be a fake because Mr. So-and-So is not signing any longer, that can blow a whole operation.

We preferred that our agents not use fake documents unless absolutely necessary, for relatively simple equipment will expose a false passport. We therefore employed every opportunity to exchange our counterfeited documents for authentic ones. How was this done? Let me give you one example. During the 1956 International Fair in Poznan, the UB had a large group of employees working in tourist hotels.

All foreign visitors to Poland who stay in hotels must leave their passports temporarily at the reception desk, thus making it easy to steal pages from them. The room behind the reception desk was often a makeshift office, where our intelligence staffers quickly removed pages from American, Canadian, French, West German, British, Scandinavian and other passports, and inserted pages produced in Poland.

There is also a process designed for visitors who stay in private homes in Poland; they are required to register with the police within forty-eight hours and leave their passports at the police station for a while—long enough to duplicate them. Thousands of foreigners who have visited Poland at one time or another are walking around with passports that are eighty percent fake.

The numbers of Americans' Social Security cards were also frequently checked—for future use. If a visitor was staying in Poland for a few weeks, Social Security cards and other documents in his wallet were often duplicated and exchanged; prostitutes, illegal entry and other methods were used to obtain visitors' wallets in order to steal driver's licenses, Social Security cards, and other personal documents.

We also had a most ingenious photo lab, which formed an extremely important part of Branch 1-A's operation. Its technicians were constantly devising new methods of code-writing and new types of microfilm. The lab utilized microdots so small that they were invisible to the naked eye when put on, or under, a stamp, or on a picture postcard. Daily, the photo lab received and processed hundreds of picture postcards that arrived from all over the world. The postcards bore innocuous greetings, but under the stamp, or on the front of the picture, in the shadows of a building or in the spires of a church, was hidden a microdot containing photographs of one or more pages of some government's top-secret documents. (The place on the card where the dot was to be put was often arranged before the agent began his mission. He was supplied with several hundred picture postcards and told where on them to hide the microdots.) It was necessary to use a microscope to find the dot, and special equipment to develop it into readable print. This was one of the lab's main duties.

Another was training agents in how to photograph documents and reduce the film to microdots—there is no point in getting a card every week from Paris or London or Washington, D.C., if you cannot read the contents of the document on the microdots.

Still another vital role of Branch 1-A was operation of a special storage area where agents were equipped with every commonplace item that they would need abroad, such as clothes, brushes, briefcases, suitcases. Everything had within it a secret hiding place known only to those administering this section. A special employee traveled abroad perennially for only one reason: to buy and bring back the many different things—from cigarettes to matches to shaving equipment— that the average person would be using in a particular country. Agents going abroad had to look like common Frenchmen, Englishmen or Americans.

We had another special group in Branch 1-A—whose members included T. Szwarc, R. Broz and K. Kraskiewicz— responsible only for training our spies who were to become residents abroad. Such agents, whose identities were deliberately kept hidden from staff officers of Department 1, usually went through one or two years of special schooling before taking up their posts as planted spies in foreign countries.

Language, of course, was crucial. We never picked out a candidate to be sent abroad unless he had a good knowledge of the language of the country where he was going. Even so, his French or English or whatever the language was generally had to be improved, and made more colloquial, by special instructors. The curriculum involved not only language training, but making this person an effective agent. Usually our illegal agents had never before had anything to do with the intelligence service. This was for several reasons. For one thing, professional intelligence operatives of Communist countries generally have no foreign background or connections. As I explained, the selection process is such that any candidate discovered to have relatives or other contacts abroad, or to have lived abroad, is automatically disqualified. This means that few Polish staff officers can speak any language other than Polish without an accent. Even after intensive language training and lengthy residence abroad in a legal intelligence position, such a person will not be able to lose his Polish accent; after ten years in the United States, I still have a thick accent.

Since an illegal agent was often infiltrated into a country as an alleged native of that country, he had to not only be fluent in its language, but speak it without a trace of foreign accent. It was therefore necessary to recruit persons who, because of their particular backgrounds, could speak the language of a foreign country like a native. Perhaps they had grown up there and been brought back to Poland by their parents. It did not matter what their original professions were—clerk, professor, plumber, journalist, etc. The challenge was to make such a person into a qualified spy. Sometimes the illegal spy eventually became even better qualified than certain staff officers.

Whatever the agent had been doing before, he had to forget. He had to take on a new personality, a new life. He had to become, in short, a professional intelligence officer. I knew several persons who were instructors of such agents. The instructors would spend months with a candidate, and the candidate would go through exhaustive testing before it was decided that he could be sent.

Naturally, the officials in charge of Branch 1 were mainly interested in the collecting of secret information. They were not immediately involved in training our spies. That was left to the special training group of Branch 1-A. The point was not only to divide the total effort, but to keep it segmented for security reasons—to have as small a group as possible (the upper echelon only) know anything about the overall intelligence-gathering operation. The supporting group, which prepared the agents and gave them knowledge of the target countries, never knew exactly who had actually been sent abroad, how or where agents were to be stationed, or what their precise duties were. The separation of this aspect of the Polish Intelligence Service into two parts was very important and, I must say, quite prudent.

There was a special radio group in Branch 1-A responsible

for contact with the agents. Usually we did not know the names of our agents or their exact locations; we knew them only by the nicknames, symbols and codes that were used in their radio communications. The members of this radio group traveled abroad—after an agent was given a radio frequency and code with which to contact headquarters, his radio communication was always checked in various ways before he started using it. It was highly important to establish the proper time for installing a transmitter, and the proper location. If there was a Polish diplomatic or other mission in the country involved, the agent often transmitted to the local installation, which relayed the information without having any personal contact with the agent. For instance, in Washington information was relayed from the Polish embassy directly to Warsaw.

Western counterintelligence was especially interested in knowing about the operations of Polish radio communications agents, who were sometimes very active against a specific country or against specific organizations in some countries. When I defected I told Western intelligence everything. A name like Kolodynski, Wozniak, Szumski or Cieslak does not say anything to the uninitiated, but they were responsible for the installation and organization of radio contact with our illegal intelligence agents abroad. Thus, Kolodynski, Wozniak, Szumski and Cieslak knew who the individuals in our illegal net were, knew their approximate locations, and knew how they were to receive their orders and transmit their information—and, in the case of radio, the wave lengths and codes used. It is obvious that the information that those four headquarters officers were obliged to possess would be of great value to a foreign intelligence service interested in picking up their agents.

Let me say a few words about Department 1's Branch 2, whose chief, Slowikowski, was later a member of the Polish delegation to the United Nations. This operation was particularly important from the point of view of the Americans. Branch 2 specialized in intelligence dealing with the United States, Canada, Middle America, and South America. Interestingly, Israel was also included in this branch. This was because Israel was considered an important place from which to move our agents into the United States. We would arrange for illegal agents to emigrate from Poland to Israel, and they would later emigrate to the United States. Partly as a reflection of this utilization of Israel as a way station for the infiltration of agents into America, ninety percent of our diplomatic staff in Israel was Department 1 officers. Our activity in Israel was very intense.

Among the names that figured in Branch 2 were those of Antoni Czajer and Slawek Lipowski, whose activities in Washington nearly provoked a breach of diplomatic relations between the United States and Poland in 1958. As far as I know, these two individuals are still stationed abroad.

Branch 3 of Department 1, whose chief was Tadeusz Cibor, later of the Polish embassy in Washington, was the most important branch from the Polish national point of view. Branch 3 dealt with those Western European areas closest to us—West Germany, West Berlin and Austria. Austria itself was not overly important to us, but we used Austria as a place from which to work against West Germany.

Sometime during 1959 or 1960 the decision was made that Vienna would be the most convenient place in which to work with our agents. We used Vienna for contact with our spies from all over the world. Every day someone was coming from Vienna or going to Vienna to meet our agents. During this same period, Rome was also used for our contacts and meetings. Even Sienkiewicz often visited Rome during this time.

Branch 4 was probably the most important component of the UB's activities from the standpoint of political operations. As I have mentioned, components of Branch 4 were France, Switzerland, Belgium, Holland, Scandinavia and Italy (the Vatican). Great Britain was initially part of Branch 4, but later was transferred to Branch 2. I worked in Branch 4 for two years, and during that time I learned exactly what it was doing, how many agents it had, and other details of its operations.

Let me mention quickly Branch 5—Emigration. To understand the role and significance of Branch 5, you must remember that there are at least twelve million Polish immigrants living in foreign countries. According to our estimates, which were based on the most conservative figures, at least 6,000,000 persons of Polish origin reside in the United States, 700,000 in France, 150,000 in Great Britain. We also have hundreds of thousands of expatriates in West Germany. There are Polish emigrants in every foreign country.

Many of our emigrants left Poland twenty or thirty years ago, or even as far back as fifty or sixty years ago. They are citizens of another country; they have children who probably don't even speak Polish. Yet these emigrants still have families and friends in Poland. In spite of their foreign citizenship and their new lives in another land, they still have deeply rooted ties to Poland. This is extremely valuable for the Polish Intelligence Service.

Our mission in Branch 5 was to recruit and exploit the small percentage of emigrants who were ready to work surreptitiously for their homeland. I am not suggesting that all Polish emigrants abroad are traitors to their adopted countries—they are not. The percentage of Polish emigrants who will work for the Communists is minuscule. Many such emigrants, after all, are self-exiled anti-Communists.

However, the Polish regime and the Polish Intelligence Service succeeded in using many of these expatriates against their wills. When a person has ninety percent of his family in Poland, you can almost always find a way to blackmail him. It takes time and knowledge, but it can be done. We would scan the Polish newspapers published abroad—in Detroit, Chicago, Paris, London—for leads. Such publications are most helpful, even though they sometimes issue warnings to Polish emigrants about the Communist agents among them. The risk of detection for such agents is high.

Branch 5 was the biggest branch of Department 1 in terms of number of employees. Between sixty and seventy persons worked for this branch in Warsaw, and hundreds more were stationed abroad. Staff members and agents of Branch 5 were very busy, for our contacts with Polish emigrants and Polish organizations in other countries were voluminous. Immigrants are sometimes hungry for contacts with the country of their father and mother. When I was an intelligence agent assigned to the Polish Foreign Ministry, I was for four years chief of the department dealing with Polish emigrants, so I know what we were doing.

Initially, Branch 5 concentrated on obtaining as much information as possible about Polish organizations abroad and their activities, if any, against the Communist regime in Warsaw. We also endeavored to provoke dissension and open battles among Polish emigrant organizations. Kidnappings and assassinations were deliberately carried out to provoke one group against another—not because we hoped to win any group to our side, but because we wanted to weaken the total leadership of Polish expatriates. We wanted to destroy them as any sort of cohesive political force.

Later, our objectives changed. Warsaw is no longer concerned with breaking up Polish emigrant groups, because they are no longer considered a potential danger to the Polish government. Today the most important mission of Branch 5 is to use the base created by Polish emigrants in foreign countries for various forms of intelligence activity against those countries.

The Polish emigrant is often in a good position to obtain interesting information for the intelligence-gatherers of his homeland. What differentiates the Polish emigrant from the native-born citizen of a foreign country? The most important distinction perhaps is that the Polish emigrant usually retains some kind of relationship, even if only psychological, with his former country, and that can be a strong motivator. Also important is the emigrant's knowledge of the Polish language. Still another factor is that the emigrant is often not completely accepted by his or her new society.

Although we had persons who specialized in working with Polish emigrants in particular countries, the operations of Branch 5 were based not on a geographical division of the world but on the emigrants' past political colorations. We divided the emigrants into groups according to their membership in different political organizations. After World War II the Polish Intelligence Service worked on the basis of the political structure that had existed in Poland in the years immediately preceding September 1939. Thus we had one section working with former members of the Polish National Party *(Endecja)*, and another concentrating on supporters of *Sanacja*, the group of political parties in power in 1939. Because Poland had had such a plethora of political parties before World War II, this section was later further divided in order to concentrate on smaller areas.

Branch 6 of Department 1 was in charge of industrial and scientific espionage. Colonel Goleniewski was chief of Branch 6 for many years, until he disappeared in 1960 during one of his trips to the West. He was replaced by Josef Bisztyga, who went on to become a deputy foreign minister of the Polish government. More than half of all the agents who worked for this branch were recruited from among Polish emigrants living abroad. Working in a variety of industries in a variety of countries, these native Poles were able to obtain industrial information—how to do something, how to make something—that was extremely valuable to both us and the Russians. This kind of intelligence is relatively easy to gather and brings quick, visible results. It is particularly useful to a country like Poland, which is backward in many industrial and scientific areas. I know several Eastern European inventions that were the result not of scientific research but of pure espionage.

Branch 7 of Department 1 was the counterintelligence arm of the Polish Intelligence Service. Branch 7 had two chiefs when I joined Department 1—Marek Fink and Martiuk. Both held the rank of colonel. Later the branch was headed by Krauze and Alaborski. This branch was responsible for the protection, in the intelligence sense, of Polish installations and personnel abroad. In that capacity, Branch 7 was responsible for the loyal conduct of every individual sent out of Poland on behalf of the government.

Branch 7's operations were called *dziurkacze*, which literally means someone watching someone else through a keyhole. Branch 7 operatives investigated and reported on every member of the Polish Intelligence Service. Branch 7 even created situations in order to test whether individuals were potentially vulnerable to recruitment by the West. Provocations were also used to check agents' overall loyalty to the government. Those working in this branch were a special type. Most of them were hated by their fellow officers in the secret service.

Branch 8 of Department 1 in effect constituted the central file of the Polish Intelligence Service. The chief of Branch 8 was Tuszynski, a colorless, weak bureaucrat with no discernible individual character; he was a complete slave of our Russian advisors. Every person involved in our investigative activity was registered in Branch 8. It was a unit in which the Russian advisors were especially interested, and quite often you could find the Russians checking the files there, especially the dossiers of former agents. It was a highly secret place, and you could never see or register anything in Branch 8 without filling out many special forms. Naturally, everybody from Department 1 was registered in Branch 8.

Actually, being registered in Branch 8 had its advantages. If a person was in its files he was always protected. Any unit of government that became interested in a particular person was obliged to check him first in Branch 8. Of course, when the other government unit checked him, the proper section of the intelligence service was informed at once. We could therefore stop any other governmental departments from harassing our agents.

Branch 9 was a special "research and study" office. Its chief, Wendrowski, was later to become the Polish ambassador to Denmark. The leadership of the government and of the Polish Communist party were usually informed of all important information received by the secret service, but we never delivered them completely raw data. Reports for the leadership had to be prepared in a special way that could cover the source of the information. The task of this research and study bureau was to prepare such reports for the leadership.

Branch 10, whose chief was Feliks Kotowski, was mainly concerned with financial and administrative affairs. I never learned what the total UB budget was, but I can say that whenever we had a need for additional funds—to finance unexpected opportunities for recruitment, for example—we would get the money very quickly. Our budget was really determined by our needs rather than by a paper-work projection. This may be of interest in view of recent discussions in the United States Congress about the CIA budget. The intelligence service of a Communist country does not really have a ceiling on its budget. As for the UB's personnel, at any given time there were 400 to 500 employees in Warsaw headquarters and 1,500 to 1,600 staff officers stationed abroad. Each intelligence-gathering branch of Department 1 was dealing with fifty to sixty agents.

We had a special branch without a number that was concerned with personal problems within the organization and with the personal aspects of recruitment. It would have corresponded to Branch 11.

Branch 12 consisted of the training school of Department 1. This school was developed in the early 1950's and continued until 1962, when it was dissolved. This school should not be confused with the one I initially attended, which was for the intelligence service generally. The Department 1 school was predicated on the premise that a modern intelligence service cannot exist without a means of not only training new personnel but also retraining veteran employees in order to keep their skills up to date. As in every other business today, in espionage there are constantly new developments in technology and methods. You have to train your people continuously; otherwise you will fall behind.

The problem with the school was that it allowed different groups of persons in Department 1 to become connected with one another. A group of twenty-five to forty intelligence officers, gathered together for six months to a year in a training course, could get to know one another not only by faces and names, but by character, background and experience. Often the trainees became friends. The leadership decided that all of this was dangerous. The group system was abolished, and since then training for Department 1 has been carried out on an individual basis. As an added precaution, the training or retraining of illegal agents is usually carried out away from UB headquarters, in safe apartments or houses in and around Warsaw. Agents do not meet anyone except their teachers, and do not even enter UB headquarters. Of course, such individual training is more expensive and time-consuming. But I personally felt that, from the point of view of the service, this was a more rational solution to the problem of training. It is better that agents about to be sent abroad on an illegal basis not know too much about one another.

It was within this organizational matrix that I began my career as a spy. And the experience continued my apprenticeship in hatred. When I had been at the university, studying the economics of capitalist countries, we were told by our professors that in a capitalistic society everyone has a price. I remember a joke told by one of the professors. He said, "In a capitalistic society, when you introduce Mr. Smaltz to Mr. Brown, and vice versa, that is only half the introduction. You are not so much interested in knowing the name of the person as the price tag he represents. If you are told that this is a man of honor, you have to ask the next question: How high is the price of his truthfulness? $10,000? $20,000? Or more?"

It was effective Communist indoctrination, and it was reinforced when I went through intelligence training. Again I was told that you can buy anybody in a capitalist society. Be that as it may, it is worth noting that the comrades in Communist countries are hardly immune to material incentives. Military and intelligence officers in Communist lands, for example, are paid much more than those in other areas of government service. In 1953–54, a good salary in Poland was 2,000 *zlotys* a month. The chief of a department in the Foreign Ministry received 4,000 *zlotys* a month. I, as an apprentice intelligence officer, made 6,000 *zlotys*. Converted to dollars it wasn't much, but in relation to the standard of living in Poland, my salary was very good. Also, we enjoyed many extras. Expense accounts were completely open—I was reimbursed for whatever I spent. While stationed in Stockholm, I received more money from the UB as a spy than from the cashier of the Polish embassy as an embassy attaché.

The Polish Intelligence Service had a reputation for paying pretty well. It was a jest among Western intelligence operatives that an Eastern-bloc agent's home country could be determined by his pay. If he was being paid a niggardly sum, he was working for the Russians, the East Germans, or the Czechs; if he was well paid, he was probably working for the Poles. For example, a Polish secret agent abroad received several hundred dollars for each meeting with his contact with Warsaw, plus bonuses, the latter depending on the value of the agent's information.

In addition to the art of making payoffs, my intelligence school mentors taught me the fine art of blackmail. Why pay if there is no need to pay? If you can find a person's weakness, you can frequently have him or her for nothing.

From the Communist point of view, the first approach should be to probe for ideological weaknesses; the Reds regularly test their own agents in this way. Approach No. 2 is to try to find sexual irregularities that can be used to blackmail. Homosexuality, the classic "crime against nature," is sometimes a possibility, depending on the country in which you are operating. In Great Britain, knowing of someone's homosexuality is not going to be important unless the individual is an officer of the British Foreign Service or intelligence service. Among the general populace in Great Britain, it isn't considered so embarrassing to be a homosexual. However, if the individual is stationed in a country where homosexuality is classified as a crime, he could get into trouble very easily, especially if you help him.

There are other compromising methods that can be used. For instance, persons in the diplomatic or intelligence service, because of the nature of their work, tend to be away from home a great percentage of the time. Often, diplomats' wives have lovers at home, and diplomats have mistresses abroad. And although they suspect each other, they don't want each other to know about their respective affairs.

Even more important, diplomatic or intelligence officers do not want their supervisors to know that their lifestyle is not impeccable. To sin is to be vulnerable to blackmail by another country. If you have been unfaithful to your wife, you are probably less afraid of her than of your supervisor. You live in fear that he is going to find out about it. It is a distinct disadvantage.

Whatever the incentive—cash or blackmail—it usually takes from one to three years, sometimes even longer, before you are ready to try to recruit a person. You have to know nearly everything about him or her before you make a decision that this individual is a candidate. You try to approach the problem from every angle. And after you have all of the information you need, you have to make a decision as to how and when to move.

These things are very important. You may be able to recruit

a person today but be unable to recruit the same person tomorrow, and vice versa. You have to find out when this person is up or down, happy or unhappy, strong or vulnerable.

A case in point is one that I became involved in early in my career. The mission concerned a Western European diplomat, B, who at the time was a functionary of his country's embassy in Warsaw. He had been stationed there for a couple of years, and had met a young woman from a well-to-do Polish family. She was studying medicine at the University of Warsaw. Since the diplomat was under surveillance—all foreign diplomats in Poland are under surveillance—counterintelligence discovered that he was dating this woman. This was enough for our secret service to look into the background of her family. They had been connected with the Polish Nationalist party during the war. Her father, a grocer, had owned several groceries in Poland before and during the war. After the war, the Communist regime took over his private chain, but he became manager of what had been one of his own groceries. His wealth was drastically reduced, but still, in relation to circumstances in Poland after the war, the family was well off. Unsurprisingly, the family was known anti-Communist; however, they did not participate in any political activity.

The intelligence service cultivated informers in the group that the woman's family moved in. One of the informers working for UB was instructed to improve his relationship with the family and especially with the young woman, if possible.

We tried to find out something about her, but couldn't learn anything of particular interest. The twenty-one- or twenty-two-year-old woman, whom I shall call Miss C, was well educated, very pretty, slim and blond. She moved in a circle of attractive and influential friends that included well-known journalists and film and stage actors and actresses. One of her friends was a prominent movie actress in Poland. Another was a noted music critic. It was the social circle in which Miss C was moving that led her to be invited to the foreign-embassy reception where she met B.

B and the young woman were eventually married, and soon afterward B was recalled home. The UB wanted to have her alone for a while in Poland in order to recruit her before she left. Because of Poland's diplomatic relations with her husband's homeland, sooner or later she would have to be permitted to leave, but we managed to impede permission for her departure. She was approached for recruitment, but she rejected the idea. She said that she would not do it for any price. After a couple of months, B's government intervened, and the UB had to let her go. She went to her husband's country, but our intelligence service never stopped working on her.

After two or three years, her husband was assigned to Paris as a member of his government's delegation to the Organization of European Economic Cooperation and Development. We were still working on them. We had a file as big as a table on them, with photocopies of every letter from her to her family, to her friends, to her relatives and from them to her. We didn't miss a single postcard sent to her or by her. Finally, after several years of intercepting her mail, the UB discovered that she had an old flame from high school who was now a Polish sports journalist.

He had learned that she was married to the diplomat and that she and her husband were living in France. The journalist and the woman started writing to each other. The letters were warm and informal. Suddenly, she decided to return to Poland for a visit, and she advised him by letter that she was coming. At the beginning she talked about coming with her husband, but her husband changed his mind and she went to Poland for two weeks alone.

Well, we had to get ready in the span of a couple of days. We had already placed one of our agents close to her sportswriter friend. We had checked the journalist's files and learned that a couple of years earlier we had tried to recruit him but he had refused, so we knew that we were not going to get any cooperation from him. For this reason we had to put someone next to him, even though we didn't like introducing one more person into the picture. Using the nickname Ikar, the agent, Fedowicz, managed to get acquainted with the sportswriter and establish a friendship with him. Fedowicz's family was close to the woman's relatives, and we used him later in another situation involving her family.

I was in charge of the entire operation. As always, there

was voluminous paperwork involved. In the Polish Intelligence Service you cannot recruit, or attempt to recruit, someone as important as the wife of a foreign diplomat without first submitting a twenty- or thirty-page report outlining everything—how you plan to approach the prospect, when, who is responsible, what kind of action is to be taken. It must be approved by the chief of the intelligence service. It was my job to prepare the report on the diplomat's wife. I planned the strategy and oversaw the operation. And my strategy was very simple. Obviously, she was not going to accept our invitation to cooperate without being compromised. So we compromised her.

Prior to the woman's arrival, our agent procured a car and camping equipment, and then told his journalist friend that the equipment for an outing was available. Ikar explained that it had been lent to him. When the young woman arrived in Poland, the sportswriter fell into our trap: he asked our agent for the car and the camping equipment for a quiet outing. Ikar said something like, "Yes, go ahead. But I wouldn't want my friend who loaned it to me to know that I was loaning it to you." He created some complications.

Then our agent said, as a pretended afterthought, "Now that I think about it, I don't want to loan the car to anybody, because my friend will kill me if he comes back and finds out. But I can be your driver."

If Ikar had been alone with the couple, it would have been inconvenient. So we also supplied a good-looking woman for our agent. The two couples went camping together at an isolated lake in an area of Poland known as Mazury. The lake that the foursome chose to camp by was near a small, beautiful town called Augustow.

We had more than ten operatives hidden in the area with cameras, tape recorders and other equipment. The sportswriter and the Polish wife of the diplomat stayed together for a week. Our photographers took pictures of the couple swimming nude in the lake. We even planted microphones in their tent—the two couples slept in separate tents—so that at night, when the journalist and the young wife on holiday were screwing each other, we would capture every word they said.

(Our agent's woman did not let him screw her. First of all,

women like this are not stupid. They are paid for what they do, and they do what you tell them—no more, no less. Our agent could have screwed her only with our permission, and that wasn't part of the arrangement. Ikar—poor bastard—was married.)

After her illicit idyll with her high school sweetheart, the diplomat's wife returned to Warsaw. There were at least two of us watching her at all times. Because of diplomatic considerations, we had to be discreet. But we were not overly concerned about this. We knew her program—her appointments and so on—through her telephone, which we had tapped. One day, when she was going shopping, we brought her in. My then-boss Wartak and I picked her up on Marszalkowska Street.

I got out and approached her, while my driver and my boss remained in the car. I said, "I am from the police, and you are to get in the car." As a citizen of a Communist country, she knew well enough not to resist. She was scared to death at what we might be planning to do with her. I told her not to worry—"We just want to talk with you. It will be a rather friendly chat."

We took her to a safe apartment. We had hundreds of apartments like this in Warsaw—hideaways used only for secret meetings with agents. In spite of my reassurances, she was visibly frightened.

We said nothing at first, of course, about our knowledge of her extracurricular intimacies with her old flame. I went into the next room, and my boss began talking to her, approaching again the subject of recruitment. Wartak was taping the conversation with a small recorder hidden on his person. Not only is this standard procedure in Polish intelligence work in order to gather information; it can also make it easier later if your supervisor says you didn't do a good job. When she refused again, my boss called me. "Stefan, may I have that folder, please?" I was waiting for this moment. The folder contained only hints of what we knew about her dalliance at the lake.

Later, when she was crying and very upset about the whole situation, I was brought into the discussion. We tried to be nice to her.

She said to us: "How could you do this! It wasn't nice, you know, to do something like that."

I told her: "It isn't nice to blame us for it. We didn't tell you to do this. Why blame each other at all? We are offering you a deal. If you want to come to Poland from time to time— do you? Your father has had three heart attacks. You love your father?" We tried to push her while at the same time showing her the potential advantages of the situation.

We had picked her up about 10:30 in the morning, and we worked on her until at least 1 P.M. We knew, better than she, that she had an appointment at 1:30. We couldn't take more of her time just then, because we did not want anyone else to be surprised by her not showing up.

So Wartak said to her, "That's all for now. But don't try to avoid the situation, and don't try to run away from the country, because we're going to stop you if you do. So go, but forget about ever seeing your father and your mother again. Never again." For a relatively young woman, such a threat is terrible.

"You can imagine the situation," I added as a parting thought, "if your husband knew. He is really a very intelligent, noble person, from a good family. He isn't going to accept it. Perhaps he isn't going to harm you physically, but he is going to divorce you for sure. And what are you going to do abroad? Of course, you can survive, but it won't be the same life, especially if you know that you cannot come back again to Poland, even to see your parents, and your parents aren't going to be able to leave the country to see you. It doesn't make sense. You're killing some kind of happiness in your own home. No Poland, no parents, no husband. Why destroy everything?"

Finally, we told her that we did not necessarily want anything tomorrow, or a year from now, or perhaps even five years from now.

She protested: "I don't know anything about your business. I'm not that type of person."

"You're wrong," I replied. "Everybody is that type of person. Let us help you. You're going to like it. I like it. My boss likes it."

We did not bother her again in Poland, and, in spite of our initial threats, we let her leave the country and go back to her diplomat-husband. But after she returned to France, we again tried to talk to her. Again she rejected our overtures. Actually we were reassured by this, because had she agreed too readily, we might have suspected her of being a double agent.

She even declared: "You asked me something like this a couple of years ago. Forget it, because I am not going to say yes—never."

"Okay, we know this," we said, "but are you interested in seeing some of the pictures?" We showed her several of our photographs from the lake.

Those morsels of blackmail she had not seen before; we had deliberately held them in reserve. She burst into tears. It was obvious that she was really frightened of her husband's reaction if he should ever see the photographs. Her husband, she was certain, would throw her out. We did not wish to show the pictures to her husband, we assured her. We wanted to compromise with her. Again she protested that she did not know how she could help us. We told her to please be quiet, that we were going to tell her how she could work.

Finally she succumbed. She promised to work for us. And she did. The last I heard of her, in 1960, she was back in her husband's homeland, still the wife of the diplomat. Whether she is still working for Polish intelligence I cannot know. You would have to ask the UB, KGB or CIA.

A very important technique, which we employed quite often, was to create situations to compromise persons against their will. But we were extremely happy when individuals, of their own volition, put themselves in compromising situations. After exploring such a situation, my boss Wartak and I would often talk to each other about it in these terms: "Look, we're nice people. These bastards put themselves in a dirty situation. We're only using it."

Why did the diplomat's wife come to Poland? She came not only to see her father, but to see her boyfriend. So, okay.

Assignment
in Stockholm

NOT QUITE A YEAR AFTER I STARTED MY CAREER in espionage, I became the first operative from the Polish Intelligence Service to be transferred to the Polish Foreign Ministry as part of a cooperative program. The purpose was to prepare me to be sent to Great Britain. I had been working on the British desk of Branch 4, under Colonel Dybala. In the Foreign Ministry, I was under the leadership of Ambassador Birecki, a former chief of the Polish mission to the United Nations and former Polish ambassador to France.

Birecki was an extremely intelligent and highly qualified Polish Jew. He had emigrated to France as a child, but had returned to Poland in 1945. At the time he couldn't even speak Polish, but in only a couple of years he achieved a masterful command of the language. He was a spellbinding speaker. After the 1967 Arab-Israeli war, his name completely disappeared from the newspapers and all other sources of public information. I am afraid that there are few in the West who know exactly what happened to him.

We did not have too many agents in Great Britain, but we had hundreds and hundreds of other persons—both Poles living in Britain and native Britons—in so-called active operation. They were, in our minds, potential candidates for recruitment as agents. Among those in this category were many politicians, journalists, scientists and lawyers. Many had some kind of connection with Poland—a wife from Poland, a brother-in-law from Poland, a close friend from Poland. Sometimes they also had had sporadic contact with so-called left-wing elements. Thus, even though our friends in active operation were not ready or able to engage in specific intelligence-gathering, they often had friends who would indirectly assist our cause.

We were not interested in outright recruitment of members of the British Communist party, or others involved in "peace movements" or left-wing groups. This is something that the CIA found hard to believe, but we had clear instructions: Never touch anybody who is actively involved in any kind of left-wing "progressive" movement. The reason for this policy says much about the Communists' strategy of subversion. If someone was involved in any kind of activity that was in the interests of our so-called socialist camp, we considered that activity too important to risk compromising the person through any secret cooperation or intelligence contact. When we were involved in particularly serious intelligence operations, we were sometimes told to keep away from local Communists even in our private lives.

Still and all, except during special operations, we were allowed to have friendly relationships with such persons. And this was valuable because of their contacts with other sectors of their society. It is difficult to imagine a Communist in Sweden, Great Britain or France who does not have friends who are not Communists. I remember that I often met very conservative individuals in the homes of Swedish and Norwegian Communists. What was especially interesting to us young Communists sent abroad was the fact that Communists in Sweden or France or Great Britain could have friends of different political persuasions. They had perhaps gone to high school or to the university together. Later their political points of view diverged, but because they had been good friends many years earlier, they remained personal friends. They visited each other often; they discussed issues; and they exchanged political views.

I recall one specific case involving a Communist in Norway who was a member of its parliament. In a public political debate in parliament, he was the worst enemy of one of his friends.

The day before, the two of them had been sitting at the coffee table, having a drink and discussing problems in a peaceful way.

Such is not the case in the "people's democracies." Political differences are a luxury that the dictatorship of the proletariat cannot afford. For the Communists, anyone who is not a friend and collaborator twenty-four hours a day is an enemy.

In any event, we never let our curiosity about such quaint Western practices as personal friendships among political rivals interfere with our seriousness of purpose. We used Communists and other left-wing elements as a means of meeting their friends and making contacts. I made many contacts at cocktail parties in the apartments of local leftists.

As things turned out, I was not sent to Britain. After a period on the British desk of the Polish Foreign Ministry, I was transferred to the Scandinavian desk. It was an extremely important and interesting period of time for our operations in Scandinavia. They were being conducted from a high level, and the business at our desk was rich in both agents and informers. We were engaged in many successful, and unsuccessful, recruitment efforts nearly every week.

I did not stay in the Foreign Ministry for long. In February of 1956, I was sent to Sweden. My cover assignment was press attaché of the Polish embassy in Stockholm. In reality, I was an intelligence officer and assistant to the resident agent of the Polish Intelligence Service in Sweden. In my undercover role, initially I was responsible principally for helping engender Communist political activity within Sweden. Later my assignment was expanded, and I became responsible for the Polish illegal intelligence network in Sweden.

As both assistant to the resident agent of the Polish Intelligence Service in Sweden and purported press attaché of the Polish embassy, I had to fulfill a wide variety of duties. I was really a double employee, because, in order to maintain my cover, I had to perform my regular tasks at the embassy as well as my intelligence duties.

Following my arrival in Stockholm, I was given a three-month period of acclimatization during which my only duty was to become familiar with the city, particularly with places that were going to be used later for contacting our agents. I had to get acquainted with Swedish police and familiarize myself with methods of Swedish surveillance. I had to prepare many havens in town where it would be relatively easy to shake off Swedish surveillance.

Sweden was an important intelligence center for us, and as I leaf through my old Swedish notebooks, many a name and face comes back to me: Lorna, Alan, Dr. F, Dr. E, Mrs. F, Ula, Olof, Sven, Goodwin, Richard, Elaina, Helen, and many, many others. Every one of these names could be a separate story.

Here I come across the name of Dave P, who was trying to convince me not to go back to Poland. Here is N, an officer and resident agent of a Western European intelligence service, who tried to recruit me. Veeda, Axis S, Comrade S from the Russian embassy. Marion, Mrs. T, Anatol, another Russian friend. I see here a couple of really good friends, Ola and Britt. Here is T, one of our former agents. And Anna V. Here I have the license numbers of the cars used by the Swedish secret police. Here I have the exact system of communications we were using to contact Polish intelligence agents in Sweden, in order to keep them informed, to leave them instructions, to arrange pickups.

In discussing our illegal agents in various countries, I am, as I have said, mentioning some names. I do not have to worry about persons who I know have escaped to Poland, where—because of the services that they have performed for the UB—they have very comfortable houses, plenty of money, and a relatively easy life. But there are individuals—in Sweden, for example—who are still involved. I cannot quite understand why the Swedish counterintelligence authorities do not know—or know and do nothing. In any event, I feel conscience-bound to be very careful with the names of many of the latter agents.

At the time of my arrival in Stockholm, Polish intelligence had two resident agents in Sweden. One was a professional staff officer, the other simply an agent. At the beginning I was assistant to the staff officer, who was the chief resident agent. Both of our agents were men, both were married, both were native Poles who had become Swedish citizens, both had jobs and contacts, and both—interesting, perhaps, to the uninitiated—were active in anti-Communist organizations. They were likewise active in various Polish societies in Sweden, had won degrees from the University of Stockholm, and had been in Sweden for years.

Our two agents had been infiltrated into Sweden from Poland in 1949 in circumstances so bizarre that Swedish counterintelligence never suspected they could be spies. They were packed in a pipe inside a Swedish ship.

Many Swedish ships dock in Polish ports to pick up coal. Polish counterintelligence had an agent on one such vessel, a Swedish sailor, who helped plant five stowaways aboard. Three of them were real defectors from Poland: a fisherman, a sailor and a young student. None of the three had been involved in any activities relating to intelligence; they wanted only to flee Polish Communism. We learned of their desire to defect. Unbeknownst to the trio, we decided to help them get out of Poland under a plan by which they would unwittingly provide a cover for our two agents. The Swedish sailor who assisted in the operation was paid by both the escaping Poles and by us, since at the same time he was helping them he was also acting for us. We had no objection to his keeping the extra money from the real defectors.

The head of this operation was none other than Dybala, who was to become deputy director of the Polish Intelligence Service, my friend, and finally a suicide. He arranged to hide the escapees in a pipe in the ship's hold that was a conduit for warm steam. It so happened that our two agents—neither of whom knew that the other was an agent—ended up much deeper in the pipe than the three authentic escapees. Moreover, the trip took longer than it should have, and the five had to remain in the pipe nearly forty-eight hours before the ship docked in Sweden. A chemical reaction from the coal caused a gas to form in the pipes during the voyage. The temperature was higher than it should have been, and all of the stowaways, including our agents, were almost killed. Our staff officer landed in particularly bad shape, and it took him some time to recover.

When I arrived in Sweden, our two resident agents had been working for several years, but had not supplied much information of importance. Upon my arrival they were reactivated. I knew these two agents only by their cover names—Slon for the staff officer, Zenek for the agent. No one else in Department 1 knew their real names either. They were registered by their nicknames in the department's control file, and only the highest officials of the Polish Intelligence Service knew who these men really were. It wasn't until five years after my assignment in Stockholm began that I learned that Slon, our staff officer, was operating in Sweden under the name Janusz D, and that the agent was using the last name Wisniewski.

In the Polish Intelligence Service, cover names are suggested by the officer in charge of an operation. But when the operations officer presents a name to his supervisor, he does not know whether the same name is being used by someone else, so the files are checked. If a name is not good, the operations officer has to find another name. I remember that during one period the nickname Zygmunt was very popular. We had seven Zygmunts: Zygmunt #1, Zygmunt #2, etc. It caused a lot of trouble in the office, since such duplication can have negative effects on secrecy. If you are in charge of Zygmunt #2 and suddenly you get something from Zygmunt #5, whom you are not supposed to know anything about, it is rather embarrassing, to say the least.

As I got settled into Stockholm, Slon and Zenek became increasingly productive. On the surface, they could have been anyone's typical next-door neighbors.

In the beginning, their activity centered mainly on the Polish emigrant community in Sweden. Slon probably had about twenty-five persons supplying him with information. They included not only Swedes, but other Scandinavians, Germans and Belgians residing in Sweden.

One of the Polish emigrants we recruited, S, was publishing a small monthly magazine in Polish. With our assistance the magazine's circulation jumped from 2,000 to 20,000. It began to reach not only a greater number of Polish emigrants in Sweden but also leaders of Polish emigrants all over the world. Little did the magazine's readers know that the Polish UB, through my intelligence operation, was behind this expansion. S was never a member of the Communist party, but was still a devout Communist. No one ever suspected that he was our man.

S was one of the most impressive individuals I have ever met. He was able to work around the clock without sleep, without food. He was always brimming with ideas and was a superb writer, even though he had had no university education.

The name of his magazine was *Nasz Znak*. In Polish this means "our symbol" or "our mark." Our editorial approach at the beginning was as follows: The Communists are very bad. Poland is under Russian-Communist occupation. Who could change the situation? If we could get rid of the Communists and our leader, Mikolajczyk, could take over, everything would be all right.

This provided a starting point of discussion—an ideological infiltration, as it were.

Then we gradually shifted our editorial position: Whatever the situation in Poland now, the Polish people are ninety percent against the system we had in our country before the war. It was worse. It was a fascist system. The problem is, would you like to have the situation you had before in Poland?

Here is where the vast majority of our readers would have to say no.

Nasz Znak used a paperback-size format. It was only one of many immigrant publications, but it had a good reputation. It was not too sophisticated, but at the same time it was interesting. For a period of two years, S and I published this magazine alone—writing and editing it, devising stories based sometimes even on World War II documents. We published documents compromising one Polish exile leader after another. The files and archives of the Gestapo, compiled in Poland during the war, were most useful in destroying the reputations of some of our exiled opposition. I cannot say that I was carrying out this operation completely on my own, however, because I was very well instructed from Warsaw.

Through this magazine, we broke the Polish immigrant movement in the West into a score or more of different groups, all fighting among themselves. Today, the 200,000 Poles around the world who are still members of this movement are justifiably concerned about the movement's future.

Interestingly, we usually had little difficulty recruiting influential left-wing politicians—those not so far left as to be considered a member of the "peace movement." There seems to be a natural affinity among those on the political left. Such persons we classified as "progressives." They tended to be strategically well positioned—as journalists, as members of parliament, as officials in important governmental institutions. These individuals were well known, and, although many of their fellow citizens did not agree with their ideas, they enjoyed respect and a certain prestige.

They were spending half of their time in places and among persons we couldn't see for any price. It was incalculably valuable for us to be able to learn from these leftists certain things that we, as outsiders, would never have known about otherwise. The information usually was not the type that would be classified as secret, but all the same it was the kind of data that we could not find in the newspapers or on radio or television. For example, it is impossible to learn from the public forum which member of parliament is homosexual—especially in a country where homosexual acts are a crime; or which important government official is having a liaison with a woman other than his wife.

Also very important are so-called unconscious informers. These are persons who are not of a mind to work as spies. If you were to suggest intelligence cooperation to them, they might angrily reject the proposition and create a scandal for you. But if you know, for instance, that such an individual gets very excited by a political discussion and likes to have a good drink, a discussion at your home or somebody else's home can be very useful. Without giving any indication that you are a spy, you meet these people from time to time and maintain some kind of friendship with them. You can gather extremely significant information—who thinks this way and that, what kinds of reciprocal hatreds exist among politicians, what is the best way to use one against another.

The calculated exploiting of human antagonisms is an intrinsic part of the spy game. Several years ago, when the Western European intelligence services wanted to recruit me, they sent a person who was quite professional. At the time, I was not interested. During the process of our discussion, I let drop a few words about the unflattering things that his agent-employees in the country where I was stationed were saying about him. (In the espionage profession, operatives on opposing sides in a particular country often know, and interact with, one another.) The emissary blew up in anger. He retorted that I should not listen to such persons because they were too mentally inferior to deserve any attention. He said a few more rather unpleasant words about his people. He was probably right in several cases. But a few months later, when I recruited one of his assistants, a native Pole, I related exactly what his superior had told me: That his assistant was a low-level guy who was good only for doing a dirty job. It was the best argument I could have had to convince this employee that he should work not for his boss, who had denigrated him, but for us—the Western agent came over to our side.

In late 1956, I was placed in charge of our illegal intelligence net in Sweden and ordered to reduce my intelligence-related contact with our embassy headquarters in Stockholm. Even the Polish ambassador no longer knew exactly what I was doing outside of the office, or how I was involved with our espionage net in Scandinavia.

One important dimension of our activities was industrial espionage. During my assignment in Stockholm, my agents and I succeeded in stealing countless confidential documents from Swedish businesses. And although it is a neutral country, it is one of the largest vendors of military strategic equipment, including weapons. Russia and Poland were always interested in Sweden's methods of steel production. No other country produces the high-quality steel that Sweden does.

All of my reports were sent to Warsaw. The material, in the form of either photocopies or coded messages, was sent on microfilm in toothpaste or shaving cream tubes. Without any difficulty you can put one whole page of a report on one small piece of microfilm. And tubes of toothpaste or shaving cream are an ideal vehicle for smuggling the information out of a country. You open the toothpaste tube, push the microfilm into the top part of the paste, cover the film with a layer of toothpaste from another tube, then put the cap back on the original tube. Needless to say, your courier does not use this tube to brush his teeth.

In an illegal espionage operation, communication with headquarters back home presents a special problem. Since we could not use the Polish embassy openly, we had to employ other means. Clandestine radio was utilized on a large scale. Instructions were delivered to us through letters, postcards, microfilm and agents who were sent from Poland to specific places. We also used go-betweens who had clandestine contact with persons in the Polish installations. Such an outsider did not know our agents; he was responsible only for picking up the stuff from the dead drop and delivering it to someone who was with the installation.

We had UB staff officers abroad who were responsible only for seeing to it that the illegally gathered espionage materials from different places were picked up on a specific day at a particular time, and delivered as soon as possible to headquarters in Warsaw. These staff officers were usually emigrants from Poland who had moved to the countries where they were working five, ten, or twenty years earlier.

The illegal net is organized in such a way that the go-betweens have no idea what is being transferred. Even I was not in direct touch with our agents. I knew exactly how they were organized, but I never saw one single Polish agent from *this* illegal net, even though I was running the whole show.

My wife Krystyna—who normally knew nothing of the details of my spying activities—helped me establish and maintain contact with one of our important go-betweens. Krystyna would go once a week to a hairdresser, B, who was a go-between for the transmission of microfilm. At this time, B was using two containers, one of them tubes of the American toothpaste Colgate, the other a Swedish shaving cream called Rakin.

During the first contact with us, B was obliged to exchange a special coded sentence. He was quite shocked when he heard my wife speak this sentence. He answered, nevertheless, and contact was established. They never again uttered a word to each other about anything having to do with intelligence. They acted the roles of hairdresser and client. My wife went to B's shop whenever we were informed that there was something for us. But she also went sometimes when we knew that there was nothing waiting. We were creating the impression that my wife was going there simply because B, whose family was from Poland, could speak Polish and she was his customer.

My wife would buy cosmetics there, and, among her purchases, she would from time to time buy Rakin shaving cream and Colgate toothpaste. The tubes that B handed her contained the microfilm. Yet B never knew Krystyna's real name or who she was. Because of the way the chain was organized, B did not know one single name from our net. One of our agents would leave a tube of toothpaste or shaving cream in a specific place, at a specific time, after an exchange of the appropriate signals, which were organized by me. At the appointed hour, B would pick up the toothpaste or shaving cream. He was obliged to hold the stuff in his shop until the proper day, then relay it to my wife. On even-numbered days of the month, she would ask for Rakin shaving cream; on odd-numbered days, she would buy Colgate toothpaste.

The whole operation was organized so well that we had no problem continuing our contact with the hairdresser B, or with transferring the microfilm in both tubes, even though my wife and I, as members of the Polish embassy, were under strict surveillance by Swedish counterintelligence. As far as I know, they did not even suspect us.

Later, toward the end of my stay in Stockholm, the communications system among our agents in Sweden was improved. We began using radio more frequently. This same system of radio contact among in-country spies for Communist Poland was also established in many other nations. The man responsible for installing these radio networks was my former friend, Stanislaw Szumski, a former radio operator in the Polish embassies in Stockholm and Washington. To the best of my knowledge, Poland's illegal agents in the United States today are operating in exactly the same way.

Radio contact between Sweden and Poland is not a problem because of the relatively short distance between the two countries. Radio contact between the United States and Poland by an agent who is not able to have at his disposal heavy, sophisticated, powerful radio equipment is organized in a different way. The agent stays in radio contact with the Polish embassy in Washington and the Polish consulate in Chicago.

This is not going to work during, for instance, a war between East and West, when Polish installations in the United States would be closed. So the solution for maintaining contact in such an eventuality is a more complicated one. Here Cuba becomes important. Some say that Communist Cuba would not exist in case of a war. That may be true. But there is still Mexico. There are those who believe that whatever the situation between the United States and the Communist camp, Mexico is never going to be under American occupation; and there are persons in Mexico who, even though they are not Communists, do not mind helping the Communists.

Helen the Whore and Other Comic Moments

FOR ALL ITS ARCANE GRIMNESS, THE SPY BUSINESS has its moments of comic relief. There was, for example, the case of Helen the Whore. Helen A was a Polish girl who grew up in Lodz. The police there have two cases full of data on her.

When crazy Swedes would come to Poland for a couple of days or a couple of weeks, they would often consort with prostitutes. Helen was a good-looking freelance whore who had been copulating since she was fourteen or fifteen years old. The fact of the matter was that she simply enjoyed it. Eventually she met and married a Swedish businessman and moved to Stockholm.

But Helen was a born whore, and she remained one after their marriage. There were very few men in town who did not screw her. She wasn't ashamed of screwing these guys, but she did not want her husband to know too many of the details—even though he was so crazy about her that he was willing to overlook to a degree her extracurricular activities. She didn't want to ruin the good business she had going with him—she had been a prostitute, standing every night on the corner in a factory town, and suddenly she had two cars, a nice house, everything she wanted. She dressed better than any other good-looking woman in Stockholm. In order to retain her freedom, she would not have children. She was traveling to Japan and other faraway places with her salesman-husband, who worked for a large electronics company.

Helen didn't like the Swedes; they were too civilized for her. On the other hand, she knew everyone in the Polish community in Stockholm. We discovered that one of our agents, Slon, was screwing Helen. But he had not told us because at the time he was married, and he wasn't permitted to go to bed with anyone except his wife without permission from headquarters—especially a woman such as Helen A, about whose background he knew very little. When we found out, we ordered Slon to lay off—literally. As for myself, I was in a professional relationship with Helen for a couple of years and spent a great deal of time with her, but I didn't screw her.

I must confess that I was involved in the preliminary scheme to recruit Helen, although it wasn't as much my idea as that of others. We waited to make our move until, after having resided in Sweden for two years, she returned to Poland to visit her parents.

One of our agents went to her mother's birthday party with a small Japanese tape recorder. He had been invited as a "friend" of Helen's father, who was secretly privy to our plans to recruit his daughter that night. Our agent was drinking with the family and their friends. Helen was a girl who after a few drinks, if she wanted to be screwed, was ready to do it in the middle of the table. He was kissing her hand when she suddenly discovered the tape recorder hidden under his arm and decided that he must be from the police.

Helen took a bottle of vodka and smashed it over our operative's head. Momentarily stunned, he staggered out of the house bleeding profusely, with Helen shrieking curses at him from the porch. A couple of other agents and I were waiting in a car in front of the house for him. We got him back into the car, and that was the end of the recruiting effort for that day.

We finally decided that Helen would not really be an effective agent because of the probability that she would get drunk and somehow compromise us. When I left Sweden I bequeathed her to my successor—to use or not, as he saw fit. I do not believe that he ever contacted her. I know that Helen A was still in Sweden at least up until 1967.

For the newly arrived spy in a foreign country, the process of orientation can be as trying as that for the rank tourist. I will never forget one incident that occurred on my first assignment in Stockholm. After having been in Sweden for only two or three weeks, I was obliged to visit Stockholm's Museum of Technical Achievements, the *Tekniska Museum,* in a suburb of the capital. I decided that it would look suspicious to the Swedes who were watching me if I went alone, so I took my son, who was then four years old. We visited the museum ostensibly to inspect a coal mine exposition. My real purpose was to check out a drop-off place for material from our agents. At the entrance to the simulated coal mine—a very dark entrance—there was a male mannequin dressed in a coal miner's uniform. We were using one of his pockets for the transfer.

As the bus neared the museum, I rang the bell to get off. The bus stopped, and my son and I approached the rear exit door. But the door did not open, and the bus resumed its journey. Finally, some Swedish passengers rang the bell and approached the exit door; it opened and they got off. My son and I got off with them. Since we were by this time far past our original stop, we caught a bus in the opposite direction. But when we neared our destination again, the same thing happened. I rang the bell, we approached the exit door, it failed to open, and the bus resumed moving.

Swedish passengers continued getting off of the bus with no difficulty. I was baffled and furious, yet too embarrassed to ask the driver or anyone else how to get off the bus. With a trace of the professional spy's paranoia, I thought: Why is the door opening for everyone but me? Only after my son and I had ridden all the way back to Stockholm did I discover what the problem was: To open the bus door, you had to put your foot on a metal plate at the edge of the exit step. Thus educated in the sophistries of Swedish urban transit, I caught still another bus to the museum and carried out my cloak-and-dagger mission—which was far simpler by comparison.

One night I attended a dinner in a Stockholm restaurant with our chief resident agent, two other Polish operatives, and a high official of the Polish Intelligence Service, whom I shall call Z. The five of us had a meal fit for royalty. Z enjoyed the drinks, the excellent French cuisine, the wine. Later on, of course, there was after-dinner coffee and brandy, and more drinks. If Swedish counterintelligence had wanted to arrest us they could not have found a better time, because all of us were completely drunk.

There was a big show going on in a nightclub next door, and Z decided that we simply had to see this show. In the nightclub Z ordered the waiter to bring the biggest bottle of his best French cognac. Our party could hardly have been more conspicuous: we walked behind Z, and behind us was the waiter carrying the big bottle of cognac. Everyone else in the place could tell that we were Eastern Europeans from the way we talked and the way we looked. And we were to become even more conspicuous. When we left the nightclub through a glass-lined lobby, Z did not see the glass door. It hit him on the forehead and knocked him flat.

Somehow we got him to the Hotel Carlton where he was staying, but Z had to finish any good intelligence operation by having an orgy with women, and this time was no exception. By now he did not care any longer about Swedish police or counterintelligence. Finally, after a couple more days of eating and drinking and swapping stories with us, he announced: "I am leaving day after tomorrow. Today is the last drinking day and tomorrow we talk seriously."

We did, and Z went back to his high post in Warsaw.

The Baggy-Britches Brigade

IT MAY BE OF INTEREST TO THE UNINITIATED TO know how the Soviet intelligence apparatus functions in conjunction with those of Poland and other Eastern European satellite states. In dealings with our comrades from the U.S.S.R., I observed that they operate through a combination of power and persuasion—mostly the former.

Before 1954, I did not know much about the Russian "consultants" or "advisors" in Poland. From time to time I had had some indication that we had some Soviet counselors, probably on a top level.

My first very limited contact with the problem occurred at intelligence school, where we encountered some instructors who had Russian accents. It was obvious that they either were from the Soviet Union or had spent a lot of time there. Later, a few weeks after I joined Department 1, I discovered in every corridor a special office where there were several men and a secretary, all of whom were Russians. They didn't even speak Polish. They, I learned, were our advisors.

I could see that my supervisor was called to one of those offices nearly every day. He had to tell the advisor exactly what we were doing. After a couple of months in Department

1, I was telephoned by our Russian advisor one day and told, in Russian, that I should come to his office without my supervisor, and bring the folder for a specific case that I was working on. I reported with my files and was obliged to reply to numerous questions. My command of the Russian language was never perfect, even though we had been taught it in intelligence school, but I responded in Russian as best I could. Interestingly, I got no advice whatsoever from him. I was simply asked to tell exactly what I was doing on the case and what kind of plan I had for the future.

On other occasions, I would be told that we had to drop a particular case. The Soviet advisor would instruct me to send a file to the archives. I was ordered several times to leave a highly confidential, secret folder with the Russians. Sometimes I would get it back the next day, or two days later; sometimes never.

Two weeks after I turned in one interesting case to the Russians, we were told to get off the case. I wondered why. On reflection it became clear to me that the Russians were interested in recruiting this person, and they did not want us involved.

Our documents, gathered and assembled by the Polish UB, were translated into Russian and sent by diplomatic pouch from the Soviet embassy in Warsaw to Moscow. The translation of a file, or of an interesting case, sometimes ran as long as 500 pages.

We were often informed by the Russians about individuals of Polish origin who were working in strategic industries abroad—in which there was a potential for industrial espionage. The Russians would tell us to try to recruit an individual if they were sure that they had no chance of doing so. Such cases usually involved Polish emigrants who had relatives in Poland.

But sometimes, after we had compiled enough information to compromise or blackmail the Polish person in question, we were forced to forgo the operation because the Russians decided, for reasons of their own, that they no longer wanted us to pursue it. A week later or six months later, the Russians would often remove the whole file from our archives, and nobody in the Polish Intelligence Service would ever know what happened to it.

The Russians' influence and power in Department 1 were absolute. We Poles didn't discuss this state of affairs, but we didn't like it. Since there was very little we could do about it, it was better to be quiet.

Twice a month or so, the UB hierarchy, up to and including Witold Sienkiewicz, chief of the Polish Intelligence Service, went hunting with the Russians over a three- or four-day weekend. One of the deputies of the UB was left in the office. In addition to hunting, there was drinking and, above all, long sessions of business talk. They stayed somewhere in the forest in an old, small castle that had been appropriated by the Polish Communist government. It was an extremely opportune occasion for the Russians to deliver their latest instructions in total privacy. This went on from 1945 until October 1956.

In the wake of the popular demonstrations that restored Wladyslaw Gomulka to power, the Russians were kicked out of the Polish Intelligence Service completely. They left their offices without even cleaning out their desks. During a meeting of the Department 1 unit of the Polish Communist party, things got so hot that the Russians were told to leave the building. They promptly did so. Moreover, they were afraid to come back, particularly since one of the department's deputy directors had decided to give all of the Polish staffers arms from our storage supply. (He was later expelled from the service for this, but that was two years after the fact, in 1958.)

But the Russians do not give up easily. Department 1 had a special hotel in Warsaw for our agents and for persons arriving from abroad whom we wanted in a protected place. The hotel was situated at 18 Belwederska Street. In 1958, our operation was suddenly transferred to a different hotel. The building at 18 Belwederska Street was renovated and given to the Russian embassy as an annex. The Russians put a small plate on the building: Commercial Office of the Embassy of the Soviet Union in Poland. All of the same Russian intelligence advisors were back, and headquartered there instead of in our office.

After the upheaval of 1956, the fact that the Russians had resumed their activities at a different address was kept secret, and they were much less blatant about their intervention. In our operations, for example, they now called in no one below the level of desk chief. Nonetheless, when our people were summoned, they still had to respond with as much alacrity as before 1956. Only now they had to take a car and drive to 18 Belwederska Street.

By 1958 our Russian advisors were no longer afraid for their lives. Business was going on essentially as it had been before 1956. They continued to tap our information; they continued to give us directives when they so desired. The situation made a mockery of what Wladyslaw Gomulka had said to the Russians in 1956: "This is the end. We're going to run our own business."

I have been asked many times by various persons, especially representatives of the CIA: Were we Poles working for Russia? I have answered that we were not working for Russia because, on the surface at least, we were managing our own business. But the problem was that the Russians knew everything we were doing. They could always halt our actions and our initiatives when they wanted to.

There was never any joking or kidding when we were talking to the Russian advisors. They were dead serious. I know the Russian people in a social way. I have met them at cocktail parties and receptions in Sweden, France, Norway and all other countries where I have been stationed. In those situations the Russians were sometimes able to kid; you could have fun with them. But at headquarters the Russians were unbendingly serious. I was always nervous when I was called to their office, because I could never be myself. For example, we Poles generally smoked Western European cigarettes if we had the occasion, but when we were called into the Russian office we were at once invited to smoke a Russian cigarette because the Russians did not smoke any other cigarettes. And it was in good taste to take their cigarette quickly and to show that you enjoyed it. Also, the advisor would get angry because of my poor Russian, and would have to call his secretary. She would translate what the officer of the Polish Intelligence Service was obliged to tell the Russian advisor. It was all very humiliating.

While I was stationed abroad as an officer of the Polish

Intelligence Service, I was well known to the Russians. When a member of the UB arrived in a particular country to take over Polish espionage operations there, he could expect that, within a week or two, the first or second secretary of the local Russian embassy would pay him a visit or issue an invitation to visit the Soviet mission. The Russian contact never said: "Listen, I'm the boss or deputy boss of the Russian intelligence operation here, and I know you're the same in the Polish embassy." He was not that obvious. The Russian would simply give you an indication; for instance, he might address you as "friend" or "neighbor," two code names for the Russian intelligence service. When a Russian offered greetings from "friends" or "neighbors," it meant that he was representing the KGB.

"I hope we're going to have a good relationship," the Russian would say, "that we're going to see each other from time to time, and if you have something interesting you will tell me."

The Polish agent was permitted by the Russians to inform his headquarters about this conversation, but that was only to protect himself with Warsaw. The Polish spy did not have much choice about cooperating with his Soviet counterpart: he knew that if he was not able to establish a good relationship with the Russian, he was going to be replaced very soon. Thus, the Polish agent had to maintain a good relationship both with headquarters in Warsaw and with a specific Russian from the Russian embassy in the capital where he was stationed.

Basically, therefore, the Russians, even if you couldn't see them very much openly, were running the whole show. The Russians knew everything that the Poles, the Czechs, the Hungarians, the East Germans, the Bulgarians and the other Eastern Europeans were doing.

Because we in Department 1 spent a great deal of our time abroad, we always dressed well in Western European style. You could not accuse the Russian advisors of that.

Even abroad, the Russians have an unmistakable style of dress. They are, to put it mildly, very conservative. A typical Russian in the Soviet foreign service, and even in the Soviet intelligence service, will wear baggy slacks, a jacket with absolutely square padded shoulders, and a Russian hat and overcoat. Today almost everyone else is wearing relatively short coats, but not the Russians—with the possible exception of the *Hassidim*, the Russians wear the longest overcoats in the world.

I remember that in Stockholm, in 1956, during the anti-Soviet uprising in Poland, the Russians' odd clothing styles caused us some problems. Young Swedish students were gathered in front of the Polish embassy shouting "Bravo Gomulka!" and "Long live Gomulka!" There were thousands of them. The Russian embassy was two or three blocks away from us on one of Stockholm's narrow streets. The demonstrators then descended on the Soviet mission, throwing bottles of ink at it and trying to destroy it.

The Polish ambassador, Jozek Koszutski, sent me to see what was going on around the Soviet embassy. He was a very good friend of the Soviet Union and was intensely concerned. We could hear windows being broken in our comrades' mission. I was making my way through the narrow streets behind and around the sides of the building when I encountered a man whom I had never seen before but who I was sure was a Russian. His quaint dress betrayed him.

He was a young fellow who had probably just arrived from Moscow and did not realize what was going on. I stopped him on the street and greeted him in Russian. I said, "Listen, don't go there, because there are demonstrations in front of your embassy. If this crowd recognizes you, you are in trouble—you could even be killed. You had better come with me." This man did not know who I was; he could hear that my Russian was broken and he may have supposed that I was a Swedish Communist. White with fear, he started to walk with me. I wanted to let him wait in our building. But when he looked at the plaque on the door, "The Embassy of the Polish People's Republic," he turned back and started running away through the park. That was the last I saw of him. He was more afraid of us than of the Swedish students.

The next day the diplomatic couriers came from Warsaw. These couriers are usually devoted Communists, but without much formal education. They are physically strong, and they can fight. If you should try to take the courier's pouch from him, he would be ready to resist and be killed. The couriers usually do not speak any foreign language, because we are not interested in their having any more contacts than necessary with foreigners.

The couriers generally do not care about being well dressed, so they tend to look like Russians.

We picked up our couriers at the Stockholm airport. They left their diplomatic pouches at the embassy, and two of them went downtown to go shopping, which—as a later scandal would reveal—was too much their wont. On the way back, the two Polish couriers were walking through Humle Garden Park, where the crowd of anti-Soviet Swedish student demonstrators had reassembled. The students decided that these strangely dressed men were Russians, and they started spitting at them. Through the long park, which stretches for approximately one mile, the crowd of several thousand demonstrators swarmed around the two couriers. Streams of spittle continued raining down on the hapless pair.

Peering out the embassy window, we saw that the couriers were in some kind of trouble.

I left the embassy and started sprinting through the streets to help. When I came close, I saw that those poor couriers were drenched in spittle.

"Leave them alone!" I shouted to the students. "They're not Russians; they're Poles."

It was enough. Had the couriers been able to explain their nationality in virtually any foreign language, the incident would have been averted. Unfortunately, they had not been able to do so.

After the 1956 revolt in Hungary, we of the Polish Intelligence Service were not permitted to engage in any kind of cooperation with the Hungarian intelligence service. Any exchange of information between Warsaw and Budapest had to go through Moscow. The same stricture was applied, to an equal or lesser degree, to relationships with the intelligence services of the other Eastern European countries.

Abroad, we knew pretty much who was responsible for intelligence-gathering at, for example, the Hungarian embassy, and the Hungarians could determine rather readily who among us was involved in the business. Yet we were not allowed to talk to each other about our mutual espionage activities. Quite often there were periods when we were ordered to keep away from one another's embassies, and the ambassadors were instructed that even their embassies should eschew a close relationship. Everybody was to act and deal on his own. And who was coordinating all of these instructions? The Russians.

The Russians proceeded on the premise that they were authorized to coordinate the overall Eastern European intelligence-gathering effort. Given our Marxist community of interest, there was perhaps something to be said for at least some coordination. The Russians did not want us spending time on the same operation that the Hungarians or the Czechs were working. And the Russians made it their business to keep very well informed on what everyone in the Eastern European bloc was doing.

I recall cases that we appealed to the Russians, insisting that certain information be told very quickly to, for instance, the Hungarians. The Russians would say: "We know what the Hungarians should know, and it isn't your problem." We were permitted only one channel of direct cooperation with the other Eastern European countries, and that was when an employee of the Polish embassy in any of the other bloc countries was involved in suspicious contact with somebody from the American embassy. Whenever this happened, we were informed by the Hungarians or East Germans or Romanians very quickly— with the Russians' enthusiastic approval. A group of our agents was then sent to the neighboring Communist country to take care of the situation.

This type of activity, incidentally—the attempted recruitment of another country's officials in the capital of a third country—forms an important part of the intelligence business. If you are recruiting a United States State Department official, you do not do it in Washington, or in the capital of your own country. You try to do it in some third-country city, where he is not under the same kind of protection as in the United States, and where your contacts with him would not be as suspicious as in your own capital. In such a third country, despite the presence of United States counterintelligence operatives, he is freer in his movements and therefore more accessible.

By the same token, Americans do not try to recruit Polish agents in Warsaw or in Washington. They realize that by attempting to do so they could compromise their own government. But the CIA is trying to recruit Polish secret service officers in Paris, Prague, Oslo, Stockholm and other third-country cities. And in trying to recruit a Polish intelligence officer or a Polish diplomat in France, for example, the CIA does not even need to use the American flag.

We had persons in our service posing as United States intelligence officers. One was an extremely clever agent, code-named Zybura, who spoke English and French as well as he could speak Polish. He had spent a large part of his life in the United States and France. Pretending to be an American or Frenchman, he was recruiting individuals in Western Europe under the American or French flag. He knew that certain persons, because they were anti-Communist, would never knowingly work for the Communists. So he duped them into working for the East.

For example, sometimes we would have a prospect who was a West German or a Swiss in a very important position, and who needed money. But he was anti-Communist—he would never intentionally work for the Communists for any price. Yet we knew that he was amenable to doing intelligence work for the United States, France or Great Britain. The problem was to recruit him ostensibly under one of these flags. Then when you had sufficient material on him and had paid him enough money, you could tell him that he was working for the Communists. And that by then it was too late for him to stop. One word to his government and he would be in prison as a spy.

Of course, you usually did not need to say anything like this to such an agent, for he wants to believe that he is working for the Americans. Even if he senses that something is wrong, that these "Americans" are not Americans, he himself knows that it is too late. Better not to ask any questions now. Better to go on playing the game. Thus there is no reason to tell him, for the outright blackmail of an agent—especially one who is actively working and producing—is something to avoid wherever possible.

The Russians implanted many of their intelligence theories and practices in us. They believe that the best way to recruit a foreign agent is under another country's flag. If you are a Russian, you don't recruit as a Russian. If you are a Pole, you don't recruit as a Pole.

It is difficult to compare the Polish Intelligence Service with the Soviet secret service. The potential and the money that the Russians have at their disposition, and the contacts that they enjoy, make it impossible to liken theirs to the intelligence operations of a smaller country.

First of all, if the Russians need help, they can call on the services of the satellite peoples and of Communists abroad (whose assistance we were denied). The Russians receive intelligence support from a tremendous number of party members and sympathizers in foreign countries who are not included in active spying operations.

Second, the Russians (and the Americans too) have separate specialists for each activity. If you are an officer of the Hungarian or Polish secret service, when you recruit an agent you usually also have to teach him code writing, the use of equipment, and other espionage skills. The Russians and the Americans may use up to ten men on a single recruit. Spying is expensive, and only large countries have a staff big enough to divide these different duties among different persons.

I personally consider the Russians very dangerous people from the point of view of espionage. I have seen many movies on American television in which the Russians are portrayed as fools. It is absolutely wrong and dangerous to create the impression that the Russians are a bunch of clowns. They have the back-up for their actions, and although they can be fooled, they are not fooled when it is necessary not to be. Russians put in a lot of preparatory effort before undertaking any action. Even if Russian agents working as individuals are not the smartest people, they are good enough to make the preparations. And when the time comes to recruit a candidate, the Russians will send a special person from Moscow. The Russians do not do anything before they are reasonably sure that it is going to work.

Nevertheless, the Russians are not immune from overzealousness—which can be a fatal failing in the intelligence business. In one case in which I was involved, it cost us dearly.

You may or may not recall the arrest in 1958 of an official of the Danish embassy in Bonn, a spy code-named Oliwa, and his subsequent sentence to twelve years in prison. The newspapers accused the Soviet Union of being behind his activities, but this was not so. The officer of the Danish embassy in West Germany was actually working for us, and only indirectly for the Russians. Oliwa was an excellent agent who had been a spy for the Polish secret service for many years.

I know Oliwa's story intimately because he was under the jurisdiction of the Scandinavian desk in Branch 4 when I was assigned there. Only I and a colleague and friend of mine, Czeslaw Drewniak, were dealing with him. We worked with Oliwa first through our commercial counselor in Copenhagen and later, when Oliwa was stationed in Bonn, through our people from the Polish military mission in West Berlin.

The FBI warns United States citizens against becoming too friendly with officials of Communist countries, and in this the FBI is exactly right. Oliwa's recruitment is a classic example. When Oliwa was working in Copenhagen, he became a friend of the commercial counselor of our embassy, Strus. At the time, our commercial counselor had nothing to do with the intelligence service. When our service found out about this contact between the two, we first recruited Strus. We simply told him that he was going to work for us. Since he was already a Polish government employee, he could do little except acquiesce. It took us several months to make him an effective intelligence person. We gave the Danish official the nickname Oliwa. We let some more time pass, in order for the friendship between our counselor and Oliwa to be further solidified. Then, two months before Strus was scheduled to be recalled to Warsaw, we ordered him to ask Oliwa to work for us.

Oliwa, of course, refused. Following our directions, Strus insisted: "Do it only for me."

And finally they found a solution. "All right," Oliwa said. "I'm going to do it, but only for you."

They exchanged briefcases two or three times a week when they lunched together. We simply bought two matching briefcases. Every time they met for lunch, Oliwa would bring one of the briefcases filled with documents and Strus would bring the other briefcase empty. They would leave the briefcases in the checkroom. When they were leaving, Oliwa would take the empty case and our commercial counselor would take the case containing the documents. The arrangement was carried out in some of Copenhagen's finest restaurants for a couple of months without anybody's suspecting anything.

Only when we were sure that we had the material we needed to blackmail Oliwa—photographs and other evidence revealing his relationship with us—was Strus recalled to Warsaw. (Strus later built a highly successful career in the intelligence service, mainly because of his continuing help in the Oliwa case.) During their last meeting, he told Oliwa, "I'm going back to Warsaw, but I hope you don't mind doing this for my successor, who is also my friend." Strus's successor as commercial counselor was not his friend. He was an experienced intelligence officer named Czeslaw Bleja.

Nevertheless, Oliwa agreed, and he kept his word to Strus. It was fantastic what Oliwa was doing for us. Thanks to him we received a briefcase full of top-secret documents from the West every week. We had a special diplomatic courier take Oliwa's material back to Warsaw as soon as possible. In Warsaw, there was a special plane from Moscow waiting for copies of the material. We would pick up the diplomatic pouch at the airport in Warsaw, develop the microfilms and make prints immediately, and deliver copies to the waiting Russian plane.

Because of Oliwa's access to top-secret documents, we were understandably excited when he was transferred to Bonn. The Russians became even more excited. As an officer of the Danish embassy in Bonn, Oliwa had access to important NATO data, mainly foreign trade and commercial documents—information that was extremely important for the Russians. Unfortunately, it was their zeal that brought about Oliwa's arrest and the resulting scandal.

At the time, Poland had only a small commercial mission in West Germany, at Kuhl, without diplomatic status. We had to use the Polish military mission in West Berlin to contact Oliwa in Bonn, which is a relatively small, provincial city and thus not a good place for clandestine meetings. After Oliwa took up his post in Bonn, the Russians forced us to meet him nearly every day. The West Germans, and probably the counterintelligence of other countries, became interested in knowing why our military man from West Berlin was going to Bonn so often without any special mission. And they got our Danish agent.

In 1958 Oliwa was picked up on a street in Bonn, sent back to Denmark, and sentenced to twelve years in prison for espionage. I hope that, since his term would have been completed by now, he is no longer in jail. He was already more than sixty years old when he was arrested. He was paid well, but never really enough for the kind of job that he accomplished for us and, by extension, for the Russians. Not only was his information important in and of itself, but we even used it to recruit other agents. The Danish authorities never knew everything that Oliwa did. Nevertheless there was a big scandal. The West, the Danish court and West German newspapers were absolutely certain that he was a Russian agent. But he was never a Russian agent; he was working for us all the time.

PART THREE

Bullets in
the Streets

WHEN I ARRIVED IN SWEDEN IN FEBRUARY 1956, I was struck by the conflict between my long period of indoctrination and the facts. I was surprised by the high standard of living in this non-Communist country, the lack of unemployment. I was looking for the starving people who I had been told abounded in the West, and I couldn't find them. When I returned to Poland on an assignment several months later, I talked about my impressions to several of my old friends who were long-time Communists, and I remember the reaction of one, Jozef Knapik, a former counselor of Polish missions in Sweden, West Berlin and North Korea.

He gave me a lecture that today strikes me as amusing.

He told me, "Listen, they shouldn't send a young Communist to Sweden, because it isn't a proper country for the first assignment. They should send you, for instance, to Great Britain or France, where you could see the differences in social classes—the wealthy and powerful people, the middle classes, the poor people. Sweden isn't typical. It isn't showing you all the social problems of the capitalists."

I remember a story he told me bearing on the difference in living standards between East and West. Knapik's formal education left something to be desired, but, having been stationed abroad many times, he knew life in his own special way.

I confided to him that before I had left Poland for Sweden,

I had never drunk a good French cognac and that, although it was an expensive drink, I did not like it. "Janusz," he said, "I went through the same experience many years ago. I didn't like brandy; I didn't like the best French cognac. But I have to tell you that now I like French cognac. And you will discover in a couple of years that it is a beautiful drink, a good French cognac."

"The problem with us," he continued, "is that we don't drink good French cognac, we don't smoke good American cigarettes. Such things are extremely expensive in a Communist country. One day we are stationed abroad, and we become used to drinking good French cognac, to smoking good American cigarettes. What happens later to some of us? We are recalled to our country. And suddenly, believe me, you miss French cognac, and good American cigarettes."

I must confess that he was perfectly right, because after Knapik was kicked out of the Polish Foreign Service many years later, he was extremely happy when, on my vacation trips home, I would bring him a bottle of French Rémy Martin cognac, or a pack of good cigarettes. Those were the greatest gifts that you could give the old Communist.

Frankly, I was to become corrupted myself. Before I was sent abroad, I too had not been able to afford the good cigarettes and good French cognac and good Scotch whiskey that I appreciate today.

In spite of the material temptations to which I was exposed abroad and the contradictions between what I had been told about the West and what I saw in Sweden, I remained a devout Communist. I continued to believe that our system, although not perfect, was going to be perfected; that it was only a question of time. If our standard of living was low, it was only because of the capitalists surrounding us and the fact that we had to pay to help our friends in North Korea, East Germany and elsewhere struggle against the imperialists. If there were no capitalists, our system would be perfect. I believed in this; it was not just the influence of propaganda and indoctrination. I really wanted to believe.

Suddenly, in June of 1956, there was Poznan. That is the name of the Polish city that for decades has been the site of a well-known international fair. Sometimes as many as one hundred countries participate.

Even though it was 1956 and the Cold War was still frigid, there were thousands and thousands of foreign visitors in Poznan. The Poznan Fair had become a gallery of competition between East and West, where both sides tried to show off their best and newest products. Whatever its significance for East-West trade, the exhibition was also very much a propaganda spectacular. From the political point of view, it was a very interesting and important confrontation for both East and West.

Because people were coming and going, it was relatively easy to get a visa to Poland at this time. Many journalists from many nations were thus on hand to witness this East-West confrontation. At this stage the Western press had not had much opportunity to visit the nations of the Communist bloc, to present life in the East or the economic achievements of a Communist country. Therefore the West was using Poznan to learn more about the East. The East, for its part, wanted to win a position in the Western market—the Communists wanted dollars and other hard Western currencies.

At the time of the 1956 fair, tension in Poland was increasing. Nikita Khrushchev had just given a speech to the twentieth Congress of the Soviet Communist party in which he had denounced the crimes of Stalin. The speech was still secret, but details had begun leaking out. Those details were shattering. What had long been suspected, but had been kept hidden by the Soviet police state and further obscured by the heroic Russian battle against the Germans in World War II, now stood bared before history—the whole period in Russia during Stalin's rule had been a nightmare of purges, concentration camps and murders.

Closer to home, we Polish Communists were slowly learning, for the first time, that the entire leadership of the Polish Communist party before World War II had been exterminated in Russia. Stalin and the Comintern (the international body which at the time ruled the world Communist movement—under the command of the Russians) had made the decision in 1937 that the Polish Communist party would be liquidated. In

Poland, the Communist party had been legal before the war. Communists were persecuted and sent to jail sometimes, but generally speaking their activities were permitted. It now became public knowledge on the streets of Warsaw that it had not been the Polish capitalistic government, or even Poland's Nazi occupiers, who had been responsible for liquidating our country's prewar Communist party. It had been the Comintern and, more specifically, Stalin personally. After accusing the Polish Communist party of having too many provocateurs in its ranks and of being infiltrated by the Polish counterintelligence service, Stalin and company simply decided to eliminate this existing arm of world Communism.

Suddenly, one day in 1937, the Polish Communist party was declared anathema in the eyes of the international Communist movement. Unsurprisingly, the Polish government, which had been moving increasingly to the right, followed suit. It said, in effect: "If their international body is refusing them the right to exist, we're not going to tolerate them either. If this party is illegal for the Russians, it is just as illegal or more illegal for us." Whereupon you had the interesting situation of the Communist hierarchy's instigating a capitalist government's liquidation of its own party in a capitalist country.

The Polish police started arresting Communists. If two Communists were found together, they were accused of conspiring. In desperation many Polish Communists fled to Russia. Some were killed in their attempts to escape from Poland, but many succeeded in getting across the border. The problem was that a mile or two after they crossed the border, they were arrested by the Russians, because the accusation, emanating from the highest level in the Kremlin, was that the Polish Communist party was at least fifty percent counterintelligence agents for the West.

The primitive local police commander would say, "You are escaping from Poland. Why?"

"Well, because I was a member of the Communist party in Poland and the Communist party there has been made illegal and we are being arrested one after another. We do not have a choice. I am escaping to the big brother, Russia, because it is the only place I can go."

"Aha, you are a member of the Communist party. Come here; we have business to talk about."

And in a few minutes the fellow would be sent to Moscow under detention, and quite often that was the last anyone heard of him.

Polish Communists were condemned to political concentration camps all over Russia. Finally, in the ultimate Machiavellian irony, they were accused of being Western spies, of having been ordered to escape to Russia in order to act as Western agents there.

Nobody ever knew exactly how many were slain. But I am certain that there is not one leader of the Polish Communist party who fled to Russia in the late 1930s who was not murdered. And until 1956, it was a secret.

How could such a monumental crime have occurred? The explanation is a complex one that goes back to the situation in Russia and the cult—and paranoia—of Joseph Stalin. It was not only Polish Communists who were murdered in Russia. During Stalin's great purges of 1930, '31, '32 and '37, thousands upon thousands of Russian Communists were murdered too.

You can find documents today confirming how a completely innocent person told a story long enough to fill several books about how he was working for the West as a foreign agent. They forced these persons to make such false confessions.

Immediately following World War II, leaders of the Communist party in other countries, such as Czechoslovakia, Bulgaria and Hungary, were also forced to confess and then killed. You can find speeches from the political trials in which they confirmed the fictitious accusations against them. A good example was the Slansky trial in Czechoslovakia. But what is not documented is that before the victims confessed their bones were often broken. These persons were beaten every day for two or three years and finally they "confessed." And when one did confess, they arrested all of his friends.

As is now well known, not even the leadership of the Soviet secret police survived; even the liquidators were liquidated. If this was the situation in the Soviet Communist party, you can imagine how it was with the Polish Communist leaders who fled to Russia.

The tension in Poland in 1956, as a result of these revelations, was tremendous. The disappointment and bitterness of the Polish working masses was deep and widespread. Poland's standard of living had been getting steadily worse, partly because an increasing percentage of the country's production was being used to help finance the international Communist movement, through propaganda and other means. Then suddenly there was this big show at Poznan, displaying the supposed abundance of life in the new Poland. The Polish people were fed up with this kind of hypocrisy. And the uprising flared.

It was not organized by the West. It was not organized by the CIA. The Polish people were so tired and frustrated—their salaries were not able to cover even the minimal necessities— that they could not tolerate the situation any longer. For impact, there could hardly have been a more auspicious occasion. There were several thousand visitors from the West in Poznan, and suddenly workers of this Communist country, which was supposed to be doing everything for the masses, were on the streets of the city demonstrating in protest. Thousands of workers abandoned their factories to go out and shout slogans against the government; they wanted bread, more freedom, and to know the truth about events.

What was the reaction of the Polish Communist regime? Unprepared and confused. So out of touch with the people were the country's Red rulers that they could not comprehend what was wrong. Predictably, the first accusation was levied by the then prime minister, Jozef Cyrankiewicz. Branding Poznan an imperialistic provocation, Cyrankiewicz declared: "We're going to cut off the hands of the imperialistic agents and the leaders of this uprising."

Russian troops stationed in Poland and in East Germany moved into Poznan. Shooting broke out between the secret police and protesting workers. The foreigners in Poznan were witnessing and taking photographs of the violence. It was a shock for all concerned—and a humiliation for the government. The next day there were pictures and stories in newspapers throughout the non-Communist world.

In Stockholm, we received no immediate word from Warsaw officialdom about what happened. I remember that the next morning I was on my way to take the subway to my office downtown when suddenly, at the underground station, I saw big newspaper headlines on the kiosks about a revolt in Poland. I began reading incredulously. I could not believe that such a thing could be happening.

I said to myself: "This is impossible. Any kind of revolt in Poland is impossible, because we're trying to do everything for the working class. If we can't do more, it isn't our error—it's the result of the international situation. This must be a provocation. We would never allow something like this to happen!"

What nonsense such a reaction was on my part. I was, of course, anxious to get to the embassy and find out exactly what had happened in my homeland. When I arrived, I found the office in a state of complete disorganization. Some of the embassy staff members were literally in tears. They were all convinced, as I was at that stage, that somebody had organized this revolt in Poland in order to compromise the Communists, not only in Poland but in all of Eastern Europe. It had to be the Americans or the West Germans or other Western provocateurs. Workers in a Communist country could not be protesting on such a scale!

And yet, there were the newspapers before us, laden with pictures of Polish workers in the streets. We could see the demonstrators with their slogans: "Give us bread," "Give us freedom," "Release all of the political prisoners." And we could see bodies of persons killed in the streets.

The Poznan uprising was the first such event in the entire history of the world Communist movement: workers were battling the police and the "people's army" on the streets of a Communist country.

We did not receive our first message from Warsaw on the subject until that afternoon. It accused the West for the events in Poznan—giving names of persons allegedly implicated, the numbers arrested, and purported proof that they had been instigators for the West, influenced by CIA operatives and other persons who had attended the international exhibition posing as journalists or businessmen. All of these accusations were false.

We were instructed to clip each and every one of the pictures of the Poznan demonstrations published in the Swedish newspapers. The same was done in West Germany, France and other countries where the photographs appeared. We were ordered to dispatch an embassy employee immediately to Poland with an envelope containing these pictures. The Warsaw regime then set about trying to identify every person appearing in the newspaper photographs who might have been involved in the Poznan riots. Some of the photographs were quite good. You could identify marchers even beyond the second row. The Polish police arrested individuals on the basis of these cutouts from the Western newspapers, and then used them again during the trials.

By October of 1956, a troubled mood had erupted everywhere in Eastern Europe. When the Khrushchev speech was finally publicly revealed, students in Hungary, Poland and other satellite countries were incensed. There was such tension in the air that revolt was expected any day.

"Kiss
My Ass"

BEING MORE PAPIST THAN THE POPE IN MY OWN
Communist fanaticism, I was at first unmoved by the reports
of Khrushchev's secret speech, and even by the subsequent
events of Poznan. I could not believe that Stalin and Communism in the Soviet Union were responsible for the deaths
of so many human beings.

But during a business trip to Warsaw in the summer of
1956—I was attached to an important radio delegation under
the leadership of Uzdanski—I was told by my friends back
home, "Janusz, unfortunately this is true." They convinced me
that Stalin had indeed cold-bloodedly liquidated the fathers of
some of my closest friends.

I went through mental agony for months. I decided, "I am
never going to be blind again. I am never going to believe any
political leader again, no matter what his party, his nationality
or his name." I convinced myself, after checking and recheck-
ing the evidence, that Stalin's crimes were not merely the work
of one man, but the result of the Communist system.

Such was the beginning of my disenchantment with Communism. After 1956, I did not bow to any kind of party in-
struction, or any kind of party policy, without questioning.
Slowly, almost in spite of myself, my political conscience was
being raised. Still, Stalin's political crimes aside, I continued

132

to believe that the Communist program made some kind of sense and was useful.

People in Poland who had been afraid to say anything, even in their private apartments, suddenly were not afraid.

Even J. Cyrankiewicz, the Polish prime minister who in June had vowed to cut off the hands of the provocateurs of Poznan, suddenly changed his tune. He now said in substance, "Well, we'll investigate this whole affair in Poznan again. We don't have any proof that it was provocation. The workers were bitter and disappointed because their salaries were not satisfactory. They have every right to protest. We were wrong; we made a mistake." It was a 180-degree switch.

Russian soldiers in Poland could no longer go into the cities; they would have been killed on the streets. The staff of the Soviet embassy in Warsaw was terror-stricken; they could not leave their building. And there were political demonstrations twenty-four hours a day. Not "against Communism"—the people were too smart. They knew that if they said, "Out with the Communists!" the Russians would start shooting. But by saying, "We must improve the framework of Communism," they gave the Russians no specific target. Thousands of workers in factories around Warsaw and other cities staged round-the-clock sit-ins. Dissent was also simmering in Hungary, Czechoslovakia, Bulgaria and Rumania.

But I was in Sweden for most of this period, and I did not know exactly what was going on, because the Polish newspapers that we received did not print stories about the situation. The Western European newspapers did, but I did not then know how much of their dispatches to believe. Only later was I to learn the details of what was happening in my homeland.

It was an extremely difficult time for everyone—the old Communists, the young Communists. No one knew any longer what to think.

Suddenly one day in October a sensation occurred. Gomulka was rehabilitated. Cardinal Wyszynski was let out of the monastery where he had been confined for five or six years. Stalinist leaders of the Polish Communist party became very quiet. The members of the central committee of the Polish Communist party were engaged in open battle. Moreover, for the first time

their speeches were published in Polish newspapers. Now it
was not only Western newspapers that were bringing the news,
it was the Communist Polish newspaper. It would quote one
member of the central committee declaring to another, in effect:
"You are responsible for everything that has happened because
for the last ten or twenty years you have been a Russian agent.
You are not a Polish Communist but a Russian agent. So-and-
so was arrested in Russia because you accused him, but he was
innocent. He spent many years in jail. You should go to jail
yourself."

The tension increased. Hundreds and thousands of Poles
amassed in the streets of Warsaw, protesting and waiting. The
building where the central committee was in acrimonious session was surrounded by crowds. Loudspeakers were installed
outside so that, for the first time, citizens of Poland could listen
to a meeting of the central committee of the Polish Communist
party.

Suddenly, Gomulka was brought to the meeting. The central
committee decided that he had been innocent of any wrong-
doing, that it was Soviet pressure that had brought about his
arrest and forced him to spend years in prison. There was no
longer any doubt that Gomulka was going to be a member of
both the central committee and the politburo of the Polish
Communist party. By now the crowd around the building was
shouting: "Gomulka for first secretary!" Gomulka, it must be
remembered, was still an ideological Communist. Probably
seventy-five percent of the people on the streets were not Communists, but they wanted him.

Then there was more news: The whole Russian leadership
was in Warsaw. Khrushchev and the entire politburo of the
Soviet Communist party had landed at Warsaw's military airport. The central committee of the Polish Communist party
drove to the airport. It was an extraordinary scene. They knew
Khrushchev. Khrushchev knew them. They introduced Gomulka to him, and Khrushchev, right in front of everybody,
said: "Never in my life am I going to shake the hand of this
son of a bitch. He was in jail. He should be in jail. What is
he doing here?"

Khrushchev then asked why the Polish leadership was considering reactivating Gomulka's membership in the Communist party. Told that the question was not whether Gomulka should be reactivated as a party member but whether he should be first secretary of the Polish party, Khrushchev retorted—and this is an exact quotation, confirmed by an acquaintance of mine who was present: "I will never let him be even a member of the Communist party."

The whole crowd drove downtown to the Polish central committee headquarters, and there was a joint session with Khrushchev and the other members of the Soviet leadership. The Polish leaders warned the Russians that if they did not allow Gomulka to be elected first secretary, there would be a revolution in Poland. Warsaw was surrounded by the Russian army, but part of the leadership of the Polish army was giving guns to the workers, and the Polish people were determined never to let the Russian army enter Warsaw.

The chief commander of the Polish army was General Konstanty Rokossowski, who had been born in Warsaw of a Polish family but who had been "Russianized." When Rokosowski* was seventeen years old, he had joined the Communist movement and gone to Russia. He took part in the Russian revolution, became a general in the Soviet army, and was jailed by Stalin and nearly sentenced to death. He was one of the very few generals who survived the Stalinist purge. Following Germany's invasion of Russia in 1941, Stalin had Rokossowski brought to the Soviet capital from a concentration camp. The next day Rokossowski was one of the commanders of the Russian army, and he participated in the battles to defend both Moscow and Stalingrad during the German offensive. He was later made a marshal of the Soviet army.

In 1951 the Russians decided to kick out General Zymierski, who was then chief commander of the Polish army. They replaced him with Rokossowski, who was a man more to their liking. And Zymierski completely disappeared from the scene: one day he was commander-in-chief of the Polish army, and

---

*After many years in Russia, he added an "s" to his last name to give it the Russian spelling.

the next day there was no news of him. Such is the surreal world of Communism.

The Polish people considered Rokossowski a traitor to Poland. He spoke Polish with a heavy Russian accent, and he mixed Polish words with Russian words. He reorganized the Polish army totally along Russian lines. Now, during the demonstrations of 1956, the crowds tried to kill him. He escaped by military plane to Moscow. We never saw him again in Warsaw.

The commander of the Polish national guard at the time was General Wladyslaw Komar. A Polish Jew and former boss of the Polish Intelligence Service, General Komar had been jailed in 1951, accused of being a Western agent. Later he had been rehabilitated and made commander of the Polish constabulary. Even after his years in prison, he was still a dedicated Communist. But he was a friend of the nationalist-oriented leaders of the Polish Communist party. Komar announced: "I don't know about the other troops, but my troops are going to defend Warsaw. And my troops are going to shoot the Russians if they try to shoot us."

As the crisis deepened, Khrushchev and the other Russian leaders in Warsaw were told to their faces: "Listen, you are out of your minds if you try to force us to do anything. You came to Warsaw without the permission of the Polish government. It is true that you came with an escort of twenty military planes and that the Russian army is surrounding Warsaw. But even so, we are telling you that you are probably not going to be able to leave Warsaw without our permission. We are not going to let you leave Warsaw if you talk to us the way you have been talking. Today things are different.

"It is our business whether or not Gomulka is going to be first secretary of the Communist party in Poland. You had better listen to him. And you had better listen to us. Open the window; look on the streets. People are just waiting. If we let you go without escort to the airport, you are going to be dead. Do you really understand the situation in Poland, Comrade Khrushchev?"

There sat Khrushchev, Bulganin, all of them. They had all come to Warsaw as arrogant masters, and now they were being held hostage and threatened with death. It must have shocked them beyond belief.

Khrushchev was further told: "You started this process of de-Stalinization. You told us what Stalin did. And now you want to stop this movement? We can only promise you that we don't want to liquidate socialism in Poland. Gomulka is a Communist, and he always will be a Communist. But don't try to force us to do anything. It's too late."

The Russians had no choice but to accept this solution. Hat in hand, Khrushchev had to go to Gomulka and shake his hand and apologize. A couple of hours later Gomulka was first secretary of the Polish Communist party. The same afternoon there were 400,000 people in the biggest square in Warsaw listening to his speech.

It was a fantastic speech. I wouldn't have had any reason to become a CIA double agent if Gomulka had been able to accept his own speech. But he did not talk or act that way after he got into power.

In his address, Gomulka told the Russians that they were no longer going to run the show in Poland, that the Polish nation was going to decide its affairs without the help of strangers. He ordered all political prisoners out of jail and promised that henceforth nobody would be put behind bars in Poland for political convictions.

It was, Gomulka vowed, the end of an old order. We were going to create, still within the framework of socialism, a completely different life for everybody. Workers were underpaid; they would have to be paid better. We would have to forget about helping Communists around the world; our business was here in our country. We would have to forget about making propaganda; the best propaganda is to create democratic freedom in Poland and show the world what kind of people and nation we are.

Gomulka spoke for three or four hours, and every five minutes there was tremendous applause from the people. And for the first time, even such a reactionary as Cardinal Wyszynski, the leader of the Polish Catholic church, found that he could support the Communist leadership in Poland.

Thanks to Gomulka, Poland had the only free election it has

ever had under Communism in January 1957. When the people went out to the polls to vote, nobody forced them to—and they voted for Gomulka. Non-Communists and even many anti-Communists endorsed the Gomulka regime. Cardinal Wyszynski appealed to the people to support Gomulka because, the prelate declared, Poland had no other choice. If the Polish people seemed to be divided in their support of Gomulka, Wyszynski reasoned, the Russians might intervene. And even the church preferred Gomulka to the Russians.

A couple of months after Gomulka took over, he was invited by the Russians to make his first trip to Moscow. He went to Moscow by train, and the train was stopped every few miles by cheering throngs. It took him two or three days to make the trip, so delayed was he by the demonstrations—not only on the part of Poles but also by Russians after his train crossed into Soviet territory. It was a startling outpouring of support.

The applause and the placards that greeted Gomulka did not please the Soviet leadership, because the demonstrators were in effect criticizing the Russians and telling Gomulka, "Don't be afraid of them. We're with you." Because he had come out of prison and gained so much independence for Poland, Gomulka had become a hero in other Communist countries. Yugoslavs were comparing him with Tito; the people in other Eastern European satellites were comparing Gomulka with their own national heroes. Gomulka could have entertained no doubt that he enjoyed widespread popular backing and that, if he chose to assert himself, the Russians would have to take him seriously as a very powerful partner.

Well, his first trip to Moscow was a huge success. Previously the Russians had been buying a wide range of products from Poland but paying us abysmally low prices; conversely, everything that we bought from the Russians was very expensive. We owed them millions of rubles, and, although we needed financial help, Russian assistance had always been so expensive for us that it was better to be without any help at all. But during Gomulka's visit they canceled all of our debts. At the same time they promised to send us flour and other goods, to build factories for nearly nothing, and to give long- and short-term credit.

When he returned from Moscow, Gomulka was welcomed like a national savior. But then the exchange of delegations and state visits became a monthly business. Gomulka was going every second month to Moscow, and Khrushchev or the other Soviet leaders were coming regularly to Poland. A great friendship was activated. Khrushchev did not deliver a speech in which he did not praise Gomulka as a brother, a friend of Russia. After many such visits, both in Moscow and Warsaw, a new procedure was started: three top officials of the Russian leadership would meet Gomulka and his two aides nearly every month at the border for one- or two-day sessions. The attendees never communicated to the public the details of these meetings.

Gradually we Poles could discern that some kind of reversal of our national liberation movement was beginning to take place. This was forbidden, that was forbidden; this was changed, that was changed. In October 1957, exactly one year after our "Spring in October," the revolutionary Polish student weekly magazine *Poprostu* was liquidated. What had it been doing? Nothing more than publishing the same kind of articles that it had published before October 1956—brave articles supporting a liberal program. The magazine had helped bring Gomulka to power.

This was the first major indication that the liberalization movement was being undercut. We suspected that it was the result of Russian pressure, that Gomulka had not made the decision on his own. Again, students and workers launched demonstrations. And it was the same story as before Gomulka. Police intervened, several students were killed on the streets in Warsaw, and the demonstrations were brutally crushed.

Soon there were more and more symptoms of regression. All the while, the Russians praised Gomulka effusively, describing him as an ever-closer friend of Russia. But he started disenchanting the Polish people; popular support for him was waning.

People started to know the real Gomulka. I am afraid he was always more Communist than Pole. He was an opportunist, too. I had friends close to Gomulka. One of them was his personal secretary, and another was a secretary of the politburo—their names were Trepczynski and Namiotkiewicz, respectively. I also had a group of journalist friends who were always somewhere around Gomulka. They were slowly piecing together, from meetings over which he presided and from his other actions, the hard fact that he had become very nasty, very tough. If a top-leval official said something that he disagreed with, he would tell the dissenter to shut up or he would throw him out of the room.

I also knew Mieczyslaw Rakowski, chief editor of the magazine *Polityka*, which is the Polish party's official weekly political journal. Rakowski, in his late thirties, was the youngest member of the Polish Communist party leadership to enjoy Gomulka's confidence.

Although Rakowski was not a party veteran, he was an authentic representative of the proletariat. For many years he had been a simple worker in a metals factory producing trains. Later he had become an officer of the Polish army. More recently, he had earned law and economic degrees from the University of Warsaw and was studying philosophy. He is one of the few persons whose combination of humble upbringing and high intelligence I will never forget.

Mieczyslaw Rakowski was present, in 1964, at the last meeting between Gomulka and Khrushchev. The meeting took place at the time when Khrushchev's son-in-law, Alexei Adzhubei, was visiting West Germany, and rumors had started that Khrushchev was going to visit West Germany. Poland's sensitivity to Germany being what it is, the Polish leadership became very worried about what Khrushchev might do in Bonn. This time, perhaps for the first time, it was the Polish leadership that demanded a meeting between Gomulka and Khrushchev, and the meeting took place as usual at the Polish-Russian border.

The session went on for two or three days. Gomulka and the other Polish leaders told Khrushchev that they were concerned about his planned visit to Bonn, and asked what he was going to do there that might affect Polish interests. There had been many newspaper reports that Khrushchev was trying to find a solution to the Soviet Union's political problems with West Germany, and that at least a part of the solution would be at Poland's expense—Russia would give Polish-occupied territory to West Germany.

Khrushchev got angry. He declared to Gomulka: "I'm telling you, the policy of the socialist camp is run not by you or by anybody else but the Russians. We are responsible; we make the decisions. And that is not only in the Russian interest but in the interest of all of us."

Gomulka replied, "Yes, I can even agree with this. But why no consultation? Why no discussion between us beforehand? Why do we have to ask you for this meeting when you know how important the German problem is for us in Poland? We aren't able to explain anything to our people, because we don't know anything."

Khrushchev did not want to give any explanation. The discussion became more and more heated, and finally Khrushchev exploded.

Two years earlier, Poland had built a factory to produce small planes for use as crop-dusters, air ambulances and the like. We had planned to exchange these planes on the Eastern European common market for goods from neighboring Communist countries.

We had invested a great deal of money and had halted many other investments in our effort to build this plant.

Khrushchev told Gomulka: "You're going to eat those planes, because nobody in any socialist country is going to buy them. If you open your mouth too much to me, I'll teach you a lesson. I'll teach all of you a lesson."

The meeting broke up with little understanding and less comradely friendship. The episode may well have contributed to Khrushchev's soon afterward being removed from the Russian leadership. There were other reasons too, of course: Cuba, his German policy, his dictatorship, his shoe-thumping at the United Nations. He had become too arrogant and dangerous for his own peers. He had been against Stalin and the dictatorship of Stalin, but he was starting to do the same.

Nikita Khrushchev was an unstable, not-too-intelligent peasant who moved first to the left and then to the right. You were never sure what he was going to do. Individuals who had occasion to be in direct contact with Khrushchev say that what

he did in the United Nations with his shoes was nothing compared to what he was capable of doing when he was among
his own people. He was drunk with power. In anger he was
perfectly capable of taking his slacks off and saying, "Kiss my
ass."

On the other hand, the name Khrushchev is never going to
be forgotten in the history of the Communist countries. His
denunciation of Stalin was a bold act of historical magnitude,
and if Brezhnev and Kosygin and the rulers of Red China have
had increasing problems in maintaining Communist totalitarianism, it was Khrushchev who ignited those problems. If we
have somewhat more freedom in Poland today, if we had—at
least briefly—Dubcek in Czechoslovakia, it is the result of a
process started by Khrushchev. I am sure that many Russians
have a warmer feeling for Khrushchev—today anyway—than
they have for Brezhnev or Kosygin.

Gomulka came back to Warsaw from his meeting with
Khrushchev very disappointed, very bitter and very worried.
When Khrushchev was toppled from the leadership of the Soviet party, Gomulka was the first in Eastern Europe to support
the decision.

Nationalism and anti-Semitism are rooted in centuries of
Polish history, and there is not room in this book to trace the
whole trajectory of these two phenomena. But I can tell you
about the wave of anti-Semitism that developed in Poland in
the wake of Gomulka's 1956 return to power—an aspect of
his regime that deserves to be more widely revealed.

Sometime during 1957 it became clear that the new leadership of the Polish Communist party was trying to place the
blame for the events of 1956 on persons of Jewish origin. Two
opposing groups within the Polish Communist party were
involved in the events of 1956: the Natolin group and the
Pulawska group. The Natolin faction was a dogmatic, old-
fashioned clique of Communists who were determined to block
any liberal developments. Their orientation was very much pro-
Stalin and anti-Gomulka.

The Pulawska group included many Jews and those long-
time Communists who supported new ideas. The Pulawska

group had been an important factor in the developments of 1956. Its members were not only interested in changing the situation in Poland; they wanted to revise and improve Communism everywhere. Thus they represented a danger to the entire so-called socialist camp.

In the history of Communist countries and Communist parties, mutual accusations of dogmatism or opportunism are familiar fare. This did not lessen the effects of the recriminations in Poland. After the events of 1956 had settled down, when Gomulka's relationship with the Russians was at a peak, the liberal Pulawska group was accused of revisionism.

Given Poland's inherent anti-Semitism, it was no surprise that the accusations about revisionism being levied against the Pulawska group began to take on an anti-Semitic tone. Moreover, during this period, a group led by the former World War II Polish underground leader General M. Moczar rose to a position of power. An orthodox Communist, Moczar directed his movement at the blue-collar elements of Polish society, telling them that the whole terrible period of 1956 was the work of the Jews who are in the leadership of the Polish Communist party.

Of course, in the beginning this anti-Semitic purge was carried out cautiously. I remember that when I read the first articles on the subject in the Western newspapers in Stockholm, I did not believe them. But by 1962, all of my former Jewish comrades were being visibly pushed away from influence and leadership. By 1964 the purge was well underway.

Poland's political pogrom was openly revealed to the Polish people during the 1967 Israeli-Arab War. For the first time in public, the leaders of a Communist country—Poland—declared anti-Semitism an official policy of the ruling government. It was a dubious first. And Poland's Roman Catholic church offered no protest. Thousands and thousands of Jews left Poland. They were lucky enough to be able to leave—as the world knows, thousands of Soviet Jews cannot leave the Soviet Union today.

Resurrecting
the Dead

IN 1958 I WAS EXPELLED FROM SWEDEN FOR SPYING. Since I enjoyed diplomatic immunity because of my embassy cover position, there was nothing the Swedes could do except order me out of their country.

Returning to Warsaw, I was assigned to Department 1, Branch 1-A, where I carried out intelligence support work from 1958 to 1960. During the two years I spent in Branch 1-A, I was involved in countless cover preparations. I concocted ingenious cover stories, the great majority of which were used by scores of our agents abroad.

I will tell you how we planted one agent. There was a man who had left Poland just before World War II. Let us call him W. He spent nearly twenty-five years abroad. When he was approximately fifty years old, he decided to return to Poland. He had United States citizenship, but had spent most of his life in South America, Central America and Canada. He had always been a bachelor, traveling from place to place in connection with his business—he was a technician—and never staying more than a couple of years in any country.

Although not a millionaire by any means, W had compiled a nest egg of $50,000. Now he wanted to return to his native country. He decided that he had saved enough money to be able to spend the rest of his life there comfortably. He was absolutely right. If he exchanged his money on the black market

144

he could be a millionaire by Polish standards, and could open his own small business. However, having been away from Poland for so long, he wanted to see the situation in his homeland first. So, while on a trip through Europe, he returned to Poland for a visit. He contacted his seventy-year-old mother, his sisters and brothers-in-law and their children.

When counterintelligence received its first message about W, reporting that this man had visited his mother in Poland after so many years abroad, we lost no time in interesting ourselves in his case. The news had reached Warsaw buried in a long list of official reports about entries of foreigners.

I was sent to meet W and casually talk to him. I had to leave everything in the office and go quickly to Gdansk, several hundred miles north of Warsaw, to meet W. I satisfied myself that this gentleman wanted to come back to Poland forever.

We then decided to attempt to recruit him. I was again the emissary. I convinced him that we would assist him in every possible way, not only by facilitating his return to Poland, but also by helping him bring in all of his possessions, including money and other valuables, and by reimbursing him for every expense that he incurred during his move. This would all be done on one condition: that W return to Poland in strict accordance with our plans.

The proposition was accepted.

"I am ready to do it," he told us. "I don't care one way or the other about Communism. I'm returning to my country because I would like to spend the rest of my life here."

I said, "Fine. You don't need to like Communism—that's your business. We're not going to bother you. On the contrary, we're going to help you.

"Listen, go back to Canada," I told him. At the time W was working in Labrador. "And don't come back to Poland without our go-ahead. But right now tell me your whole life story. And when you go back to Labrador, be a nice guy to everybody. A couple of months from now, give up your job. Don't mention to anybody that you have any idea of returning to Poland. I'll give you money and you'll travel. You'll work one month here, two months there, to lose track of your present friends completely. And nobody should know that one day you are returning to Poland. You're going to be here for the rest of your life, Mr. W, so cut off all of your contacts abroad. As far as your friends are concerned, you have just disappeared."

He was smart and did exactly as we told him. We developed a fantastic story based on his life that was so detailed it could have accommodated five imposters posing as W in various parts of the world.

First of all, he supplied us with two Canadian passports—he "lost" one and asked for another—plus a United States passport, a Venezuelan passport and old passports from other Latin American countries. He had a beautiful life story, extremely difficult to check. If somebody had wanted to track the path of his life, it would have been extremely complicated, for he had been in too many countries. And he could speak several languages, but none of them really well, so it was difficult for anyone to tell where he was really from. Moreover, W had an excellent memory. He was able, for example, to give us a detailed description of an apartment house that he had lived in ten years earlier. He had no difficulty in reconstructing names, places and circumstances of five, ten, twenty years before.

The painstaking task of piecing together virtually every day of W's life took six months. His life history, when completely pieced together by us, took up several hundred typewritten pages.

Then he was informed of what we now wanted of him, and he proceeded to follow our instructions. He went to the United States; he left the United States for Canada; he left Canada for Switzerland; he stayed in Switzerland for a while, traveling from there to various countries. Then, when everything was ready, W completely disappeared from the Western world, at least in his original form.

He was replaced by a reasonably good look-alike who duplicated W's mannerisms, had complete knowledge of W's life, and had become acquainted with all of the places where W had been. Our agent just got in W's shoes and continued W's former life. As a result, our imposter was able to evolve virtually any kind of contact he needed in Venezuela or Canada or in any other country where W was well known, including the United States. Our plan was not to use W's past or present contacts or friends, but to develop new ones. Although W was just a normal guy, his story was extremely valuable to the Polish Intelligence Service.

We re-created countless like histories, many of them in collaboration with Canadian citizens. We much preferred to send an imposter abroad with a family. How better to look like typical next-door neighbors? But it is not always possible to put together an ideal situation. Whenever we could, we would make an arrangement with a whole family that wanted to return to Poland. At first their friends in Canada or whatever other country they had been living in would receive letters from the family postmarked from all over Europe, then the letters would slow down, and still later the information would be spread that the family had moved to Australia or to some other faraway place because the man had a new job.

Such fictitious transfers and travels were organized in order to separate these families from their old friends by thousands of miles to decrease chances of the friends' attempting to visit the family. The families used temporary addresses to make it even more complicated for anyone else to follow or find them. But at the same time, it was important to be consistent, in order not to have any breaks in the story that could arouse the suspicions of United States, Canadian or other national authorities, because our agent who had assumed the identity of the head of the family would be obliged in a couple of years to contact his consulate abroad in order to renew his passport. He had to look similar but not necessarily exactly the same. United States passports, which are valid for five years, are extremely good in this respect. Who looks exactly the same today as five years ago?

Whenever possible, the United States passport was not used in the United States, or the Latin American passport in Latin America. We wanted the pseudo-American citizen to operate in Europe, the European citizen in Canada, the false Latin American in the United States. For example, a pseudo-American might operate in any of several Western European countries, just playing the role of the American working abroad. How many thousands of Americans are doing this? If only a couple of them are our agents, who is going to discover this?

Some of our agents were also sent abroad in the guises of persons who had been killed in accidents. This, of course, could only be done if the individual did not have a closely knit family or close friends.

However it is contrived, the creation and infiltration of imposters is a large and important part of the work of the Polish Intelligence Service. These doubles were sometimes more valuable than the best agents recruited on the scene. Naturally, an agent recruited on the spot was exactly what we were looking for when he had access to top-secret documents. But if we did not have people to contact him and work with him, he was of no value to us. This was often the task of the imposter.

When you send such a person abroad, his "background" must be as complete as a finished jigsaw puzzle. Naturally, your imposter must speak the language of the country to which he is going at least as well as the person he is replacing. And if he is forty years old, you have to piece together a story for the forty years that he has lived since he was born, based on facts that can be checked and rechecked, day after day, year after year, his relatives, friends, associates, and contacts. It must be a complete story. Say a close friend of the person whose life is being re-created was killed in a car accident in the United States on July 12, 1930. You—and your imposter—have to know the circumstrances of the accident, whether the victim was a single man or a married man, whether or not he had children, what he was doing at the time, how many relatives survived him, where he was studying or working. Otherwise your imposter might be unmasked by the most innocuous of conversations.

In order to fulfill our task of duplicating human beings by putting imposters in their shoes, we and our Russian advisors gathered a plethora of birth certificates, wedding certificates, death certificates, old passports, etc. You must have a tremendous number of papers and documents in order to create one or two people. In Branch 1-A we were producing thousands upon thousands of fake foreign passports, particularly West German, French and Canadian. The Canadian passport was our favorite—it was easy to make and very useful. For a spy, it is better to be Canadian than American, French or West German. I don't know why, but people pay less attention to Canadians. They don't consider them dangerous. Americans are, well, Americans; as for Germans, there are a lot of people in the world who don't like Germans; and Frenchmen are still another story—there is a great deal of prejudice against them in different parts of this world.

Branch 1-A would supply Branch 1 with a folder containing the story of a person's whole life, confirmed with documents. Branch 1 would then match a folder with a candidate. It would sometimes take one or two years of training to get our candidate to actually begin to think of himself not as Kowalski, but as "James Brown."

When our imposter would finally leave Poland, he would leave surreptitiously so that nobody would know that James Brown had been in Poland at all. The duplicated Brown would go to Paris or London as Mr. Schwartz, a West German tourist with a West German passport. Somewhere in Paris or London, someone would be waiting for our agent, probably someone from the Polish embassy. And he would have a briefcase with him. There would be a meeting, and after a few minutes there would no longer be a Mr. Schwartz. "Mr. Brown" would have become Mr. Smythe, a Canadian. He would leave Paris or London the next day and go to Latin America, but this time in the guise of a Canadian who had gone from Canada to France or Britain as a tourist or on business. From Paris or London he would go on to Latin America.

In Buenos Aires or Rio de Janeiro, as soon as prudent, this "Canadian" would go to a Canadian embassy and say, "I lost my passport" or "My passport has expired—may I get a new one?" And after a few days he would receive a new passport from the Canadian embassy. Our forged Canadian passport, containing its stolen pages, would no longer be used once he had an authentic Canadian passport. And how easy it was to do things like that!

After another waiting period, our agent would move on to Canada, with the help of his authentic Canadian passport. Ultimately, another clandestine meeting would be held, at which he would exchange his Canadian papers for United States documents identifying him as James Brown. He would then enter the United States as an imposter and a spy.

Of course, you could always unmask Mr. Brown, but it would require an extraordinary effort. Even if the FBI or the Canadian counterintelligence service had reason to suspect him, which is unlikely, it would be a difficult job to break apart the carefully pieced together jigsaw puzzle of his life.

What we did not like about the United States was that it is a very bad country from the standpoint of fingerprints. In no other country are so many fingerprints of non-criminals on file. And if you have his fingerprints on file, you can identify a person—or unmask an imposter—quite easily. Therefore, when infiltrating an agent into the United States, it was important to ascertain that our original had never been fingerprinted.

We had specialists who were able to falsify anyone's signature. As I understand it, every signature has at least eleven principal characteristics. No one in the world is able to write his signature exactly the same way twice, so if there is a slight difference, that is good. But the specialist must find and identify the eleven telltale characteristics that must be found in the false signature.

We had a special agent in Washington doing nothing but supplying us with the signatures of various persons. He was a full-time employee of Branch 1-A. His first name was Henryk and he was listed as an attaché of the Polish consulate in Washington. He was picking up parking violation tickets from cars, stealing mail from mailboxes, going to all of the public offices in Washington and buying or stealing every piece of paper bearing a signature that he could get his hands on. Such random signatures were extremely important to us in the preparation of necessary documents.

Before an imposter was deemed ready to be sent abroad, he was exhaustively tested, and sometimes we in Branch 1-A participated in his examination. One wrong answer meant that he had to go through more training. The agent had to be able to stick with his story so well that there could not be the remotest possibility of a miscue.

Branch 1-A carried out a variety of other activities. For example, we supplied Branch 1 with necessary personal effects and technical equipment. We provided coats, shoes, briefcases, suitcases, pencils, pens and everything else that our agents going abroad would need. Our officers setting out for assignments in foreign countries were always properly dressed. We maintained a storage room where you could find suits of different colors and styles in every size, as well as American, French and German hats. We furnished codes, special kinds of paper, Minox cameras. We bought Western European goods and remade them. We outfitted shoes to carry money and coded messages. We had shaving equipment and toiletry items that were really tools of our trade. For example, we designed a hairbrush in which was hidden a small Minox camera.

We also operated highly efficient photo and radio labs. From our building in Warsaw we maintained contact with agents abroad, utilizing our branch's own radio transmitter and receiving equipment.

As you can see, my assignment in Branch 1-A was a highly specialized job. I enjoyed it, but at the same time I did not like being cut off from the outside world. What I was doing was important, yet it was a support task, and I preferred to be in operations.

My problem was, I later discovered, that when I returned from Sweden in 1958 I was under suspicion. It was for this reason that I was assigned to support activity. They suspected me because the West had tried to recruit me. Of course I had refused and had reported everything to Warsaw, but they were suspicious.

I remember a Polish agent whom the French tried to recruit. He refused and reported everything. What happened? He was called back to Warsaw immediately, and kicked out of the intelligence service. Why? Because there always remained a percentage of suspicion. So he refused, the reaction went. Perhaps he was wise and informed us, but how was it really? Did he really refuse? Perhaps he told us the whole story with one exception—that he finally accepted.

Or even if he did not accept—why hadn't the French tried to recruit someone else? Why did they pick him out? They did not approach him because he has a short or long nose. Perhaps they discovered something weak about his character; perhaps they discovered that he is not happy at home, that he had a bad relationship with his wife, or is a drunkard or a homosexual. They had to have something on him before they started talking with him. And if they tried once, they are going to try again. And perhaps another time our agent will not report it. So why take the risk?

It was like this with me. I informed Warsaw that I had been approached, that I was going to have a meeting, and asked for instructions. I received instructions, and I reported everything that happened.

A certain person in Stockholm wanted to convince me that I should never go back to Poland. I said, "Listen, Mr. P"—he was an Israeli Jew originally from Poland and a former member of the Polish Communist party—"you like Israel; it is your country now. Whether you like our system or not is another story. But for me it would be impossible to think of not returning to my country."

"Bullshit," he replied. "I don't care about Israel, about Sweden, about anything. I spent the whole war in Russia. I know what socialism is. Don't tell me what socialism is, because when I left Russia in 1946 I weighed eighty pounds. Don't tell me how good socialism is."

I said, "Okay, but I just can't do it."

He continued: "Sweden, Israel—any country is good for me if I can have peace and quiet. I make a good living, and I'm happy. It's bullshit to talk about any country in itself being better than another."

All of this of course was highly suggestive. He was a very interesting guy.

When we finished the discussion, I said, "We'll have a drink from time to time and see each other, but you're not going to convince me that I should abandon Poland."

"Listen," he implored, "I have a job for you. You can work. I don't have any political reasons for suggesting this. I think what you're doing is stupid."

Then he added: "Janusz, you know the consul general from Poland is a Jew. I know him because he's buying gold from me. And we're friends. He's a smart fellow. I tell you, if I wanted to cook you, I could tell him tomorrow that you're spending time and money in restaurants with girls, and so on. I could create a situation that he would have to report to Warsaw, and you know what would happen in Warsaw? There would be four or five guys. One would get this report and say, 'We have information that so-and-so, an attaché of our embassy in Sweden, is spending time and money in good restaurants in Stockholm with girls. First of all, how come he has so much money that he can spend his time like this?' And another would say, 'So-and-so is a good guy, a good Communist, why shouldn't he? These rumors aren't true. We trust him; we believe he isn't doing things like this, or even if he is, he's okay—we know him.' And they'd talk about you for an hour or two, and they'd come to the conclusion that you're a beautiful guy, that there's no reason to suspect you.

"At the very end of the discussion, though, one of them would say, 'Oh, absolutely, I believe Mr. So-and-so, I trust him. He's a good comrade. But if something should happen to him tomorrow or a year from now—well, we were informed, we discussed it, we trusted him. There will be a report that we discussed this story and we rejected the accusation. If something happens to him, we're going to be responsible for it. So in order to cut off these rumors, what about calling him back to Poland? We don't lose anything; we don't hurt him. Why not call him back—just cut it off? Rumors aren't good.'"

P must have done what he threatened to do—and he was damned correct at the reaction in Warsaw.

Since, coincidentally, I was expelled from Sweden about this time, there was no need for Warsaw to recall me. Nevertheless, when I returned to Poland I could fell the eyes of Witold Sienkiewicz watching me. Although I was not accused of anything, there was a suspicion that I had been involved in too much in Sweden. Slon and Zenek, our agents there, were under complete cover, and suddenly Western European intelligence had tried to recruit me. Why? Even I did not know.

Even though most of Branch 1-A's work consisted of support activities, it did carry out certain intelligence operations inside Poland, and I was involved in several of them.

In one case, a group of foreigners from twenty-five countries, chiefly scientists, visited Poland, and as a Pole who had lived in Sweden, I played the role of a guide in their party. (They of course had no idea what I had really been doing in Sweden.) I was with them for a couple of weeks, traveling, researching and so on. Some of them we recruited by utilizing really dirty tricks, and others we spied on and stole papers from.

We knew that one of the visitors was not a professor of Russian and Polish languages in West Germany, as he purported to be, but a West German staff intelligence officer. We also knew that he carried everything that was worth anything on his person. How to get it? Well, we simply drugged him into unconsciousness for a couple of hours, removed the belt containing his documents, instructions and money, copied everything of importance, and put it back on him.

We used prostitutes to compromise members of the group. These women didn't know that I was a UB officer—they thought I was a foreigner too. Even the group's official hosts, who included the minister of higher education and the deans of the University of Warsaw and the University of Krakow, were not informed of my affiliations. I just joined the crowd and became one of them.

I played my role so well that several of our other agents were reporting about this Polish guy from Sweden who drove a car with foreign plates. It was my car, and I had replaced my Polish plates with my Swedish plates because I was told to do so as part of my cover for this operation.

Believe me, I was in real trouble a couple of months later. By then Polish counterintelligence had received all of their reports from their informers and agents about this foreign group. And they had picked out a very interesting guy—he could speak Swedish, English, Polish and Russian and he drove a car with Swedish plates. Counterintelligence (which was Department 2 of the UB) put me under serious investigation—because of a lack of communication, they had not been informed of my role. Suddenly my mail was censored, and I sensed that I was under surveillance.

It reached the point where a good friend of mine, who

worked in the personnel office of Department 1, came to me one day nearly in tears.

"Janusz," he said, "you're in serious trouble. They're accusing you of being a Swedish spy."

"Who?"

"Department 2. Counterintelligence."

"You must be crazy."

"No, Janusz, I could show you. A folder like this with pictures and reports against you."

At first I could not believe it. But he went on, "Don't say anything to anybody because they'll kill me. I shouldn't say anything like this to you. But I know that you could even be arrested tomorrow, it's so serious."

I ran to Witold Sienkiewicz and demanded: "What's going on? You must be crazy, all of you."

He looked at me and asked, "Why?"

"I've been working for a couple of months with these foreign groups," I said. "We have been concocting dirty stories to use against them. These prostitutes, informers and agents have reported against me because they don't know I'm from UB. And now somebody has fabricated a story against me."

Sienkiewicz started to laugh and said, "Well, it makes sense—you're probably right." He picked up a telephone and said, "I'd like to see the file on Janusz, because I'm afraid that somebody made a terrible mistake." After studying my file, Sienkiewicz informed Department 2 that there was no reason to suspect me as a result of the material they had collected. He explained my infiltration of the foreign group. Shortly afterward my troubles with counterintelligence ceased.

All the same, one day Sienkiewicz called me in and advised me that I was going to be transferred from Department 1 to an undercover assignment in the Foreign Ministry. The transfer may have been, at least in part, a further manifestation of the doubts about me that had developed when I was in Sweden. By that time I was just as glad. I wanted very much to be moved. Life in Department 1 was terrible. Department 1 headquarters was twenty miles from downtown Warsaw and had its own shops, so there was rarely any occasion to go downtown. Of the several hundred persons working in the department, the vast majority were men. None of the few women, including the secretaries and typists, were even good-looking. They didn't want beautiful girls, for they would have been too distracting and even dangerous. In this special kind of job you were cut off from anything resembling a normal life.

Another factor involved in my transfer from Branch 1-A, I have no doubt, was that I was elected secretary of the Communist organization in Department 1. This was quite an honor, but Sienkiewicz understandably was not too happy about it, for I got 286 votes to his 270. He was not particularly interested in being secretary of our party unit, but it was a post to which the director of the department was traditionally elected. It was soon after the election that he announced his decision to transfer me to the Foreign Ministry. I could hardly protest, because as an elected party functionary I had to do my duty—to say nothing of the fact that I was a career intelligence officer. Sienkiewicz at once picked a man to replace me who was much more to his liking. His name was Ryszard Smusz. So much for internal democracy in the Communist party.

The Two Faces of Communism

IN JULY 1960, I WAS TRANSFERRED TO THE CONSU-
lar Department of the Polish Foreign Ministry and, as my initial
cover, made responsible for press affairs in the department
dealing with Poles living abroad. My new job was not unin-
teresting.

At the time, there were a hundred and fifty Polish-language
newspapers and weekly magazines being published outside of
Poland, all of which I was to be interested in. Of that total,
a score or more were daily Polish-language newspapers being
published in the United States. Further, there were a great
number of publications being printed in Poland only for export
to emigrants—books, weekly magazines, monthly magazines.
Propaganda films were also being produced. These books and
movies were not distributed in Poland because people in Poland
would laugh at such caricatures—the publications depict the
country in a way that bears no relationship to reality.

I began traveling abroad every month. I had not had any
occasion to travel since my return from Sweden in 1958, and
thus had not bought any good cigarettes or good cognac.

In France, the authorities permitted us to organize a special
publishing house. We started printing a good-looking weekly
magazine. Millions of francs were involved in the deal. Unfortunately, the man in charge of it, a colonel of the Polish
Intelligence Service, disappeared one day with all the money.

After a period of time, in accordance with the agency's plan, I became chief of the Foreign Ministry's Department of Poles Living Abroad. It was in this position that I first began to taste the fruits of real power in a Communist society—and to me they were both sweet and bitter.

The assignment was a rewarding one in many ways. It paid more money than I had been making while working directly within the Polish Intelligence Service. And the position carried prestige. I participated in high-level meetings. I was invited to cocktail parties at foreign embassies in Warsaw. I gradually became a public figure. The CIA has in my files a book of newspaper clippings that show me appearing at openings of exhibits, welcoming delegations. I was on the radio; I was on television. People were saying, "You're making a tremendous career."

They did not know that I was being pushed forward by the UB because they wanted their intelligence officer to be a public figure with whom the Polish expatriate community would identify. By assuming such an active, public role I was also helping to create the impression that I did not have anything to do with intelligence.

The perquisites of the position only continued to feed my growing intellectual corruption. When I went abroad, the local Polish ambassador came to the airport to welcome me. He was scared of me. For my part, I was a bastard. I had too much power for my own good, and I began using that power to feed my own ego. When I went to Paris or London, I did not have to stay in a hotel because the ambassador gave me his apartment in the chancellery or invited me to stay with him at the embassy residence. At the age of thirty, after so many years in the Communist movement and in Communist intelligence, I was finally discovering socialism's good life.

I had a first-hand look at the people running my country. I could see them not only in their official appearances but in their private lives. I could see their real faces, and I came to despise those faces.

They were not the people I had thought them to be when I joined the party. They were worse than the Catholic priest who had been instrumental in my rejection of the church many years earlier. He had his morality, his rules; I discovered that the Communists had no rules. There was only power, money and the exploitation of the system by a small privileged group.

The Communist system is used by, at most, two percent of the people—those at the top—for their own benefit. They are worse than the worst capitalists of the eighteenth and nineteenth centuries, who, even though they might have been earning large profits, at least had employees whom they had to pay. And today, capitalists pay their employees quite well.

Under Communism, you have to work, but they do not pay you enough for bread. Under Communism, where the factories and everything else theoretically belong to you, you cannot afford your own car, even if you save for fifty years. But if you are a member of the central committee, they give you a car—a Mercedes, not a Polish or Russian car. And you can exchange it every second year for a new one. You have a paid-for maid and a rent-free apartment. You even have a charge account paid for by the government. You have a special department store and a special hospital. They import good French, British and West German shirts for you. You are part of a privileged caste in a country where a ticket to the movie theater is a luxury for most people.

My disillusionment with Communism continued to grow. I became ever more sensitive, ever more eager to listen to new ideas. I began to reflect upon the ideals expressed in many speeches by John F. Kennedy. I thought a lot about Kennedy's humanistic approach to problems, to people, to peace, to co-existence, to justice, to equal rights for blacks. I said to myself: "This is the way it should be. Our Polish leaders don't have a program like this at all. Nor are they going to, because they don't care. What they are saying and what they are doing are two different things."

Gomulka, by then firmly settled in power with Soviet support, was a case in point. He was not a reformer. International Communism was more important to him than Poland. Permit me to recite an incident that offers a measure of the man. Gomulka has a sister in the United States. In 1960, Gomulka was in New York to attend the fifteenth General Assembly of the United Nations. His sister and her family traveled to New

York to see him. When he received them, his sister began by saying, *"Wladziu,* who would imagine that you would be the leader of a Communist country?" Whereupon Gomulka ended the reunion. He had wanted to see his sister. I know this, because his secretary Trepczynski told me. But even his sister could not talk to Gomulka the Communist in such a familiar, anti-Communist way.

How could a man who had spent years in prison under a system once again make himself part and parcel of that system? The explanation lies partly in Gomulka's character and partly in the fanatical mindlessness of Communism—the fact that to the dyed-in-the-red Communist, everything else, even yourself, comes second. Those who say that Poland is not really a Communist country, that its party members are not true Communists, that one cannot tell who is for sure a Communist in Poland are in error.

My experience abroad helped me understand the type of Communist that Gomulka is. He is akin to the old dogmatic, conservative leaders of the Swedish, Norwegian and French Communist parties. Life for them stopped years ago with *laissez-faire* capitalism and its accompanying unemployment and poverty—the capitalistic oppression that forced workers to labor ten or twelve hours a day without proper pay benefits, that permitted sweat shops and child labor. Of course, this type of unreconstructed capitalism exists in very few countries today, at least in the industrialized world. But for these old-guard Communists, all capitalists are still the same.

Such individuals deliberately wear blinders. When Gomulka came to the United States to visit the United Nations, he did not want to see anything outside of the UN building and the Polish mission to the UN.

I was able to witness the growing influence of General Moczar, who at the time was minister of international affairs. Moczar's political cunning is not to be underestimated. I know him well, and had the opportunity to observe him and to listen to him on several different occasions. I remember one day Moczar spoke at an organizational meeting conducted in Department 1. He told us how we were going to clean all of the

Jews out of the Foreign Ministry, how they couldn't be trusted, how we in the intelligence service were going to run the country firmly.

I was one of the few persons present at that meeting who was also present at a meeting Moczar had the next week with the Communist party organization in the Foreign Ministry. Before the Foreign Ministry audience, Moczar was a completely different person. He talked about friendship, about unity, about the need for a family-type relationship among all of us in the Polish government. He denied accusations that the Warsaw regime was anti-Semitic. Our Polish Jewish comrades, he declared, are members of the same family. I remember my friends in the Foreign Ministry, some of them Jewish, marveling over what a tremendous man they thought Moczar was.

While talking to us in Department 1, Moczar had said, "Comrades, nobody is permitted *Rozkraczac sie.*" *Rozkraczac* refers to the way very poor women of many years ago who didn't have any underwear would simply stand and spread their legs to urinate because they didn't have anything under their skirts. He was telling us that our feet and our legs had to be together; that if anybody tried to pull one leg this way or that way, that person was no longer with us. And he who was not with us was against us. Therefore, we had to stand fast, with our legs together.

But in the Foreign Ministry, Moczar talked about the need to be flexible, to take an occasional step back. The reason for Moczar's change of face was transparent enough. He wanted to carry popularity and influence in the Foreign Ministry, and he knew that—the differences between spies and diplomats being what they are—he could not talk to the people there the way he had talked a few days earlier to the intelligence service. He was a real political bastard.

But Moczar's political effectiveness should not be underestimated. Today there are few if any Jews in the Polish Foreign Ministry, and Moczar's followers are sprinkled throughout Polish embassies. Probably half of the people in the Polish Foreign Service today are Moczar's people. Moczar has also put his stamp on the Polish Intelligence Service.

Seeing him in action was but one more nail in the coffin of my ideological dreams.

In Department 1 intelligence, I had functioned on the periphery of life at the top. But in the Foreign Ministry I was meeting with cabinet ministers and other high members of the government, drinking coffee with them. And I became completely convinced that they did not care at all about the workers. The government leaders are pure bastards, I concluded.

I decided to play their game by their rules, but I would try to be the smartest one and the dirtiest. I determined to forget morality. From the moment I took on my high position in the Foreign Ministry and felt the kind of power that I had at my fingertips, I was always well aware that what I was doing was not nice. But I said, "This is the game, unfortunately, and it was not my invention." I went sort of crazy. I continued working hard as a Communist and as an undercover intelligence agent, but I was not the same person.

As its name implies, the quite important *Wydzial do spraw Polonii*, or Department of Poles Living Abroad, is responsible for maintaining contact with the 12,000,000 persons of Polish descent who live outside of Poland. The department's job is mainly "political culture" activity—propaganda. Millions and millions of *zlotys* and dollars are spent on this effort to convince expatriate Poles that their homeland's Communist system is the wave of the future. At the same time, the department is a key link in Poland's chain of espionage.

The department was closely connected with Branch 5 of the Polish Intelligence Service, which is called simply "Emigration." I was in daily contact with the chief of this intelligence branch.

The Department of Poles Living Abroad consisted of an office of approximately twenty staff members. Department members coordinated relationships with various Polish social organizations that are involved with emigrant Poles. There is, for instance, the Polonia Association, a large Warsaw-based organization made up primarily of professors, journalists, Catholics and activists. The Polonia Association presents itself as a non-Communist cultural group and does nothing other than maintain contact with Polish emigrants residing in foreign countries. To do so, the Association utilizes a variety of channels. For example, the Polonia Association supports a youth movement among Polish emigrants. There are also Polish children's schools and Polish publications abroad that are run by local organizations with the help of the Polonia Association and other Warsaw-based groups. These local organizations—and their Warsaw backers—are, if not openly Communist, at least pro-Communist.

There are also several outright Communist organizations that endeavor to maintain contact with Polish emigrants. One is the Union of Former Combatants, headed at this time by the ambitious General Moczar. His organization has a special department for keeping up communications with Polish World War II veterans abroad. Even the Polish government openly gets into the act—every year the regime sponsors a meeting in Poland of delegations of Poles living in the United States, Canada, France, West Germany and Great Britain. The Polish communities of those countries are of special interest to Warsaw.

In short, the Warsaw regime uses every means at its disposal to attract Poles living abroad, in the hope of using them. Even diplomatic niceties do not stand in the way. We had a Polish organization in South Africa, for instance, even though we did not have diplomatic relations with South Africa.

The Polish Foreign Ministry is, of course, very much in favor of this kind of activity. You can imagine, for example, how helpful it is to the Polish embassy in Washington or to the Polish consulate in Chicago to be able to contact the local Polish residents through the Polish ethnic associations. Indeed, it can be said without overstatement that Polish diplomatic missions exist principally to monitor and exploit the local Polish community, for purposes of Communist subversion and espionage.

Who else is interested in watching these people? The Polish Intelligence Service. The intelligence service always wanted to have someone controlling the Department of Poles Living Abroad, and I was that someone.

* * *

A man who has lived far away from Poland for twenty years or more often still feels that there is no other place in this world where he can die happily. In spite of the war, the political situation, Communists, fascists or whatever else may have pushed him out of his native country, he senses that somehow he can get a revenge of sorts against life by dying in his homeland. He is not a homosexual or an alcoholic, but he has a weakness: he must die in his native country. We wanted to use this weakness in Polish expatriates—to recruit them in return for arranging for them to spend their last years in Poland—but to do so we had to have contacts in the Polish community. Even though someone may feel this way, he does not talk about it to everyone. He may confide it to only one or two close friends.

In 1961 we sponsored a congress of Polish emigrants from all over the world. A total of eighty-six countries were represented, including the United States. During the affair, which took place in Warsaw, officials of the Polonia Association and staff members of Poland's foreign propaganda publishing houses circulated among the delegates and reported everything to me.

Just around the corner from the congress, headquartered in the next hotel, was a special group from the Polish Intelligence Service and Polish counterintelligence. They occupied an entire two floors of the hotel. We suspected that some of the Poles from certain foreign countries were CIA agents, so we kept them under special surveillance. The Polish Intelligence Service was also interested, of course, in recruiting possibilities. They wanted to know exactly what was going on at the congress—name by name, hour by hour. They had one person funneling them the information, and I was that person. Depending on my needs at any moment, I had from fifty to a hundred persons working at the congress under me.

Moreover, as chief of the department of the Foreign Ministry dealing with Poles abroad, I was the official host, and so I was introduced to everyone. If the UB wanted to know whether a man spoke good Polish, whether he was intelligent, whether he drank, I was the one who tested him out.

When the UB was interested in a particular visiting Polish

emigrant or a delegation of Polish emigrants from abroad, obviously the chief of intelligence could not go to the airport to welcome them. There had to be someone who could arrange to come into contact with them in a more natural manner. That was the role of the Department of Poles Living Abroad. You went to the airport with flowers, and then there was an official dinner. If the visitors were from the United States, there were representatives from the American embassy on hand as well. If they were not invited, they became anxious.

Similarly, Warsaw's Communist regime also keeps an eye on its lost countrymen through Polish consulates. Their routine paperwork notwithstanding, Poland's consulates abroad spend the vast majority of their time and efforts pursuing information about Polish organizations, Polish emigrants, Polish professors, Polish scientists, Polish workers. Every person of Polish origin living in a consul's area is of great interest to the consulate. And, of course, among the consulate staff members you have intelligence officers. During my tenure as chief of the Department of Poles Living Abroad, the consulate in Chicago, for example, was staffed completely by intelligence personnel, with the exception of one or two clerks dealing with commercial problems.

Nylons,
Anyone?

IN 1960, THE CHIEF OF THE SCIENTIFIC DEPARTMENT of the Polish Intelligence Service, Colonel Goleniewski, failed to return to Poland from one of his foreign trips. Goleniewski traveled abroad quite often, mainly to meet our agents working for Scientific Intelligence. We suspected that Goleniewski had become a traitor, that he had disappeared somewhere in West Germany and was in the hands of the CIA. Goleniewski would surely have been assassinated by his former colleagues in the UB if they could have got their hands on him, but they could not.

This incident occurred at approximately the same time as the assassination of Mroz for treason. The apparent defection of two such important agents of the UB within such a short span of time was something that had never happened before, and it threw the service into an uproar. In any bureaucracy, success has no enemies, but failure has no friends; the UB is no exception. There were recriminations on all sides. It was charged, belatedly, that Mroz had known absolutely too much to have been sent abroad as an illegal resident. It was charged, belatedly, that Mroz's face was too familiar. He had traveled abroad many times before as a diplomatic courier under cover names, carrying out contacts with our agents; the files of several Western European countries, it was now said, were probably full of his pictures. There were rumors that Sienkiewicz had sent Mroz out of the country simply to get rid of him. It was true that Mroz knew too much about Sienkiewicz and could have compromised him.

As a consequence of all this, morale in the intelligence service sank to an extremely low ebb. Week after week it was expected that Witold Sienkiewicz, the cool and canny master spy who had headed Poland's intelligence apparatus for almost a decade, would be removed. But the prediction never materialized at the time, perhaps because Sienkiewicz was without doubt a Russian smypathizer and a KGB agent.

The shock and confusion amid the ranks of the intelligence service added fuel to my own growing doubts. Why would such men as Mroz and Goleniewski defect? In my heart I had begun to understand, but the growing understanding was not yet strong enough to determine my own actions.

Then, in 1961, while I was still attached to the Foreign Ministry, came The Great Courier Scandal.

In Poland, as in any other Communist country, you cannot find a better middle-level job than that of diplomatic courier. These persons enjoy more than their share of privileges, especially in the financial realm. They are traveling constantly, and they make a tremendous amount of money by Communist standards.

To be a diplomatic courier for Poland before 1961, one had to be either a good friend of Witold Sienkiewicz or well connected in the Communist party. One of our best-known couriers, Arciszewski, who worked for a dozen or more years before the scandal broke, was married to the sister of the then vice prime minister, Piotr Jaroszewicz. The diplomatic couriers usually were persons with some Russian background. They were either former trainees in various Russian schools, or former members of Poland's underground Communist movement who had been affiliated with the Soviet Communist party. All were classified as UB officers.

In addition to the good salaries that they received, the couriers were paid a daily travel allowance in United States dollars, French francs or British pounds. But since the couriers spent ninety-five percent of their time on duty, and they spent much of their duty time quartered in Polish missions, waiting sometimes for days or weeks to pick up packets, the travel allotments paid them in hard Western currencies were really never used for much except—as it was discovered one day—currency speculation and black market operations.

When The Great Courier Scandal suddenly erupted, nearly all of Poland's diplomatic couriers were arrested, including some who were stationed abroad and had to be brought back by our agents. A diplomatic courier usually had a contact or two abroad who helped him engage in currency speculation or black market deals, for he would be abroad for only a short time on each trip. For example, the courier would arrange with someone in Rome, Paris or Chicago to help buy goods that he would then pack into the next diplomatic pouch and sell back home.

The scandal broke in a manner that had comic-opera overtones. One day one of the Polish couriers, W, disappeared. He had disappeared once or twice previously, but had always been lucky enough to come up with an explanation that something untoward had delayed him. This time he vanished for a longer and definitely suspicious period. Although he was not on active duty at the time, W was still a diplomatic courier and thus had to be kept track of. An order was given to the secret service to find him.

It was not very difficult to locate him. He was living it up in the most expensive hotel in Lodz. It was discovered that he had been going to Lodz often, and everyone there who knew him thought that he was a high-ranking government official. W never bought anything worth less than fifty dollars or one hundred dollars, and was always surrounded by the prettiest women in town. He was playing the role of a millionaire playboy. It was impossible to imagine that a citizen of a Communist country could have the tremendous amount of money he was spending.

W was brought back to Warsaw and given special treatment. During one night session he broke down. He confessed that his job as courier and as a UB officer was little more than a front for a complex chain of black market operations. The chain involved the smuggling into Poland of goods that could be sold easily and for an exorbitant profit.

Of course, the confession of W, whom I knew very well, immediately implicated great numbers of persons. Those compromised included individuals responsible for Poland's diplomatic links with her installations abroad. Caught in the sweeping investigation were many friends of Sienkiewicz who were stationed in Polish embassies in positions such as code clerks, radio clerks and attachés. The Polish Intelligence Service and Foreign Ministry were authentically shocked at how huge this illegal organization had become. The scandal involved millions of *zlotys* and dollars. The diplomatic couriers had become do-it-yourself capitalists.

During the forty-eight hours after W's confession, nearly every diplomatic courier who happened to be in Poland was arrested. But the diplomatic courier business is going twenty-four hours a day, three hundred and sixty-five days a year, so you always have at least half of them out of the country. Those abroad were jailed upon their return. The ones arrested named others involved. Individuals in nearly every foreign Polish installation had been accessories. The couriers also had collaborators within Poland who had helped sell the contraband quickly. Some of the couriers who were reluctant to mention too many names were threatened and beaten. Speed was of the essence. If the investigation dragged out too long, guilty persons would disappear.

Ruling officials in both the UB and the Ministry of the Interior—secret police from the latter were involved in the probe inside Poland—were stunned by the revelations gathered in the investigation and interrogations. Many couriers frankly declared that they did not participate in meetings of the Communist party because they did not have the time, that they considered everything the party said bullshit, that what was important was making money.

Many of our intelligence operatives were recalled from their posts in foreign missions for questioning. In order not to arouse their suspicions—and possibly encourage their defection to the West—they were given couriers' pouches to bring home. The pouches were filled with bricks or other useless material, and the agents were arrested upon their arrival at the airport in Warsaw. All were jailed and investigated. Poland's then vice consul in Chicago, B, was sent back to Warsaw with two bricks. Interestingly enough, B was later sent back to the United States and stationed in Washington, D.C., as first secretary of the Polish embassy and chief resident agent of the Polish Intelligence Service for the United States.

Other suspects were trapped in their own act. In one typical case, the third secretary of the Polish embassy in Rome was called back to Poland with the explanation that he was about to be promoted to a very important diplomatic post. He brought two diplomatic pouches with him. When he arrived at the Warsaw airport, he was arrested. Police opened the pouches and found them stuffed with nylons, expensive underwear, cosmetics and so on. It became obvious that nine out of ten Polish diplomatic posts had been links in a well-organized chain of smuggling.

The whole affair was Poland's Watergate. As more and more names emerged, everyone knew that Sienkiewicz was finished. Now he could not be excused by anyone, not even the Russians. How much he may have been involved was another story, but he was responsible. Those implicated were his friends; he had made them diplomatic couriers. During the investigation it came out that the couriers had had to pay with gifts and money in order to get their lucrative jobs. It was the worst scandal that Poland had seen since the war. The consequences were, of course, grim. People were sentenced to jail terms, usually between two and seven years. Still, the retribution could have been worse. For a very small political crime, such as publishing a clandestine criticism of the government, you could get ten to fifteen years, so for a scandal such as the couriers', two to seven years was not so bad.

The president of Poland and the vice prime minister were acutely interested in the scandal, since it reflected on their administration. Some of the guilty had to pay, but not all of them. The party and the government did insist on Sienkiewicz's retirement, although he was only some fifty years old. In spite of the scandal, I can say that I had never met a man of such shrewdness and intelligence, or with his special ability to deal with people and make correct decisions.

Many other persons who were inconvenient for one reason

or another, or too closely tied to Sienkiewicz and his group, were also let go on pensions. A special law applying to the Polish secret service lets you retire after ten years of service.* Others were simply fired outright, which meant that they were cut off from any pensions. Hundreds and hundreds of staffers from Department 1 and its affiliated organizations were out on the streets. Suddenly, you would meet many of them sitting in Warsaw's coffee shops, doing nothing.

Of course, our ever-present comrades—the Russian advisors—were also interested in The Great Courier Scandal. So too was Zbigniew Dybala, my former boss. In 1955, Dybala had become deputy director of the Polish Intelligence Service. He was therefore an old-timer in the intelligence-courier business. In 1957 and 1958 in New York, Dybala himself had used the post of diplomatic courier as a cover under which to organize intelligence-gathering connections among diplomatic posts in North and South America. Dybala used the name Jaworsky when he was in the United States; his assistant with him in New York was Henryk Kornowicz. Dybala returned to Europe with a car and various other items, but he was not involved in any black market operations. Unfortunately, some of his friends, diplomatic couriers, were involved in the scandal. During summers these friends had invited him and his family for long vacations in their very expensive homes, so it cannot be denied that Dybala was well aware of the above-average standard of living of the diplomatic couriers.

At a special meeting of Department 1, Dybala was informed of the situation and the fact that the Russian advisors had supplied information alleging that Dybala was one of the dogs

---

*The Polish Intelligence Service retirement policies are extremely liberal, compared with those prevailing in other Communist countries. In most nations of the socialist camp, you are lucky to get forty or fifty percent of your former salary, even after many years of government service. Of course, it helps to be a hero of the working class. There is a system in Communist countries under which, if you have received one or more medals by the time you retire, you get an added percentage of your pension for each medal that you hold. With or without medals, the Polish Intelligence Service will pay up to a hundred percent of one's salary upon retirement. Not that it matters now, but I won several medals.

who had been paid off by the couriers. Dybala tried to defend himself, but both the Polish officials and the Russian advisors refused to listen. Dybala was completely broken in spirit. His whole life was suddenly going to pieces. Even though he was still a staunch Communist, he suspected that he was going to be kicked out of the secret service. Further, he had suddenly discovered that his best friends were involved in this dirty business, and that they were accusing him of being paid. This was not true. I know for sure that Dybala was not personally involved. He was a self-made man with principles. Whatever I may think about his principles today, he was a person who could never have taken a step back from them.

The decision was made by Dybala. Before he left the office after the special departmental meeting, he prepared his reports, cleaned out his safe, and ordered a bottle of good French cognac from the UB's well-stocked commissary. He took only two portions of poison from his safe. He went home and told his wife Helen, who was also a friend of mine, the whole situation. His wife understood that he was bitter, very disappointed and very hurt, but she didn't suspect anything else. He asked her to go and buy him cigarettes. She left the apartment for only a few minutes because there was a tobacco shop in their building. During this brief time, Dybala swallowed the poison. When Helen came back, her husband was dead.

Dybala had had many friends in the service, but unfortunately in this situation he had very few. His best friends were accusing him. He may have overlooked the obvious, but I believe that Dybala himself was never guilty of any dishonorable act.

Dybala's funeral was a manifestation of respect by the persons who loved and admired him. At the time of his death, his daughter was fourteen years old and his son sixteen or seventeen. At the military cemetery in Warsaw, there were approximately 1,500 mourners, among them his few loyal friends—employees, officers, individuals who had been dealing with him for more than twenty years. One of those present was I. It was a snowy, winter day. Nobody moved until the last moment. Dybala was buried with military honors—the regime now had no reason not to honor him. The minister of the interior made a speech, but he was cut off several times by the widow screaming, "You killed him! Murderers!"

For many of us it was a tragic day. The suicides of many persons have really shocked me, but it was Dybala's that was the hardest on me. Not too many years afterward, his wife Helen killed herself.

From Opposition to Resistance

BY 1961, THE CONFUSION, DISORGANIZATION AND deterioration of morale in both the Polish Intelligence Service and the Polish Foreign Ministry had reached serious proportions.

I became more convinced than ever before that the situation in Poland was the reverse of everything that Gomulka had said in 1956, of the reforms that had been initiated in '57 and '58. I arrived at the certainty that the regime as now constituted was not going to work. They were again trying to make us politically blind. They were again forcing us to bend our beings to the will of the state. I was disenchanted. I was bitter.

Impelled by this conclusion, I joined a group of Foreign Ministry employees, most of whom were between twenty-five and forty years of age, who had decided that we would have to change our country's form of Communism. We did not desire to be anti-Communists, but we were convinced that Polish Communism had to be improved very much and very quickly. We wanted to do what Dubcek was to attempt later in Czechoslovakia—to create a "Communism with a human face," with justice and real concern for the working people. We did not want to worry about Viet Nam or international Communism. We felt that becoming a Communist should be a free decision, and thus that we should not export Communism to any other country.

We wanted Communism to speak for itself. If we could create a good standard of living for people, a democratic system in which people could live their own lives more or less in the way they preferred, then there would be no reason to change the system. We did not want big industry to be in private hands. We did not want to return to the situation that had existed in Poland before the war, with eight million persons unable to read or write, without jobs, and starving. But we argued that our Communist system would have to be transformed internally in order to demonstrate to the world—by example and not by propaganda—that Communism was the right way.

Again, this was an idea which I know today could never be realized.

One after another, members of our group got into trouble for expressing such heretical ideas. A man would be kicked out of a good job, or transferred to a menial job, or encounter difficulties finding a job. He would find himself on some kind of a blacklist. Even if he was the person most qualified for a position, he would never be appointed. We were the victims of an invisible persecution. Of course this was better than going to prison. Nobody was knocking on our doors at night and saying "Come with us," but there was no doubt that we were paying a price for our revisionist thoughts.

Gradually we moved more and more underground. We began publishing a variety of pamphlets on a primitive press. In a Communist country, because of censorship, you cannot print even your own visiting card without permission. Even if you are a high official in the Polish Foreign Ministry, the matter has to go to the Central Censorship Office. If you are a journalist, your newspaper or magazine has to write to the Central Censorship Office for permission. If you are a craftsman or a private person, it is ninety percent certain that you are not going to receive approval for a card at all because you are not going to find a sponsor.

So you can imagine the risk involved in printing illegal pamphlets. In a Communist country citizens are sentenced to prison for a crime no more heinous than publishing something without permission. The material does not even have to be anti-Communist. Naturally it does not help your case if the authorities think that they discern an appeal for freedom or for reforms in the name of improving Communism.

There is no government in the world more paranoic about the printed word than that of a Communist country. The party newspaper is enshrined as the fount of all truth. This puts an understandable strain on the editors responsible. If even one sentence in one article is not to the government's liking, the entire article has to be changed or thrown out, even if it means that the paper will be late in appearing and production costs will skyrocket.

The party is no less fearful of the foreign press. For instance, every issue of *The New York Times* is studied in Warsaw and Moscow by experts. Sentences are underlined and analyzed. Undoubtedly this is also done in Washington by specialists charged with studying Communist newspapers. But in the socialist camp the internal repercussions are far more serious. You can cause a lot of trouble for many persons in Warsaw or Prague or Moscow by a simple, single sentence in *The New York Times* or *Washington Post* or any other important United States publication.

I was still attached to the foreign service, as head of the *Wydzial do spraw Polonii*, and still traveling abroad often. At the same time, I was by now in touch with numerous countrymen at home who were also engaged in the kind of reformist activity being carried out by our group in the Foreign Ministry. One of my contacts was the son of a former Polish cabinet minister. Another was a professor of Marxism-Leninism at the University of Warsaw. The latter was finally imprisoned in 1966 and released only in 1970.

What our dissident group was trying to believe was that there are rules and morals that apply to human beings everywhere. But our group gradually came to the conclusion that to try to relate such an ideal to Communism was a contradiction in terms. Communism, by the very nature of its philosophy of totalitarian collectivism, cannot allow any real concession to individual dignity. If you are in any measure an open-minded person, you cannot be a devoted Communist.

No longer was I interested in straining to see Communist

"progress." There is no such real evolution. True, the standard of living may increase, textbook education may increase, health care and sanitation may improve, and there may even appear some Western-style luxuries. But the basic dictatorship continues; the totalitarian apparatus, enforced by the secret police, remains in place. In trying to encourage such "progress," our group had been talking in highly theoretical terms about a kind of Communism that did not and does not and cannot really exist.

One by one, many of us were prosecuted and sentenced to prison. Nevertheless, we decided that there was nothing to do but keep on fighting.

We still did not like the capitalists. We were still absolutely opposed to the system in the United States or in France or in West Germany. But by now we had evolved to a point where we were at least trying to be somewhat objective—which in itself is heresy in the Communist catechism. We were in favor of picking the good things from other countries.

One might ask whether it is possible for Communism to accept such eclecticism, whether the movement's economic and political dogmas are such that it cannot by its very nature permit any opposition or free importation of workable ideals from other systems. My answer is this: The doctrine which holds that the Communist party should run the show implies that no opposition should be permitted. But it is also part of classic Communist doctrine that the Communist party should be in close touch with every other social and political group in the society, and that the party should control those groups in the society not by force but through mutual understanding, cooperation and persuasion. The movement should give leadership to the masses, but it should lead the masses the way they wish to go. This should occur under the leadership of the "workers" and their party, which of course means the "Communist" party.

You can find this philosophy in any book by Marx or Engels, but I defy you to find the idea today in any book written by current leaders of the Communist countries. And you cannot find such a philosophy reflected by Communism in practice. Whatever the Communist movement is doing in any country is usually against the interests of the working masses. Marx

and Engels believed that the classless society could not be
brought about by destroying any social class. They considered
the task a long one of gradual acceptance and adaptation, of
taking two steps forward and one step back. The terror, killing,
extermination in Stalin's and Mao Tse-tung's books are not
Marx and Engels. It was Mao who wrote that all power comes
out of the barrel of a gun.

Communism's most important credo is that the means of
production should belong to the whole population, and more
and more persons in the world are coming to believe that this
is right—persons who are against Communism, but who think
that the capitalist system needs refinement and improvement.
In Western society, although more and more production is
being controlled by fewer and fewer large corporations, there
is a move toward public representation on corporate bodies,
and toward more government control of private industry.

Marx and Engels said that everybody in a Communist society is a stockholder, or part-owner. Of course, management
in a Communist country is the Communist party. But in practice
these Communist managers are not really managers; they are
killers. They kill their own industries and the public economy,
because they are professionally blind and usually unskilled in
effective management techniques. A riot in Chicago is more
important to them than the semi-starvation of their own working
people. It is more important for these "managers" to spend a
disproportionate amount of their budgets to fight "American
imperialists" in Viet Nam or Black Africa than to tend to the
authentic needs of their own people.

I went through the whole process of reanalysis, and came
out with the calm conclusion that I could not bear the system
anymore. I had tried to help improve it, but it was impossible.
Others shared my conclusion. Our group decided to withdraw
from open activities and act behind the scenes.

Although I was a high-ranking official of the Polish Foreign
Ministry, whatever I was doing openly in this role was always
a game; I was first and foremost an undercover intelligence
officer. Having spies double as diplomats is a standard Communist technique—several Polish professional staff intelligence officers are at this writing ambassadors of Poland to

foreign countries. For example: Sweden—Stefan Staniszewski; before him, Bejm, also a UB officer; Denmark—Stanislaw Pichla; before him, H. Wendrowski, also a UB officer.

My double role, however, caused some problems in my resistance activities. One day my fellow dissidents in the Foreign Ministry discovered who I was. I was involved in this activity because I believed in what the group was doing and I wanted to be with them. I had not considered it necessary to announce to them that I was with the Polish Intelligence Service. I did not want to scare them. But finally one whom I shall call N, my closest friend in the group, confronted me and said, "Sit down; you have to explain to us. Are you a provocateur here, or are you with us because you want to be?"

It was very difficult for me to convince them that I was not a provocateur. I pointed out that because I often had occasion to travel outside the country, I could be a contact man with the West. Most of the members of the group had little chance to visit the West.

Either because of the sincerity of the argument or because of their own youthful naïveté—after all, I could have been an infiltrator—they accepted my explanation.

And I was of special help to them. When I was sent on government missions abroad, I carried a diplomatic passport, which meant that customarily nobody opened my luggage on my return to Poland. Therefore, on several occasions I managed to smuggle into my homeland prohibited publications and parts for printing equipment. (A private citizen cannot buy or import printing equipment in Poland. Nor can you purchase or bring in a photocopy machine or similar duplicating equipment. In the most modern offices in Warsaw, you will not see one photocopy machine. If they are used, they are kept in special places and guarded like a military arsenal.) It was an exhilarating if dangerous turn in my life. I was now in active illegal opposition!

Moreover, because I was traveling abroad, I had contacts with a strong and influential group of Polish emigrants in London and in France. There are many prominent Poles in exile in Western Europe. They may or may not be active in the politics of their new countries, but you can be certain that they are doing everything they can, each in his or her own way, to change the situation in their homeland.

The best Polish publication anywhere is printed not in Warsaw but in Paris. The Communist regime in Poland fears nothing so much as this monthly publication, which is called *Kultura*. Every unauthorized issue of this publication is confiscated. If you send an issue of *Kultura* into Poland by mail, the postal authorities will tell the intended recipient that they are ready to close their eyes to many things, but not this publication. Citizens who are discovered trying to subscribe to *Kultura* are at once put on blacklists. Merely for reading *Kultura* one can be sent to jail, on the official charge of absorbing "propaganda of an anti-government printed publication." Numerous Polish youths have been sentenced to five to seven years in prison for nothing more than reading this publication or attempting to distribute it.

During my time as chief of the Foreign Ministry's Department of Poles Living Abroad, I had sole responsibility for the highly restricted distribution of the one hundred copies of *Kultura* that were permitted to arrive in Warsaw. I always retained five copies for my office use, and, believe me, every copy was in pieces after several months because it went through hundreds and hundreds of hands. Not only were the hundred copies widely smuggled, but *Kultura*'s content was spread by word of mouth. Thus, despite the fact that *Kultura* is published abroad and restricted at home, the journal has an important influence on the life and politics of Poland.

My active resistance could not be termed part of an anti-Communist movement, because we were too loosely organized to be called a movement. We were trying to bite the Communists here and there, to blunt their power where we could. Our resistance group of thirty or forty individuals was also trying to attain control of as many positions in the Foreign Ministry as we could. We wanted to change the style of the Polish Foreign Service, to force out some of the persons who were trying to block the development of new ideas.

Our efforts were, of course, quite dangerous. We were careful not to set up any formal organization. We played bridge, we talked, we decided informally what our actions would be next week, next month. There was no voting, no election, nothing that the regime could use to prove that we were a conspiratorial organization. After two years, nevertheless, the government got wind of our group, and one day in 1964 all of us were suddenly promoted. One was promoted to first secretary of the Polish embassy here, another the second secretary of the Polish embassy there. Within a few weeks, there was not one of us left in Warsaw. One of us was in Tokyo, one in Berlin, one in France, one in Latin America. As for me, I was sent to Oslo.

It was a clever way to get rid of us. After three or four years abroad, you come back to find a completely different situation. There are new faces, your friends are still abroad or are in different positions. It is very difficult to re-create the group. Thus, our pathetically small resistance effort fell apart.

We may not have been the best, but we had tried to improve the system. The hard truth is that there is no chance of really improving the situation in Eastern Europe until this process of humanization that is going on in Russia takes hold. We know that it is going on from the arrests and trials of dissidents, from the sending of scientists, writers and other intellectuals to "psychiatric hospitals" and new kinds of concentration camps. Only the liberation of the Soviet Union can bring about the liberation of Eastern Europe.

I had come full circle. Now I was at the point where I was not only disenchanted with the system; I had come to despise it. I realized that I would not be able to accomplish anything by continuing to work in informal groups. I would have to take more direct action—on my own.

Others took different routes. Many members of our group stayed on in the regime, resigned themselves to it, and are today ambassadors of Poland abroad. Others committed suicide. Why? Because they too discovered that their professional lives had been wasted, and they were not able to find a way out of their dilemma.

I did not give up. I still wanted to fight. But how?

By now, I had been a member of the Polish secret service for more than ten years. I knew the anti-Communist politicians and other influential Poles who were organizing in small groups, publishing pamphlets against the central committee. But so what? Perhaps ten or twenty individuals read what these dissidents published before the pamphlets were seized by the UB. Their authors went to prison—for what? *The New York Times* might write two lines about how Professor So-and-so was arrested because he had opposed the regime. But the professor would spend five or ten years in prison, and then be put on a blacklist so that he could not work at the university or publish a book or really do anything for the rest of his life. And the readers of *The New York Times* will forget about him the next day, or the next week.

You cannot overthrow the Communists outright. Perhaps we could have in 1945. Perhaps the Russian people could have sixty years ago in Russia. But not any longer. The Communists are too powerful. There is an army of secret service agents, uniformed troops, Russian tanks; there is terror.

Still, the system can be hurt from within. I reminded myself: "You're a staff officer of the intelligence service. You can really hurt them. And if you hate them so much, you should want to hurt them as much as possible."

By 1964, I had no illusions left and no expectations for the future.

For the first time since I began my gang activities on the streets of Warsaw, I began to see the meaning of human dignity.

In November 1963, I suffered what was diagnosed by my Polish doctors as a heart attack. Actually, as I learned years later from physicians in the United States, the illness was the beginning of a problem with my spinal cord that was complicated by incompetent doctors whose wrong treatment only provoked changes in my electrocardiogram. In any event, I was extremely ill and immobilized. My illness occurred just a couple of weeks after I had been advised that I was to be sent to Washington as Polish consul-general, which would be the cover for another intelligence assignment.

It was in a hospital in Warsaw early one morning, eight days after my collapse, that I received a newspaper announcing that John F. Kennedy had been assassinated. I liked his ideas, especially, "Don't ask what your country can do for you, but what you can do for your country." This was and is a reflection of my own philosophy of life, and remembering Kennedy's words added further fuel to my determination to do what I knew I had to do.

I was hospitalized for many weeks and convalescent for seven months. While still in the hospital, I was devising my program. My long period of convalescence gave me plenty of time to think about my developing crisis of conscience over the system of which I had become an accomplice.

One day the chief physician of the Foreign Ministry visited me in my hospital room and announced: "You cannot go to Washington after your recovery. The climate there would kill you."

I got a little worried. I then discovered that several of my friends had been arrested. Nobody had questioned me, but there were subtle indications that I was not as good a Communist as I had been in the past. I sensed that they had decided I was not sufficiently trustworthy to go to Washington, so they invoked my supposed heart attack.

There was very little I could do or say. But I knew that wherever I went, my mission was firm. Had the Polish regime known me better, it would not have sent me anywhere, except perhaps to Tirana. I was fed up with and sickened by my life as a Communist intelligence agent. I simply was not a Communist anymore.

PART FOUR

Everything but
the Furniture

IT WAS IN THE SUMMER OF 1964 THAT I WAS OF-
fered the position of secretary of the Polish embassy in Norway, which of course was another intelligence cover. I was
surprised when I was told I was being sent to Oslo. In spite
of my suspicions that I was not completely trusted, I frankly
had expected a more prestigious assignment. I consoled myself
with the thought that Norway was a quiet country, and the
Poles had had little business there, at least up to that time.
Since I knew Swedish, it would be relatively easy for me
to learn Norwegian; the two languages have similar roots.
And it was good enough to carry out what I had in my mind.

The climate in Norway was indeed good, and the country
turned out to be beautiful. Yet my new post was hardly a
holiday. I was living in the mountains, and driving up and
down between my home and the city was not good for me.
Furthermore, that quiet embassy suddenly became anything but
quiet. I found myself with a lot of work, a lot of responsibility.
In such a small embassy I had to do everything. In addition
to my covert activities, I was responsible—as part of my front
position—for all of the embassy's cultural and consular affairs.
They had sent me to Oslo ostensibly to recover, but the volume
of my work proved exhausting.

*   *   *

I am never going to say precisely when my decision to work for the West was made, in what year. I want the Polish authorities to be forever confused on this point, to make it more difficult for them to assess the damage I did to them.

When I made the decision, I was determined to establish my own contact, to be certain that I was going to work for the Americans, not some other government. Although I had arrived at the point where I was ready to make a deal, I could hardly go to the United States embassy, knock on the door, and announce, "Listen, I'm here and I'm ready." I could have been the most important person in the Polish Intelligence Service, but if I had gone to the American embassy and said, "My name is so-and-so; here is my passport; I want to work for you," I would have received a kick in my ass and that would have been the end of the story. You do not do things like that in this business.

I therefore worked for months before I was able to get in touch with individuals I was certain were from American intelligence. To make my first contact with the Americans, I went through a Norwegian businessman. I shall call him T. His wife was British, and when T was in the Norwegian army he had gone through training in the United States for a couple of months. I understood—he did not say it directly, but I understood—that he knew many Americans. I decided that T was the potentially proper channel. I invited him home, he invited me to his home, and we became friends.

I let T make some money by selling us some of his merchandise for the embassy. I let him make more money than he should have. He helped me, and I helped him. I liked this man. (I still like him, and was sorry to hear that he has since been burned completely.)

Finally, one day T casually mentioned to me that he knew several persons at the American embassy, but I did not buy it. Later he told me that a former friend of his, an American army colonel, was coming to Oslo the following month and would be stationed at the United States embassy. I did not buy this immediately either. I was testing T to make certain he was not a UB or KGB agent.

My Norwegian friend was a follower of the horse races. He invited me to the track many times. I do not like gambling, but I went along. I ultimately assured myself that T could be trusted. After his American acquaintance, the United States Army colonel, arrived in Oslo, I met him too several times at the racetrack. We spent several hundreds of dollars betting together. The colonel and I loaned each other money; once he was short of money, another time I was short of money. We had a few drinks. We played bridge. Nothing else. I was watching him. I wanted to make him sure that I was I, and I wanted to be sure completely that he was he.

I came to the conclusion that this colonel really was an American military man and not an imposter. I was certain that he was indeed a colonel in the United States Army, stationed in Norway and working at the American embassy as an assistant to the United States military attaché in Oslo. And I didn't want to waste too much time, because I was equally sure that others in my embassy, as well as the Russians, would sooner or later discover my contact with the American colonel. I cut off the relationship for a couple of weeks completely. All the while I had been careful not to let my Norwegian friend know anything about my interest.

One day I simply called my American friend and told him, "I want to see you." We saw each other privately, without any witnesses. I said, in my Polish-accented English, "Listen, I need somebody from the CIA quickly."

He said, "John, I have nothing to do with the CIA"—which did not surprise me.

"I know it, but you have to help me. And one day you're going to be promoted for doing so. Don't tell me what you're going to do—I don't want to know. Just do it quickly."

It took him only twenty-four hours. To the best of my knowledge, he is still stationed in Europe as a deputy military attaché with an American embassy. I do not want to compromise him because he is an official person, performing his duties for his country. And besides, he did me a tremendous favor.

My decision to become a double agent for the West was a shock to the Americans. They had not expected this of me. They suspected me of being a double agent for the Communists.

It took me a long time to convince them that I was not trying to doublecross them. One problem was that I did not want money. After I came to the United States, a CIA agent confided to me: "John, you don't know what kind of troubles you created for us because you didn't want money. You were the first guy who didn't."

I merely told them what I was going to do for them and asked them to promise that they would do certain things for me. Later on I was paid, but they never completely fulfilled their part of the agreement on promises that meant more to me. It is easier to pay. And Americans pay pretty well, too.

Once the Americans were convinced of my authenticity and we had begun working together, I could ask for any amount of money for expenses and get it at once. Moreover, they sent first-class people to work with me. And we were working like crazy. I had never worked that intensively with my own agents in my life. We had meetings every day. Most of our meetings, training and briefing sessions took place in a central part of Oslo. The building was new and modern, and the apartment used for the meetings with me was rented, probably by the CIA.

The Americans wanted everything from the Polish embassy but the furniture, and I did my best to give it to them. There was nothing that came into the embassy—no code from Warsaw, no secret information, nothing that was being dealt with in the Polish Foreign Ministry or in the central committee of the Polish Communist party in Warsaw or in the Polish Intelligence Service—that I did not try to get out. Papers from the files, documents, instructions, keys, combinations to the safe—everything. Whatever went through my hands I was copying for the Americans. I used every friend and every enemy.

I was also buying people in every possible way. I discovered again that you can buy any of these "great Communists," these beautiful people who claim that they live only for their political "ideals," for a bottle of French cognac, a carton of American cigarettes, a stupid watch for their wives. They ask only that nobody know. Day after day, I was confirming what I had long

since realized: corruption is an integral part of the Communist
style of life.

I had an affair with the wife of one of the employees in the
embassy—not because I loved her or was even seriously interested in her, but because all of the codes used by the Foreign
Service were in her husband's office. She brought me everything.

Embassy staffs often tend to be lazy, or at least not to bestir
themselves unduly in their far-off assignments. But I was working like hell, sometimes even twenty-four hours a day. I was
spending mornings, evenings and nights at the embassy. My
ambassador liked to travel. I had the keys to his safe, to his
desk, to his files. I saw everything that was sent from Warsaw
to the Polish embassies in Washington, in London, in Paris,
as well as to our embassy in Oslo—the most important instructions go to all of the embassies.

The Americans have many agents in the Polish Intelligence
Service. They wanted to know, in general terms, how those
agents were doing. I did not know these agents at the time,
and I do not know too many of them even today. But I was
informing the Americans about the functioning of every person
in our secret service, from the topmost to the lowest level,
and among them were United States agents. They did not tell
me who their agents were, and I did not ask. But sometimes
I could figure it out.

According to what I was told at the end of my work for the
CIA, I supplied the Americans with approximately 1,700 de-
scriptions of very important persons in different areas of the
Polish intelligence apparatus. Approximately 800 of them were
prominent functionaries of the Polish Foreign Service. Most
of the others were stationed in less conspicuous legal and illegal
positions abroad—hundreds and hundreds of agents who had
no inkling that the CIA knew exactly who they were. As I had
vowed, I hurt them like hell.

Decision
to Escape

DURING THE SUMMER OF 1966, I TOOK A VACATION
in Poland. If I had had any doubts, I returned to Oslo without
any.

All of my friends in Warsaw were pessimistic. I had never
seen the situation in my country painted in such dark colors.
I left Poland crying inside. People were truly suffering from
this blind, inhuman system which did absolutely nothing con-
structive for ninety-nine percent of the Polish population. I was
now convinced that I would never see Poland again. However,
in accordance with my private plan, I was still hoping to be
able to work and fight against the Communists, from within
their ranks, for many years to come.

But although you can act in various ways against the Communist totalitarian system from within for varying periods of
time, you cannot do so forever. There are too many factors
operating against you. As I have said, to create any kind of
lasting underground organization is impossible. The Communist police state, with its network of informers, is too efficient.
More than two persons and the organization is finished. In
order to hurt the Communists, you must do it on your own and
alone. It demands a lot of nerve, courage and sacrifice, but it
can be done, and effectively—witness how Solzhenitsyn shook
up the Soviet Union before his expulsion. Sooner or later,
however, the system catches up with you.

In December of 1966 I received a cable from Warsaw. It advised me that I was being recalled to Poland. The cable explained that I was soon to receive an important new assignment.

I was understandably concerned. It struck me as suspicious that I was being reassigned so quickly. I had been in Oslo for only two and a half years. By now I had become first secretary of the Communist party in Oslo, acting underground, of course. As such, I occupied an influential position in the covert Communist apparatus in Norway. To be called back to Poland so quickly was enough to arouse suspicion that something was very wrong. Had they discovered that I was working for the Americans?

I was told by my new friends in Oslo—operatives of the United States Central Intelligence Agency—that I should not go back to Poland. The time had come, they said, to stay in the West with my family. I had reached the point where I was ready to make this kind of decision. But on a personal level, I knew that my wife did not want to abandon her country, and I did not wish to take my son away from his mother. Because she was still a devout Communist, I had kept secret from her the fact that I was working for the West. I wanted to find a solution that would be good for all of us. And I did not actually believe that my retaliatory activities against the Communists could have been discovered by the Warsaw regime. For all of the determination with which I had been working, I had been very careful. After several days of thinking over the situation, I decided to take the risk and return to Poland with my wife and son.

The Americans were unalterably opposed. They feared, of course, that if the Warsaw regime had discovered that I was a double agent for the West, I could be broken and made to divulge the key information that I had supplied the CIA. There was also the danger that I would be forced to reveal my CIA contacts in Norway. The Americans told me: "Leave everything. The military plane is waiting for you. Go to the West."

I said no.

The Americans beseeched me, "John, you're wrong.

There's tremendous danger for you in returning. You'll probably go to jail. They know something."

By this time I was becoming more stubborn than sensible. I obtained a gun. They said, "Janusz, you'd better kill yourself. It's that bad."

I told them: "I'll kill anybody who tries to stop me. I'm going to Poland."

Thus I returned to my homeland strictly because of family considerations. I went back trusting in my luck. But this time, as I was to discover, the odds were very much against me. The Americans had been right. My battle from within was finished. I did not know it at the time, but the Polish regime had compiled a dossier of charges against me. As it turned out, they were false charges that had nothing to do with my work for the Americans. Still, I was finished.

It was not without some sadness that I left Norway. I liked the Norwegian people. They are very honest and very modest. I had made many friends there. I still miss them quite often, even though most were left-oriented radicals who, when they later discovered what I had done, considered me a traitor to the cause. I know that many of them think that I sold myself and our ideas for American money, which is of course not true.

On the way home, my family and I visited Sweden, West Germany and Berlin. I tried to delay everything. I had several meetings with friends of mine. I will never forget a dinner in an apartment house with an ex-chief of the Polish military mission in West Berlin, Wladyslaw Tykocinski, who had escaped to the West in May of 1965. It was very interesting—especially given my situation—to listen to his stories of the repercussions that had followed his escape. Everybody in the Polish government had called Tykocinski a son of a bitch, and slanderous tales were circulated about him. I am proud of him and everything he did.

While traveling back to Poland, a trip that took several days, I had as my constant companion my contact man from the West, who was always close to me, right up to five or ten minutes before I crossed The Wall into East Berlin, at Checkpoint Charlie.

In East Berlin I stayed for a couple of days at the Polish

embassy. I received a shock when a friend of mine said, "Janusz, you're here? Everyone is saying that you defected."

It was the first confirmation that all was not well for me at home.

"I defected? Never in my life! Who's spreading these bloody rumors?"

After my arrival in Warsaw, I received another shock from friends in the Foreign Ministry. "You came to Warsaw! What's wrong with you? There are rumors you defected."

I said, "I?"

I also talked to individuals who were responsible for the decision to call me back and, as I later learned, to arrest me. Even they were surprised that I had indeed returned. They greeted me with "You in Warsaw?"

I had the impression that many persons were not being completely honest with me. While expressing surprise at seeing me, they never told me exactly what my problem was. It seemed that everybody had been saying I would not be back in Poland. Of course, I tried very hard to express my surprise. Why? Who said it? What was the reason? Couldn't I leave for even twenty-four hours without such wild rumors? What's wrong? But no one would give me a straight answer.

Some of my friends were so amazed at my return that they were too embarrassed to ask me questions about my situation. Some of them, damn sons of bitches, knew that I was under suspicion, but would not tell me for what. As far as I could learn later on, the regime suspected me of political cooperation with Polish emigrants in the West. For reasons unbeknownst to me to this day, they had come to believe that I was the author of several political articles in Polish emigrant magazines, notably *Kultura* in Paris, about the situation in Warsaw. Even with the grimness of my situation, I could not help finding this suspicion amusing; in spite of all my surreptitious work for the West, that was one activity that I had *not* been engaged in. The regime did not suspect that I was an American spy. But what they did suspect me of was serious enough to send me to prison for a few years.

Unsurprisingly, I never received the "important new assignment." Things turned out to be as bad as all of the eyebrow-raising by my friends had suggested.

The arrest procedure was set in motion against me. After fourteen years as an officer of the Polish Intelligence Service—between 1960 and 1967 I had been promoted twice, from captain to major and from major to lieutenant colonel—I was summarily fired and simultaneously discharged from my cover position in the Foreign Ministry. The next day I was called to the Communist party headquarters and informed that they had taken away my party membership. And what was to be the next step? They were obviously going to arrest me. They never arrest a Communist party member before they fire him from his job and strip him of his party membership. The theory is that if you have done something bad enough to go to jail, you cannot possibly qualify as a Communist any longer, especially if the case involves political heresy.

But I had good friends, and they took care of me. When the director of the personnel department of the Foreign Ministry (a really stupid type named Kazimierz Szewczyk) was shouting at me: "We'll teach you a lesson! We'll get every piece of shit out of you! You'll never see the West even in a picture!" I was saying to myself, "I'd like to see your stupid face again in forty-eight hours, when I'm going to be in the West, sitting somewhere in a cool place and enjoying a good drink in nice company."

February 17, 1967
Warsaw Airport

FEBRUARY 17 IS THE DAY ON WHICH I SHOULD celebrate my birthday, not June 17, which is my original birthday. For February 17, 1967, was the day I was born anew.

I shall never forget the events of this day, even down to the most minute detail. In Warsaw it was a beautiful sunny morning; there was still snow on the ground, but spring was in the air. I departed from home around nine o'clock. I was virtually certain that I was walking out my front door for the last time. The developments of the preceding weeks—I had now been back in Warsaw from Oslo for exactly thirty-six days—had left little doubt that I would have to abandon my country, my wife, my son, my friends.

On this day, I had an extremely important appointment with the No. 2 person in the Foreign Ministry, Jozef Winiewicz. He had been the Polish ambassador to Great Britain and the United States, as well as chief of the Polish mission to the United Nations, and was a longtime acquaintance of mine.

I had been looking forward to this meeting for at least two weeks, in the hope that Winiewicz might at least clarify the nature of my troubles. Even though I had been fired and stripped of my Communist party membership, I still had not been officially advised of the accusations against me. In the back of my mind was the faint hope that my old acquaintance Winiewicz might help me work out a solution. Winiewicz had given me an appointment several times but had canceled it at the last moment. I had never had a problem seeing him before.

That morning, however, I was philosophical about his having avoided me: If I should see him, fine, we would talk; if not, I was going to leave Poland. The appointment was scheduled for ten o'clock. I arrived at the Foreign Ministry at twenty past nine, saw some friends, and at exactly ten A.M. I was in Jozef Winiewicz's office. I do not need to underline how important a person he was, given his position, or how important he was to me, given my situation.

Looking across the desk at Winiewicz, I could not help feeling a certain pity and even sympathy for him. He was at once a slave to and commentary on the system. Comrade Winiewicz, as a student, had been a member of the Polish National party, a political group with ideological links to Nazi Germany. The party had sympathized with Hitler and had been responsible for the pogroms inflicted on the Jewish population in Poland before the war.

In spite of his early association with fascism, Winiewicz spent the whole war in England as a Polish refugee. He had been a member of the Polish government-in-exile.

His return to Poland was engineered by his cousin, the widow of a wealthy German who had owned several factories in Poland before he died during the war. She had enjoyed protection from the Germans because of her former husband.

Nobody will ever understand exactly how or why she did it, but during the war she played a key role helping the Polish Communist underground. Wladyslaw Gomulka and other Communist leaders had hiding places in her apartment and in several houses that she owned scattered across Poland. Suddenly, in 1945, after the Communists came to power, she recalled that her cousin Winiewicz, who was twenty-five years her junior, was in London. She chartered a plane to London and two days later brought him home.

That was the beginning of his career. A few weeks later he was consul of the Polish embassy in London; a few months later he and his cousin were married. He was to become the Polish ambassador to the Court of St. James and to the United States. His past links to fascism had been very much against him when he joined the Communist regime, but his wife was able to provide a good enough guarantee of his loyalty. During the worst of the Stalinist period in Poland, Winiewicz was suspected of being a Western spy and was pushed away from any influence. He was lucky because his case never came to a political trial. Afterward he moved up again, and eventually reached the No. 2 spot in the Foreign Ministry.

Now I was seated in Winiewicz's office, listening to what he had to tell me. Our discussion went on for forty minutes. Since we had known each other for many years, there existed a measure of understanding and friendship between us. I had had occasion in the past to talk with him about various problems.

But this meeting was different. I was hoping that this gentleman—perhaps I shouldn't call him a gentleman, but I shall anyway—was going to tell me something that would be truly informative. Instead, the discussion went like this: "Janusz, I'm really upset at seeing you in this kind of trouble."

I replied that if I was in trouble I did not understand why myself, and that therefore he must know something that I didn't, and I would be very interested in hearing it.

"You expect too much from me," he intoned, "because I can tell you only that you're completely finished and you shouldn't ask me why because you probably know pretty well yourself."

"Frankly speaking, I don't know."

"Janusz," Winiewicz repeated, "you expect too much from me. I'm not entitled to tell you everything I know, but you have to leave the foreign service. And I am afraid the situation is even worse than that. We know each other well enough that I would be really surprised if you expected me to tell you anything else, because we aren't children and you should know very well the reason for your troubles."

The discussion went on more or less in this vein. I was now completely certain that he knew something that he did not want to tell me or was afraid to tell me. For his part, he doubtless suspected that I was only playing a game. In spite of his powerful position, he was careful not to say anything that could later involve him in any kind of trouble. He left me no hope that there was anybody in the party or in the government who could help me or give me any kind of protection.

At the very end of the discussion, Winiewicz concluded with the scarcely reassuring thought that he was really worried about what was going to happen to me after I left his office. There was nothing more to be said by either of us. I could not expect anything more from him. He had been nice enough, and had not tried to cover any more than necessary. (After I left Poland he was forced to retire, poor comrade.)

It is not easy to get out of Communist Poland under any circumstances, much less to escape clandestinely. My dilemma now was how to organize everything in a couple of hours.

After I left Winiewicz's office, I encountered several of my friends, and some of my enemies, in the Foreign Ministry building. I attempted to talk to everyone. I tried to say quite openly what I thought about many different things. I considered it important to leave a verbal record of at least some of my feelings. At the same time, I was afraid to leave the building openly. I was certain that somebody was waiting to follow me or arrest me. A friend of mine, Stefan Zwirski, was in charge of furnishing transportation for all of the important persons in the ministry. I decided to use Stefan's friendship, and he—not knowing what I had in mind—gave me one of the chauffeured cars used by deputy ministers.

I left the building a little more than two hours after I had arrived, departing through a special gate reserved for the kind of car that I had borrowed. I had the driver take me to the headquarters of the central committee of the Polish Communist party. I got out, walked through the building, and left it at the other end. It was a very short walk from there to the Scandinavian Airline System office.

My problem was that although an individual can reserve a ticket on SAS, Pan American or any other Western airline in Warsaw, the airlines are not permitted to take any money. To pay for the ticket you have to go to the office of the Polish airline LOT.

I made a reservation at SAS for a flight leaving that afternoon at half past two for Copenhagen, with a connection to

Oslo. I went to one of my favorite places for lunch. I behaved calmly. Everywhere I went, I tried to leave something behind me. For example, I gave an extra high tip to the waiter and the bartender so that they would remember me. I had no idea what the culmination of my situation would be, and I wanted to leave impressions of myself.

After lunch, on the way to the office of the Polish airline LOT on Constitution Square, I unfortunately ran into Ryszard Witke, a champion ski-jumper of Poland, and his new wife. Witke, whom I had known for several years, had been in Norway a few weeks earlier with the Polish team, and he was surprised to see me in Warsaw. Even though I was in a hurry, I had to spend a few minutes talking to Witke and his bride.

After they went on their way, I decided to drop into the post office. I bought big money orders with virtually all of the cash I had on me—several thousand Polish *zlotys*—and sent them to members of my family. I kept only the dollars I had.

I then entered the Polish airline office. I was certain that this was going to be the most difficult moment for me. First of all, I did not have a valid passport, for my diplomatic passport had been invalidated. However, I did have a false diplomatic passport that had been prepared many months before for just such a situation as this. But even with a diplomatic passport you generally cannot buy an airline ticket in Warsaw without a special letter from the Foreign Ministry giving you permission to do so, never mind how much Polish or American money you have.

I went to one of the clerks selling tickets. When I gave her my forged passport and the slip for the reservation from SAS, she asked me for the required letter giving me permission to purchase the ticket. I explained to her that I was going to buy the ticket with dollars. She said, "Fine, passport and dollars, but where is your—?" I knew that one telephone call to the Foreign Ministry could destroy my whole life. However, I had anticipated this and was ready to give her the name of an individual she could call.

Suddenly somebody touched me on the shoulder. I turned around and found myself face to face with another good friend

of mine, Zygmunt S, a former staff officer of the Polish Intelligence Service.

"Janusz, what are you doing here?" he asked. "You're not
in Oslo?"

"No, I'm here for a very brief visit. I came a few days ago."

"Well, it's nice to see you after such a long time. We must
talk."

I was trying to make casual conversation, but it was difficult.
I knew that S was no longer with Department 1, since he had
been involved in The Great Courier Scandal. But I sensed that
I had been followed for the past couple of days, and feared
that S's greeting might be a prelude to the regime's trying to
stop me. I asked him, "What are you doing here?"

"It's funny," he said, "but I have to tell you that since last
Monday I have been the executive director of this office."

It was then Friday. He turned to the female clerk and instructed, "Prepare a ticket for him and bring it to my office."

Turning back to me, S continued, "Let's go to my office
and have a talk. We haven't seen each other for a couple of
years."

Walking to his office I was expecting that I would be picked
up at any moment, but there was no one. Such paranoia is part
of life in a Communist country. I opened my briefcase and
gave S a good cigarette. I left some packages of cigarettes on
his desk. We started to talk, and he asked my reason for coming
to Warsaw. It was on official business, I lied. He was very
nice to me. After five or ten minutes, the woman clerk arrived
with my fabricated passport and my ticket. At his desk, I paid
for the ticket, and she wrote me a receipt.

I said: "Zygmunt, you know I have only forty-five minutes
to catch my plane. I'm sorry, but I have to leave."

"Have a good trip," he told me, not knowing the irony of
his words.

I took a taxicab from his office. I became involved in a
political discussion with the driver, and gave him a good tip.
Again I wanted to be remembered. When we reached the airport
I had still twenty-five or thirty minutes to wait. Unfortunately,
at the Warsaw airport I knew nearly everybody and nearly

everybody knew me. So my first act was to go into a toilet in the men's room and lock the door.

When they had called the plane twice, I decided not to wait any longer. I emerged from the restroom and went directly to the passport officer. He was a man who had known me for years.

His first question was, "Janusz, when am I going to see you again?"

"Well, I hope June or July."

I was required to fill out a special border control card. He told me, "Don't worry. I'll fill it out for you."

And he was again asking, "Are you sure you're coming back in June or July?"

"I'm not sure it's going to be June or July, but it's going to be this summer."

Even at this advanced point in my ordeal, I feared that I was still being followed, that this man knew I was trying to flee Poland. Only someone who has gone through an experience such as this can understand the fear with which it is fraught. I was terrified that the immigration officer might recognize my false passport, but he did not. On the outside I managed to appear very calm, but inside I was quaking.

A moment later, after getting through passport and customs control, I found myself in the departure lounge. There were businessmen from Sweden, as well as businessmen from other countries. A moment later my friend the immigration officer and a friend of his left their posts and came to visit with me. It was a visit that I did not need. We had a drink at the bar. They were very friendly and did not seem to want to leave me for a moment. In my state of near-panic, I was fearful that they had a special reason for being so convivial.

It was not having the drink that worried me, because the immigration officer, his friend and I had had drinks together many times before and I had always paid for them. But they had never appeared so excited—or so it seemed to me in my agitated mental state.

I decided that, if worst came to worst, I did not want to go to prison without anybody outside Poland knowing about it. So after the immigration officer and his friend finally left, I looked at the group of Swedish businessmen. One of them was walking toward the restroom of the departure lounge. I followed him into the restroom and, speaking in broken Swedish, asked whether he was a Swede.

He said, "Yes."

"Businessman?"

"Yes."

I beseeched him: "If you don't mind, take my business card. I'll give you two, one in Polish from the Polish Foreign Ministry with my official title, and the other in French with my name, my address and my title of secretary of the Polish embassy in Oslo."

Taken somewhat aback, he looked at my cards and said, "All right. But what am I supposed to do with them?"

"Nothing," I responded. "I'd simply be very much obliged. I hope I'll be able to explain it to you later on. In the meantime, I'd appreciate it if you would keep those cards in your pocket and watch me very carefully the whole time before departure. In the plane, if I'm there, we'll talk, or in Copenhagen, Stockholm or somewhere else. I'll explain to you everything you wish. If you don't see me on the plane, I have only one further request. Go to the Swedish authorities or a newspaper, and tell this story of what has happened just now at the airport between you and me."

He was a little confused and more than a little frightened. He did not understand anything that was going on. But he said, "All right. I'll do it."

After we came out of the men's room, I could see that he was watching me the whole time. Fifteen minutes later, there came an announcement; the flight was being delayed. Fifteen minutes after that, there was another announcement—a further delay. Ultimately it was not until half past three, an hour after the originally scheduled departure time, when we were told that we could leave the departure lounge for the plane. It was a Swedish-made plane of the Scandinavian Airlines System.

While we were boarding the craft my friends from the immigration service said good-bye to me again at the stairwell. Again, their affability threw fear into me. The plane taxied onto the runway. But then, just as we were ready to start our takeoff roll, the pilot cut the engines. Suddenly, I could see through my window two black Mercedes automobiles speeding down the runway toward our plane. My heart froze. *They are coming to arrest me,* I thought to myself. It is the precise moment to prove that I am really trying to escape. They really set me up well.

The cars' doors burst open, and I saw a squad of many of my ex-friends. Some of them were from the Polish secret service, some from the Polish Foreign Ministry, and some from the Foreign Trade Ministry. I had a Polish newspaper in my trembling hands. Next to me was another Swedish fellow, completely drunk, who kept bothering me to share a bottle of brandy with him. I could not get rid of him.

Then I glanced at the newspaper. I saw a story reporting that the Polish Commercial Foreign Trade Delegation was scheduled to leave that day for Japan. I looked out the window again at the men piling out of the two cars. I recognized the chief of the Foreign Trade Ministry, Professor Trampczynski, who was later to be appointed Polish ambassador in Washington. It was the damned trade delegation! They had obviously been delayed, and the plane had almost taken off without them.

When the delegation boarded the plane, one of my ex-friends, Brudzynski, recognized me at once. We nodded to each other. Again I was afraid—perhaps he knew too much and at the last moment I would be arrested. But no such mischance occurred, and in five minutes we took off.

After twenty or twenty-five minutes in the air, I asked the Swedish stewardess: "Are we still over Polish territory?"

"Wait a moment," she said.

She returned and reported, "No, we left Polish territory five minutes ago."

A few minutes earlier the drunken Swede in the next seat had tired of me and said, "You're not friendly; you're not like most Poles are," and had left his seat. After the stewardess assured me that we were no longer over Polish territory, I walked over to the Swede and said, "Now we can have your brandy, if you don't mind."

* * *

After perhaps a forty-five minute flight, we landed in Copenhagen. Now my problems were that I had only five or six dollars left, and although I was ticketed to Oslo, my real passport was not valid and bore no Norwegian visa. This time, for certain reasons, I was planning to use my actual passport instead of the forged one.

To my chagrin, virtually the entire staff of the Polish embassy in Denmark was on hand at the Copenhagen airport to greet the Polish trade delegation, which was scheduled for a twenty-four hour stopover in Copenhagen before continuing to Japan. I knew that I would be recognized by nearly all of the delegation from the Polish embassy. So I pretended that I did not feel well. The stewardess became worried that something might be wrong with my heart, and she brought me water. Meanwhile all of the other passangers left the plane. I gained enough time for the embassy delegation to bestow the ritual wreaths of flowers on the members of the trade mission, escort them to waiting limousines, and leave the airport.

I then debarked and ran quickly toward the telephone to call my American friends in Norway. I had only a thirty-minute stopover in Copenhagen before my plane to Oslo. But on the way, I was halted by my new Swedish businessman friend who had accepted my calling cards in Warsaw.

"Could you tell me now what this was all about?" he asked. It was not an unreasonable question.

"Listen," I replied, "I know that I promised to tell you. I can't tell you much because I'm in a hurry—I have to make a quick telephone call. But I can tell you at least that I have escaped from Poland, and I was afraid that at the last moment I would be arrested and nobody, at least for a long time, was going to know anything about my arrest. So I wanted you to relay the information that I had disappeared at the airport in Warsaw. And you helped me a great deal, because I was very close to big trouble and it was very important that you accept those cards from me. Now everyting is all right, and thank you very much. And please keep this whole story to yourself. I have to run to the telephone."

He said, "Do you have money?"

"Well, several dollars. I don't know whether I can pay for this call, but I'll try anyway."

"Don't worry," he assured me. "If you don't have enough money, I'll help you."

I thanked him again. I still do not know the name of this Swedish businessman, but if he should be reading these lines today, I hope he is aware of how much his help and understanding meant to me.

As it turned out, I had enough money to make the call. I telephoned a friend of mine in Oslo, a high-ranking officer of the American embassy there. I told him what I had done, and asked him to meet me at the airport and help me because there might be trouble.

Fortunately, I had no complications at the Copenhagen airport. Since I was an in-transit passenger, no one bothered to check my passport or visa status. Within a few minutes I boarded a plane for Norway. Only then did I realize that, except for my briefcase, I had not one piece of luggage—all I had with me were the clothes on my back.

During the flight to Oslo, my mind flashed back to my wife Krystyna and my son Jarek. I looked at my watch—still on Warsaw time. Normally, I would have been home long before now. They had to be terribly worried about me. What were they thinking? What were they saying? As my thoughts dwelled on them, my heart was heavy.

When I landed in Oslo, I arranged again to be the last passenger to leave the plane, and so I was the last in line before the immigration officer. I was one of the very few passengers, if not the only one, from Eastern Europe. Again my luck held. Upon reaching the window, I discovered that the officer was an older gentleman. He commented to me that he had been transferred from another unit and that this was his first evening at the airport. He was surprised to find that I was from a Communist country. My passport was thick, there were many different stamps, and the man was confused. He did not know what I had or did not have. And he did not really know what kind of cards he should fill out, what kind of cards I should fill out. So I helped him, cheating him just a little. (I am sorry to say it, old boy, since you were nice to me.)

While this was going on, I spotted two of my American friends, Robert and Bill, waiting for me. But they gave no sign of recognition, and did not move toward me. They were simply observing my arrival. When I emerged from the airport terminal, I could see that Robert and Bill were keeping away from me. I realized that they doubtless anticipated that Polish counterintelligence may have been watching me, and did not want to compromise me or themselves. They were right, of course. I could have been caught in a trap laid by Polish embassy officials waiting for me.

Yet I had less than one dollar in my pocket. I could not even take a taxicab. I had to run after the Americans because I could see that they were going to their cars and I was being left behind.

I rushed up to Bill in his Volkswagen and said, "Bill, don't leave me, because I don't even have enough damn money to get into town. Take me downtown."

He asked, "What happened?"

I said, "I have escaped from Poland, and there is no problem any longer with conspiracy, carefulness or anything like that. Take me to the proper place where we can talk."

He took me to the apartment where we had had all of our previous meetings, and after half an hour or more of discussion he left to organize some action for me.

In an hour Bill came back and drove me to the post office, where I called my family to tell them that I had left Poland and was not returning. It was a tragic discussion. I remember that the cost of the call was about two hundred Norwegian crowns, which at that time was about thirty dollars that I did not have. My American friends paid for that.

We went back to the apartment, had some food and a few drinks. I was extremely tired and fell asleep.

At five or six o'clock the next morning, I was again visited by Bill, along with some other American friends. They told me that I must leave Norway as soon as possible. At four o'clock that afternoon, I left by a Norwegian ship for Copenhagen. I had to depart as soon as possible, because I had not applied to the Norwegian authorities for any kind of political asylum or permission to enter, and if the Poles had discovered that I had come to Norway, they could have demanded that the Norwegian government turn me over to them.

I arrived in Copenhagen the next morning by ferryboat from where the ship had docked. Bill was waiting for me there and helped me get off the ferry. I understand that, by that time, there were discussions about my case underway between the United States embassy in Copenhagen and Washington. That afternoon Bill and I stayed for a few hours in a Copenhagen hotel, and then I went to the American embassy in Copenhagen for the night. The next morning I was informed that I was to go as soon as possible to Frankfurt.

I arrived at the Copenhagen airport with an officer of the United States embassy who was to accompany me to Frankfurt. An inspector of the Danish police was expecting me. He invited us into his office, and there an interesting incident occurred. I casually asked the inspector whether he would mind stamping my passport. At this, my American friend jumped up and exclaimed: "No! No! There's no reason to do that." The Danish officer was momentarily startled. He looked at me, he looked at him, and he said: "Well, what's the problem?"

I said: "I don't know exactly what's going to happen to me tomorrow or the day after tomorrow or a week from now. I would like to have some kind of record, and I would appreciate it very much if you could do this for me."

The Danish inspector looked at the American officer and asked: "Why don't you want me to do it? If he needs this, it's all right with me. There's no problem. If he wants it, why not? It doesn't cost me anything. Perhaps he has a good reason for it."

He took my passport and put two stamps on it. My American friend was nonplussed. He had not expected me to make such a request, and he was surprised that the Danish officer had granted it. But I had my reasons. I really did not know for sure what was going to happen to me. How did I know that the Americans would not liquidate me if my situation became too inconvenient?

In a couple of hours I was in Frankfurt. I was taken from the airport in an American army jeep, driven by a military policeman, through a special exit used only by the United States

Army. We drove to an apartment in downtown Frankfurt that had the name of a United States Army colonel on the door. Waiting for me in the apartment was a delegation of individuals representing virtually every United States intelligence and counterintelligence agency, and also including a psychiatrist, a physician, a security officer, and two bodyguards. (The latter were to become my permanent companions during my entire stay in Frankfurt.) It was the first time since my escape from Poland that I was truly scared. I could easily have been killed without anybody's even knowing about it. It was the first time in my life that I was on my own, face to face with "American imperialists" and at their mercy. The subconscious indoctrination from intelligence school was coming back. I felt very much alone.

I went through a very friendly but a very exhausting initial discussion with all of them. Many questions were asked. I was given a medical examination. Even my suit and the few other personal belongings that I was carrying were checked and re-checked. Everything was done in a nice way, but it was done.

Guns at
My Side

I STAYED IN THE FRANKFURT APARTMENT FOR
several weeks, until March 25, when I left for Washington,
D.C. Of course I went through a very tough debriefing. The
questioning continued endlessly and exhaustingly, in relays,
hour after hour, day after day, week after week. I filled up reel
after reel on the tape recorder. We worked sometimes ten or
more hours a day. But we took many breaks, because we were
also traveling to different countries.

The purpose of the trips was to recruit more defectors. (I
knew probably ninety percent of the Polish intelligence agents
stationed abroad.) I was going principally to West Germany
and to West Berlin, but also to Sweden, Norway and Denmark—this time under proper cover and disguises.

I always returned to the same apartment in Frankfurt. It was
a three-bedroom apartment, relatively small for the number of
persons occupying it. Among the occupants were two bodyguards, with guns under their arms in shoulder holsters. The
guards were usually changed every second day. They remained
at my side when I was called out for lunch with some American
official for a briefing, or when our motley group went out to
the movie theater. I usually went to dinner with several CIA
officers, and later on with Roger, who arrived one week after
I did from Washington and was to become my constant companion. On those occasions, my bodyguards withdrew. But

otherwise I was always with my two guards. They were protecting me, but at the same time I knew that if I should try to run away or cause any other kind of trouble, they would probably not hesitate to shoot me like a dog.

It was not really very pleasant at the beginning. For instance, I was told that I could never open a door if somebody knocked, because this was against regulations. I was told that when I was on the street I should not separate from my companions, that this was for my protection. But it was also clear to me that there remained some percentage of doubt about me in the minds of my American friends, that they were not really sure what I planned to do.

After a few days, when I had become friendly with everybody, the atmosphere became more relaxed and there were several amusing incidents. For example, the Americans decided that although I was reasonably well dressed by Western standards, I should be dressed in a different way. The Americans were afraid that someone might recognize me, that the Poles would send photographs of me to their people abroad and that they would find me. My new friends decided to dress me.

They sent a Jewish officer who could speak fifteen languages but none of them well, including English. He got rid of my suit, my coat, my hat, everything. This fellow went to department stores with me, spending as much as was necessary to dress me in his special style of dress—which I can only describe as tasteless. We shopped for two or three days, arguing the whole time. The shoes he wanted me to buy I did not want; the hat he wanted me to buy I did not want. Perhaps what he told me was good stuff really was, but I could not even look at it. The clothes were terrible.

Between excursions, the serious business continued without letup. My exhaustive debriefing was carried out by individuals from many branches and services. By people from Berlin, by people from Eastern European capitals (including several who were obviously CIA officers in Warsaw), and by people from Moscow.

I took my new friends to places that I knew in order to be able to explain them better or to confirm their information. By giving honest answers and information, I was at the same time making a demonstration of goodwill and cooperation.

West Berlin was of special importance. Then as now, West Berlin was an active center for intelligence operations of many countries. At this time Poland had only a military mission in the divided city, for there were no diplomatic relations between Poland and West Germany. Naturally the Polish military mission in West Berlin was loaded with Polish intelligence officers. And of course there was a large group of Americans doing nothing except keeping an eye on the Polish mission and the persons working there. I gave the Americans a great deal of help in this center of surveillance.

My most dangerous trip during this time was a mission to West Berlin. The Americans had asked me to meet some of my former friends from the UB there. There were several face-to-face confrontations with the Poles, with everybody keeping a finger on a trigger. With the tension emanating from both sides, an accident could easily have occurred.

I almost suffered a silly accident myself while staying in one of the American compounds in West Berlin. One day, when I had some free time on my hands, I decided to take a stroll through the garden. Without even a coat—even though it was still only March, the weather was nice—I embarked on my walk. Suddenly one of my young American bodyguards bolted after me with his gun out of his holster, yelling, "What are you doing? Why are you leaving the building?!" To be sure, in West Berlin anything can happen. But I did not see any reason for everybody to be so excited about my taking a walk in a garden.

Nonetheless, this is a small illustration of the atmosphere around me and the situation to which I was exposed in West Berlin. Of course, when, at the Americans' request, I began approaching my former colleagues with the idea of recruiting them, this was the beginning of additional troubles. Not all of my overtures were positive, not all of them were successful, and the reports started filtering back to Warsaw that I was not only a defector but a traitor.

I visited most of West Germany's important cities with my new friends, mainly CIA officers. We always had a pretty good time, and we were never overly concerned about how much money we spent, because everything was paid for by the United States government. It was an interesting if arduous time for me.

One week after my arrival in Frankfurt, I was informed by Bill, who had accompanied me from Norway, that he was to leave me and that somebody was coming from Washington. It was Roger who came. From the first moment I saw Roger, I did not like him. He probably did not like me either. However, later on we began to work pretty well together, and did so for more than a year. I eventually came to the conclusion that Roger was a nice person. Perhaps the real reason that I did not like him—I must confess—was that he looked almost exactly like one of my worst enemies in Poland. I never told Roger about that.

I never told Roger that I knew his full name and his home address in Maryland, either, but I learned it very quickly after just a few days in Washington.

I did this in a number of places with CIA officers. In spite of their nicknames, I knew their real names pretty well because they just were not careful enough. One CIA man even absentmindedly left an envelope containing top-secret U-2 photographs of Warsaw on my dresser! Sooner or later I was able to check most of their wallets and ID cards and be sure who was who. For instance, there was a very nice guy named Bob, and some others called Danny and Henry. In a few cases I even removed blank checks from their checkbooks because there were names and addresses printed on them. I really did not enjoy doing this sort of thing, but I was in a special situation and I wanted to know who was around me. I was dealing with a variety of "friends" with the same first name—Bill One and Bill Two, Roger One and Roger Two—and I felt that I had to know something more about them than that.

America
at Last

MY AGREEMENT WITH THE AMERICANS, WHEN I first began working with them as a double agent in Norway, had been that if at any time I was forced to leave Poland, political asylum would be given to me in the United States. But after my arrival in Frankfurt, I was told there was nothing to do except wait. They told me, "Our people are doing everything they can in Washington to get permission for you to come—but we can't guarantee anything." They had guaranteed it before, but not just now.

Finally, upon our return from the last of several trips to Berlin, I was informed that political asylum in the United States had been granted me, and that in two days I would be in America.

My first trip to the United States! My arrival was arranged to arouse no suspicions. There was no publicity surrounding my entry into the United States; indeed, this book is the first complete revelation of my defection. When I approached the United States immigration officer at Dulles International Airport outside Washington, in front and behind there were people protecting me, and there were more people waiting for me at the airport.

The immigration officer had probably been informed that I was coming and that I still had a Polish diplomatic passport without a United States visa. There were a few questions. They were very funny, because doubtless he did not believe my answers and I could not believe that he was seriously asking me such things as how long I was going to stay.

I had an American suitcase that I had bought in the PX in Frankfurt, plus another one that had been bought for me in Oslo. The United States customs officer, who had also probably been informed about me but betrayed nothing of it, asked: "Is this your suitcase?"

I said, "Yes, this and this," pointing to two.

"Do you mind if I open them?"

"Go right ahead. I don't mind." He opened one of the suitcases—and I discovered that it was not mine. Suddenly, a man nearby in the line pounced on the suitcase and protested: "Don't touch that suitcase! It's mine."

In a moment we learned that he was a diplomatic courier from Cuba en route to the United Nations in New York, and that his suitcase looked exactly like mine. No one had a right to open his suitcase. From the quick glimpse that we got, he did not seem to have anything in it except personal belongings, such as underwear and shaving equipment. The customs officer said, "I'm sorry. I thought I was opening this gentleman's suitcase, but his is the same as yours so I made a mistake." I don't know whether he made a mistake or not, but the whole episode was pretty funny.

While being driven away from Dulles Airport by my new American friends, preparatory to embarking on a new life in a new land, I reflected on my past. Those days between February 17, 1967, when I escaped from Poland to the West, and March 25, 1967, when I landed at Dulles Airport in Washington, were the end result of some fourteen years as a Communist intelligence agent. They had been the most important years of my life, but they had also been my most tragically wasted years. I had wasted them by being a part of a political ideology and bureaucracy that had corrupted my mind and my sense of humanity. Life is too precious for such a waste. I hoped I was now on the road to recovery.

I was taken to an apartment house in Alexandria, Virginia, where I stayed for several weeks.

Our apartment was on the top floor, the eighteenth or nineteenth, and had several nice bedrooms. The building itself is near Washington National Airport. We arrived at the apartment on a Sunday evening around seven o'clock, but because of the jet lag from Europe it was one o'clock at night for us. A group of us—including Terry, Roger and Bill—went to a Charcoal House restaurant across the street from the apartment house for dinner. I really did not enjoy it much; I was dead tired and wanted only to go to sleep.

After a day or two of relaxation, we resumed my debriefing. My renewed debriefing was as intensive as my first sessions in Frankfurt. And I felt as much a prisoner. Sometimes as many as ten to twenty persons trooped into the apartment in the course of a day to interrogate me. All but one of the debriefers were men. The one woman's name was Helen. She was about sixty years old, and gave the impression of being a very experienced official.

After several weeks of these goings-on, one morning we discovered that a security guard at the reception desk of the apartment house had called the building management and expressed concern about what was occurring in this apartment on the top floor. The fact that there were a bunch of men constantly coming and going had aroused suspicions that we were a nest of homosexuals. To avoid any kind of further trouble, we got out of this apartment in a matter of hours.

We moved to a house, probably rented by the CIA, in McLean, Virginia, not far from CIA headquarters. It was a nice new house, and I stayed there until October of 1967.

What happens to an ex-Communist spy in the United States? Or an ex-capitalist spy, since during the last few years of my career I was a double agent working for this side, not for the Communists. I must say, it has hardly been a bed or roses. First of all, it takes a long time before you are completely free.

From the time that I arrived in the United States until the following October, I was surrounded by quite comfortable accommodations—I might even say luxurious conditions—but I was never alone, even for a couple of minutes. I was going nearly every evening to beautiful restaurants and other places in the Washington area, but there were always two or three men with me.

Notwithstanding my permanent entourage, during this period I had occasion to meet some other persons and to make some friends, even some girlfriends. However, the latter relationships never prospered because, as you can imagine, it is rather difficult dating a woman with another man always chaperoning you—usually a different man each time.

Confining as such a situation is, it is not without its amenities. First of all, you are paid a comfortable salary. You take part in various exchanges of ideas, which can be stimulating. You stay busy working eight hours or more a day. Even later, when you are on your own, you are still paid a salary. The Agency wants your time at its disposal. You always have to be ready for the possibility that a sudden telephone call may change your plans for that day or the next.

But you are, for a period of time, a non-person. You do not have a name or any other kind of authentic identification. You know that the United States Attorney General has not even confirmed that you are in this country. For one year, sometimes two, you have no life. You are cut off from a normal existence by very special and suspicious kinds of people who are always investigating, questioning, never trusting you completely. Sometimes defectors change their minds. Every intelligence officer who goes over to the other side is always suspected of being a double agent, or a potential one.

One reason that those working in the intelligence business are cut off from normal life is that they are not really very normal themselves. The CIA people are funny in many ways. By and large, I never saw a bunch of bureaucrats so scared to death of losing their jobs. They would not survive one year in a Communist country. Given the importance and prestige of being a CIA man, to say nothing of the nature of the work, you might expect them to be not only honest but of strong character. You might also expect them to be fighters. But many of the CIA men whom I met did not really represent any kind of strength that I could appreciate or admire.

One example was an agent whose code name was Henry. He had a big mouth, but when the chips were down he was a small person. He would tell me what I should do, how an operation should be carried out. But he himself was afraid to make a move because of his boss. He was interested only in getting his promotion and preserving his retirement pension.

I must say that in spite of my truncated social life during my period of seclusion in McLean, I was provided with opportunities for feminine companionship. I would be driven to some hotel in downtown Washington or in Baltimore, usually in the company of several persons. In the beginning, I remember, there would be as many as seven or eight. There were guys from the CIA, from other intelligence agencies, from the FBI, and from a private protection service. But it was done in a very sophisticated and tasteful way. Usually we would have a nice dinner, and in the process we would meet a couple of women who had been set up for the occasion. They would be asked to join us for dinner, and it would go on for a couple of hours. And finally I would be told that I could pick whichever girl I preferred, and go with her to a particular room and do whatever I wanted to with her.

However, I would be told that we all had to get home before one or two o'clock in the morning. In the room, I would find, beside the bed, buckets of ice and Scotch and a bottle of gin and all of the necessary mix. Sometimes there would be a very small flower.

It was all done beautifully, but no chances were taken. The next room would be occupied by one of my friends. If I encountered any kind of problem, I had help at once. I was told that they had had some very bad experiences. One of the Russians had tried to kill a girl, and another one had tried to commit suicide, probably drunk or crazy and upset about the development of his situation.

Well, they did not have any problem with me. It was always peaceful and quiet and nice. There were some interesting moments, though.

I recall that one of the women, who was convinced that I was a Russian, told me, "Listen, Joe, you know they paid me a hundred and fifty dollars to spend this couple of hours with you. And do you like me?"

I said, "Yes, I like you."

She continued, "If you like me, I could be around again next time."

And I said, "Yeah, why not?"

She said, "If you promise to tell them that you really like me, I'm going to give you fifty dollars back. Because this is good business for me. It's not easy to get even a hundred dollars for only a couple of hours. You tell them that you like me very much and you don't want anybody else but me, and every time you see me, you'll get fifty dollars."

I remember that I really laughed like hell, especially later on when I told the guys jokingly, "Listen, I have a good business going, and I would like to stick to this business, if you don't mind." And I told them the whole story. But from a practical point of view, I was not interested in seeing this girl again. She had made herself inconvenient, and besides, why not still another one?

PART FIVE

The Travels of Enrico Kaminski

AFTER I MOVED TO THE UNITED STATES, I CONTINUED to travel all over the world, trying to persuade my former friends in the Communist camp to work for the West or to defect. In some cases my conversations were successful, in others they were not. In the latter cases, I was often able to convince the candidates that they should keep our meeting secret, since reporting our conversation to Warsaw would mean that they would never again be completely trusted by their fellow comrades. Two of my ex-friends, one in Berlin and the other in New York, did report their meetings with me to Warsaw, and very soon afterward both were recalled to Poland and removed from public life.

While carrying out this worldwide recruiting mission, I traveled as Enrico Kaminski, a citizen of a Latin American country. I have no idea why they picked Enrico Kaminski as my cover name or the Latin American nation as my cover country, for I cannot speak more than ten words in Spanish. Be that as it may, I managed to get around this way. My headquarters abroad was usually Frankfurt.

I was always surrounded by one or more CIA officers, but our agreement was that no matter what happened, I would never turn to them for help—in order not to compromise them. Instead, I would play it cool to the very end, and they would try to get me out of whatever trouble I was in as soon as possible. Fortunately, that was never necessary—we never experienced any major difficulties.

Because I had by then pretty well proved my dependability to the Americans, I was given more and more freedom (except in London—the British never did permit me to be unsupervised). I was visiting restaurants and meeting women without any escort and without any help. Needless to say, it was much more pleasant not to feel constantly suspected and "protected."

I realized that the Americans knew that I was now too deeply involved with them to go back to the other side. Not that I had any intention of doing so. But from now on, it was a one-way street. There was no return.

During one of my trips to Frankfurt, I was staying in the Inter-Continental Hotel, and Roger was lodged in the room next to mine. One night I picked up a woman in a bar and took her to my room. Of course she was some kind of prostitute, but she was a good-looking woman all the same. An hour or so later, I received a telephone call from the reception desk informing me that, according to the rules of the hotel, lady visitors had to leave by ten P.M. and it was just then ten o'clock. The woman and I had just started on a couple of fresh drinks and were preparing to go to bed.

I replied, "Okay, okay," and proceeded to ignore the call. Fifteen or twenty minutes later there was a knock on the door. When I opened it, I was confronted by two men from the hotel. One of them said: "Mr. Kaminski, you'll have to leave this room, because you have a lady guest and this is not permitted."

The other added in a rather nice way, "You know, this woman's reputation is well known."

I told them to go to hell and not to bother me.

But these same gentlemen came back a few minutes later with a plainclothes policeman. The long and short of it was that, after some more arguments, they kicked me out of the hotel, together with the woman. Being a little under the influence of liquor, I was not ready to give up anything to the Germans, least of all a pretty girl.

I drove the woman to her apartment and, after screwing her a couple of times, called Roger.

"Roger," I said, "just pack your stuff and get out of that hotel."

"Why?" he asked sleepily.

I said, "I was just kicked out of the hotel. And if you want to stay with me you'll leave too, because I can't go back there."

You can imagine Roger's state of mind. He didn't believe me, and he was furious.

"Impossible!" he exclaimed. "What are you telling me?"

"Go to the reception desk or call them and ask them. They just threw me out an hour ago."

Well, there was no other solution. Roger had to pack his stuff and move to another hotel with me, and we could never again stay at the Frankfurt Inter-Continental. Such are the trials of a CIA man.

Moscow's ritual accusation that West Germany is under American "occupation" is of course ridiculously primitive, since West Germany today is a nation that is hardly under anyone's hegemony. Nevertheless, after being involved in a variety of situations in West Germany, I must concede that in some operations the Americans conduct themselves in West Germany in much the same way as the Russians do in Poland. For instance, the arrangements for many of my meetings in West Germany were kept secret from the West Germans. As far as the Americans were concerned, it was intelligence business as usual.

When it comes to intelligence operations, it is difficult to find any country that uses "honest" and "decent" methods. Such terms are really irrelevant as far as spying is concerned. In saying this I am not condemning anyone; I am simply saying that in this kind of business the big powers do not always care about the niceties of friendly relationships with another nation when they need to use that country for intelligence purposes. They simply do whatever they think they must do, and do everything they can to keep it secret. And what they do is quite often far from honest in relation to the other country.

Just as Russia takes advantage of military bases in Poland, the Americans make the most of their bases in foreign countries—and not only for military purposes. A plane can bring people in and out of the base without the knowledge of the host country. Moreover, when you are engaged in an operation in the host country, it is sometimes very convenient to be able to disappear for a few days behind the guarded fence of the base, and then re-emerge from the base.

What I especially liked about the American military bases was their extremely good American food and their very cheap drinks. Frankly, I was afraid that I would have few occasions later to savor such good American cooking as I enjoyed on the American military bases in Western Europe. It was also at military bases that I first made contact with that addictive drug of the American character, the one-armed bandit, or slot machine. At the time, I was informed by my American friends— and I could see with my own eyes—that these one-armed bandits are a serious problem on many of the bases. Not so much for the American servicemen stationed there, but for their wives.

I also had the opportunity to exchange comparisons about the respective quality of the American post exchanges abroad. The reaction of visiting Americans was, in some cases, comparable to that of my Polish, Russian and other Eastern-bloc friends when they traveled abroad—all enjoyed the opportunity to buy cheap goods without paying duties. How very practical they were about comparing the prices abroad to the prices in their home country, and discussing what was good to buy and what was not good to buy.

I also had some rather amusing discussions with the Americans I always had around me. Young fellows usually, GIs stationed for a period abroad. They appreciated this time with me, I think, when they were relieved of their regular duties and could enjoy restaurants, movies and other diversions.

More often than not, the American soldiers at Frankfurt did not speak German. Nevertheless, in private the GIs complained about how nasty their German friends were. The collective view was "The Germans don't like us." One said, "I'm not surprised that you Poles don't like them, because I don't like them either." These young men also complained that ten years earlier a gift such as a package of cigarettes had been enough to make friends in Germany, but that now you needed a long list of goods. Not even human friendship, it would appear, is immune to inflation.

Such comments by my young GI friends brought back memories. I could remember, many years earlier, Russian soldiers telling us Poles that we did not love them. They had come as liberators, and we did not appreciate them. It may seem odd, but the situation of the soldier on foreign soil, whether he be a Russian in Poland or an American in Germany, is very much the same.

"Enemy of
the People"

AS PRODUCTIVE AND INTERESTING AS MY TRAVELS
for the Americans were, they did me no good back in my home
country. In the summer of 1968, I was sentenced to death by
a military court in Warsaw. High among the charges leveled
against me, at my trial in absentia, was the allegation that I
had endeavored to recruit Polish agents abroad for the CIA.

From the information that I have been able to glean, it
appears that my trial was held behind closed doors in a military
courtroom in Warsaw. No members of my family were allowed
to attend, except on the last day of the trial, when my wife and
one of my brothers were invited to sit in to hear the sentence
declared.

The chief witness for the prosecution was a functionary of
the Polish embassy in Oslo, who testified about what I, in a
private discussion, had said about the system in Poland. Actually I had not told him too much, but I had expressed some
of my feelings with a certain anger which he evidently reported
to Warsaw and then confirmed at my trial.

Also entered into evidence were some letters I had written
after I left Poland. One letter had been mailed to the secretary
of the Polish Communist party, and another to a former friend,
the Polish ambassador in Vienna. I had explained to them my
reasons for leaving, what I intended to do, and what would
have to be done in Poland before I could accept the situation

there. Also introduced into evidence were letters I had written to my family explaining the reasons for my defection. The letters had been intercepted by the authorities.

Later in the trial, two of my ex-comrades, Lucjan Lik from West Berlin and Babinski from the New York office of Orbis, the Polish government travel agency, testified that I had tried to recruit them to work for the CIA. The Polish *chargé d' affaires* in Moscow, Wladyslaw Napieraj, was likewise called as a government witness. In a Communist country, all of this was enough to merit the supreme penalty. I was pronounced an "enemy of the people" and condemned to death.

There is no denying that I was a traitor to the Polish regime, but I had not expected the maximum sentence. I was frankly surprised that they paid so much attention to me. Either I had underestimated myself or I had hurt them more than even I had realized.

My death sentence in absentia really did not mean anything to me, but of course it was quite upsetting to members of my immediate family, to my other relatives, and to my former close friends in Poland. From then on any kind of contact with me could be considered treason by association. Moreover, having this official sentence on my record meant that not only my name but those of members of my family went on various blacklists. The regime would now have more legal excuses for subjecting my family to hardship and possibly prosecution.

My wife at that time was exposed to considerable pressure. I must report that Krystyna and I had had our marital problems and had been separated from 1958 until 1960. We were later reunited, and when I escaped from Poland we were still married. At this point my wife and I had not even thought about any further separation or divorce. But for practical purposes, I advised her in my letters to get a formal separation, which in Poland has to be in effect for at least six months before one can apply for divorce. I told her that that was the only way she could get out from under the pressure they were putting on her.

I wrote, "Condemn me and do whatever else you want to do in order to disassociate yourself from me. Go even a step further and get a divorce as soon as possible, because not to do so is only going to hurt you."

My wife decided to follow my advice, and she was perfectly right in doing so. But during the divorce proceedings some faceless official inserted in the divorce decree the statement that one of the reasons for the divorce was that I had abandoned my wife and my son—without any mention of the reasons for my leaving. Another reason cited in the decree for granting the divorce was the fact that I had been tried by a military court in Warsaw for a criminal act—again without any explanation of the nature of the charges.

During one of my trips abroad from the United States, I sent four hundred dollars to my mother and my ex-wife. I sent the money through a special bank in Warsaw that handles funds from abroad. Krystyna picked up the money from the bank, but the next day she was visited by a very upset young woman from the bank. She begged Krystyna to return the money because otherwise she was going to be fired for failing to check a special list before paying out the money to my former wife. The money was returned. My mother was not even able to pick up her money, which to this day is still blocked in Warsaw. I hope that some day I am going to collect interest on this four hundred dollars which I cannot get back and my family cannot receive.

Of course the Polish regime took the position, to my mother, that this money was sent to you by your traitor of a son, and you are not going to touch it because it is CIA money that he received for committing treason.

Nevertheless, I managed later on to help my people in Poland through the assistance of friends. But I never again tried to send anything through the foreign exchange bank or by other legal means.

Still later, my mother began receiving abusive telephone calls at home. A voice would tell her, "We got him, your son! You're never going to see him again! He's dead." The caller would then hang up. Shortly after the phone calls started, one of my relatives, a married aunt who had lived in the United States for several years, decided to visit our family in Poland. I saw her off at Kennedy International Airport in New York. She arrived in Warsaw only a few weeks after my trial and saw my mother, who was understandably upset. My aunt explained to my mother that I had been seen just a couple of days earlier, and that I was alive and well.

Retribution against my relatives—for what I, not they, had done—was carried out in other ways. My mother's brother, who at the time I fled Poland was a colonel in the Polish army and an officer with considerable influence in the German-speaking Breslau region of western Poland, was kicked out of the army after I left. However, he didn't really care that much, because he too was fed up with the whole situation. He was one of the very few officers in the Polish army at this level who were not party members.

One of my brothers who was working in Polish counter-intelligence was removed from his job. Another of my brothers, who had a position in the central passport office, was also fired. My ex-wife, who was an officer in the censorship section of the Polish secret service in Warsaw, was likewise dropped. And because of me, my son—who can speak better English and Norwegian than I—was not accepted into high school.

As if this were not enough to satisfy my ex-friends in the Polish UB, one afternoon in May 1970 my son arrived home to find their apartment virtually demolished. The drapes, carpets, everything had been cut to pieces. Even the floor in some places was destroyed, as if by a sledgehammer. My son's phonograph records had been smashed, his coin collection stolen—along with everything else of any value.

Jarek telephoned his mother, and she rushed home by taxi. The police had arrived ahead of her, and their reaction was intriguing: "Oh, you were very lucky."

My ex-wife, gazing at the wreckage that was once her apartment, asked: "What are you telling me? What am I so lucky about?"

They said: "Well, if your son had arrived home half an hour earlier he could be dead now."

I do not have any proof, but there is no doubt in my mind that this criminal act was committed by the UB. For one thing, the building where my ex-wife and son lived was partly under governmental occupancy—their apartment had once been a safe apartment for Department 1. Thus the building was hardly the easiest in Warsaw to break into in broad daylight. Technically, it was not really even a break-in, since the doors had been opened with keys that fit the locks.

It was several weeks before I found out about the incident. In the meantime, my ex-wife and son managed to recover from the wreckage of their apartment and the loss of most of their material possessions. It was several months before I was able to get help to them. There was nobody going to Poland immediately who could take in material assistance from me. It was terribly depressing to know that persons who were so far away, but at the same time still so close to me, were in a tragic situation, and that although I possessed the means to help them, I could not.

Most difficult of all has been knowing that my relatives have gone through these hardships as a result of what I did. I feel that I owe them a lot. But they have never asked for moral compensation or added to my sense of guilt.

On My
Own

IN THE WAKE OF MY DEATH SENTENCE, SECURITY precautions were undertaken by my new friends to protect me against my former comrades, who, at least at the beginning, may have been prepared to look for me and execute me as they had done in 1960 in France to Wladyslaw Mroz. But I was not unduly concerned about the danger to my life. Eliminating me would not be good business for my ex-comrades, for if anything happened to me, the FBI's suspicions would fall on Polish officials in the United States—as the Polish embassy in Washington undoubtedly realizes. Besides, the UB knew that I had given all the information that I could to the West. They might still have killed me in Paris or London or somewhere else in Europe, but such things are more difficult in Washington. In any event, I am still alive—but I take prudent precautions. I am wary in my movements, and do not use my original name. With a death sentence hanging over one's head, one can never take life for granted.

The CIA kept me in the house in McLean, Virginia, for approximately six months. During this time I was allowed out a bit in order to attend an English school for foreigners in the Washington area. In addition to studying English, I was going to evening classes in other subjects. Such outings were very useful to me, as well as a psychological tonic. However, I couldn't really communicate with my classmates, since I couldn't tell them what I was doing in the United States. I had a cover story according to which a "rich uncle" was financing my education—which, come to think of it, was not too far removed from the truth. I would have liked to be a friend, and I would have liked to have friends, but it could not be. A person cannot go on indefinitely under such circumstances. Sometimes depression sets in. I know of many cases of individuals who reached the point where they were incapable of starting a normal life again.

It had to be this way at the beginning. But finally it could not continue, or I would have ended up as a vegetable. Finally I just told the CIA: "Now I'm going to live my own life."

By that time they were amenable to the idea. They said: "John, from time to time we'll need you; not as before, day after day, but maybe once a month, twice a month. But the main business is over; you can start your own life. Work, do whatever you want to do." My remuneration as stipulated by the financial agreement signed by me and by them when I came to the United States had been doubled. I had not asked for an increase, but because of my services they just gave it to me. And when I left to go on my own, I got an extra check for $20,000.

I entered the Graduate School of Business Administration at a major Northeastern university, where I studied for one year. Even during the time I was at the university, I was regularly in touch with CIA officials from Philadelphia and Washington, and also with the FBI, which obtained a great deal of information from me.

Because of my year in school, I did not begin a new professional life until July 1969, almost two and a half years after my escape. When I started looking for work, my friends offered to help me. This I rejected. Henceforth I wanted to do everything on my own, without official assistance. My first regular job in America was that of an accountant with a Washington, D.C., business corporation. It was my first opportunity to become acquainted with Americans in an open and honest way.

Being out on my own, and mostly in from the cold, to use John LeCarré's term, also set me to thinking about my national loyalties. Technically, I was still Polish. But in fact I belonged to a new country, the United States of America.

My growing feeling for my new country did not, however, take my mind off my struggles with the regime in Warsaw.

In an effort to get my son—who had been denied a passport—out of Poland, I made two attempts to approach representatives of the Polish regime on this side of the Atlantic, once in Canada and once in Washington. Both efforts proved futile.

In both cases, I was asked to work once more for my homeland's Communist regime. I was told that I could return to Poland any day I wished if I would vow to rejoin the Marxist ranks. I was promised repeatedly: "Give us the name of one American agent in Poland and your son will be with you in a week."

Each meeting lasted at least two hours. I had wanted to talk with a non-intelligence representative, such as an embassy staff member, but in both cases I confronted only a resident agent of the Polish Intelligence Service. In May 1969, I met in Montreal with Wieslaw Bednarczuk, who was then chief of Polish intelligence for Canada and who is at this writing in Washington.

The other meeting took place in Washington in May 1970. There my encounter was with Dyonizy Bilinski, first secretary of the Polish embassy in Washington—in theory. In practice, he was chief of the Polish Intelligence Service for the United States.

I had been so angered by the break-in of my ex-wife's apartment that I arranged the meeting on my own, and did not inform the FBI until half an hour before the scheduled encounter. I was certain that if I had advised the FBI any earlier, they would have tried to stop me. I did not want to be stopped— I was doing it because I believed that I was right and I was frantic.

The meeting took place at a restaurant in Washington called Adam's Rib. The session had its aspects of comic relief, since there were so many interested parties around. The FBI was on hand watching the Poles. Polish intelligence agents were watching me. There were even Russian operatives lurking about watching everybody. All of these shadowy observers of course tried to appear terribly casual in such a public place, while Bilinski and I talked across our table.

But for the fact that we were now official enemies, it might have been a reunion between two old friends. We had known each other for the better part of twenty years. His wife had worked with my wife in the censorship office of the Polish secret service in Warsaw. But at this encounter the tension was high.

At the meeting I told Bilinski: "Listen, I may not see my son for ten years. But all of you know me—one day I'll get desperate. I know that if I kill somebody I'll go to jail, and I'm not going to do that today, tomorrow, or the day after. I'm only afraid that what you're doing to my son in different ways may upset me so much that one day I'll decide that I don't have any choice but to take my revenge on you."

Bilinski asked: "Are you threatening me?"

I said: "No, try to understand me again. There is no deal between us. I'm not selling out an American agent in Poland for my son. We have known each other for a long time; you know I'm smarter than that. Why did I come here to talk to you? I want my son, and you're doing everything possible to prevent me from having him. You can ensure that I will never see him again, but remember—and tell this to Warsaw—one day you're going to pay for it."

Bilinski knew perfectly well that I meant what I said. His instructions from Warsaw had been to buy me for any possible price. He had started out promising me that I could drive with him to the Polish embassy and be in Warsaw the next day. I was not buying it. He listened, and I am certain that he relayed everything I said to Warsaw.

When we left the restaurant, there must have been ten or fifteen operatives from the Polish embassy waiting outside. I wanted to separate myself from Bilinski inside the restaurant, but he wanted to walk out with me. Outside I recognized many of my former friends, among them Zygmunt Sobczynski, Bilinski's deputy. They took moving pictures of us.

My American friends were in front waiting for me in a rented car. But the Poles tried to trail us, and it took several hours to shake them. I was afraid that if they found where I was working and living, even if they did not kill me they could bother me in other ways—through visits, telephone calls, surveillance and similar forms of harassment.

Clearly, they were not going to give my son back to me easily.

Notwithstanding President Carter's worldwide encouragement of human rights, including those of dissidents in the Soviet Union, it amazes me the way some United States government agencies often appear to be doing everything they can to stop persons such as myself from performing any actions on their own that could hurt the Communists.

I realize that behind this official reluctance is a desire to improve, or at least not to exacerbate, relations with the Soviet Union, Poland and other Communist countries. From a practical point of view, I have nothing against improving relations with any country. I would not like to see my homeland ravaged by another war, and I do not think that war—in our era of potential nuclear Armageddon—could result in liberation for Poland or any other country. Such a holocaust would be at the price of millions of innocent lives, and the ensuing chaos would be unthinkable.

Nevertheless, the mere existence of the Communist international totalitarian apparatus, and its subversive and expansive designs, is in itself a continuing threat to world peace—as has been demonstrated recently by the Cuban military infiltration of Africa. There are practical reasons why the non-Communist powers should maintain pressure on the Red bloc to ameliorate its system, and exiles from Communist countries could play a far more effective role in creating such pressure if they were allowed to.

My case is a classic example of the halters that are placed on exiles who would like to do more for their homelands. During my original dealings with the Americans, I told them: "I am going to do my best for you under one condition—that you do your best for me later on when I'm in the West." What I meant was that I wanted to continue to fight for change in Poland.

Under my understanding with the American authorities, they were to help me launch anti-Communist activities that could contribute to changing the situation in my homeland. That such has not been the case has been my greatest disappointment. On the contrary, I have been told many times by important persons that I should refrain from any kind of activity directed against the Polish regime. I have even been paid to be quiet.

I have had long, long discussions with them. They have sent brilliant people to me to try to convince me that I should remain silent. "If you need something more," they said, "we'll help you. But peace and quiet is best for you and for us." This was the fundamental subject on which we never reached agreement. And that is perhaps one of the reasons why I am writing this book.

I feel that I could do much more to serve my new country. But, as Enrico Kaminski might put it, it takes two to tango. It is up to them to decide.

My friends in the United States were indeed very interested, soon after I left Poland, in making my defection public for propaganda purposes. At the time I objected. I did not want to hurt individuals back home who had been associated with me any more than they had already been hurt. I decided to wait. As a consequence, I was one of the few high-ranking Communist intelligence officers—if not the only one—whose defection was not reported in any newspaper (as far as I know).

On several occasions I was invited to give lectures to American officials from the Foreign Service Institute, the CIA, the Sino-Soviet Institute, and the State Department. My audiences were always interested in knowing things that cannot be found in books or official publications. They wanted an understanding of the Polish situation as seen through my eyes. I appreciated the opportunity to share my experiences with these listeners, but such lectures were not the kind of anti-Communist activity I had in mind.

I consider it a tragedy of sorts that American diplomats who are to be posted in Poland are often trained at the Foreign Service Institute by Poles who do not know nearly as much about their homeland or its system as I do. The Institute employs Polish ex-housewives to brief American diplomats. Such women learned what they know from reading the newspapers in Warsaw and listening to the rumors. I spent nearly twenty years on the inside of government. It was my hope that the Institute people would be interested in proffering to me a part-time post—not for the money, because I already had a job, but because I knew the inner workings of the Polish regime.

I tried to get a job with the Voice of America on the editorial staff of the Polish desk. I passed all the tests, but I was not accepted. They played a game with me for several months, until I demanded a reply to my application. They called me on the telephone to say that they had no openings. A couple of weeks later they hired a less qualified person for the job that I had wanted.

There were other incidents of doors being shut in my face. I did not understand it and still do not understand it. I am well aware that those involved in the United States intelligence business tend to be very careful. One misstep and they lose their pensions. Furthermore, they think that since they are paid to combat the Communists, it is their exclusive duty, and they do not want anyone getting in their way. I did not want—and never will want—to compete with them. I regarded myself as offering cooperation and help. But they could not see it my way.

Communist intelligence people are also careful about making political decisions. But the few CIA or FBI agents who have defected to the Soviet Union, Poland or any other Communist country have been utilized by the Communists to the fullest.

There have been many more defectors from Communism to the United States, but the CIA seems interested in using very few of them on a long-term basis. I have at least three former Communist friends who had an extremely good relationship with the CIA, except for the fact that the agency wanted to shut their mouths.

One friend of mine, Wladyslaw Tykocinski, the former chief of the Polish military mission in Berlin who defected in May 1965, died in Washington of a heart attack. Tykocinski, whose CIA nickname was Walter, was a tremendous person. He knew six or seven languages and was a professional diplomat. He could have been head of the political science department at any university. But the CIA kept him in an apartment in Washington for more than two years, without letting him do anything, until he died.

I am still in close touch with the CIA. I work for them from time to time as a consultant. However, this occurs less and less often now, and I am not really that interested any longer.

Among other things, I should like to work with the six million persons of Polish descent in the United States. It seems to me that such a national minority from what is today a Communist country presents a fascinating opportunity for social and political communication.

I have spent many days, many evenings, with elderly Polish immigrants in Wilmington, in Philadelphia and in other places. Even though I was once in charge of the Warsaw regime's relations with Poles living abroad, I now realize that I did not understand the Polish expatriate community. I discovered it in America when I went to see these people. They wanted me to visit, to sit, to talk. Most of these Poles have little row houses in the poorer areas of cities, yet they usually have a lovely small garden and neat front steps that are swept very clean.

When they began to speak English, I discovered that my imperfect English was beautiful compared to theirs. When it came to exchanging names or telephone numbers, I was ashamed that they often could not write, either in Polish or in English. And they do not understand their old country. They would ask me about a small village here or there in Poland. What the Polish-American immigrant remembers about his own country after fifty years is a peasant village that never had electricity or running water. He pictures a tiny church and his house and a dirt street to play in (for in most cases he was a child at the time). That is his whole picture of Poland.

He is apt to express the impression that under Poland's Communist rule, the Communists are raping women, the country is a disaster. He would not be able to go to church—"It is awful what our country has come to." He doesn't know that his village probably has electricity, a school, a social house and a paved road, and that especially in a village one can attend church without fear of reprisal. Of course there is a Communist party organization in the village, but only a couple of people—peasants, typically—belong to the organization. Life in the Polish village still is not perfect, and indeed the whole system in Poland needs to be changed. But it is not the country that the Polish-American immigrant is talking about.

I tried to explain to these American Poles the true situation back home, both the pluses and the minuses. They listened, but they did not understand. However, I believe that, with the proper backing, my knowledge could be applied in their best interests and in the best interests of the United States.

I have also discovered some other realities about America. I expected a modern nation in every aspect, and a commensurate style of life—but this was not exactly the case. There are a tremendous number of things about the United States that I like, and there are quite a number that I do not like. During social occasions if someone asks, "Do you like this country?" I am simply not able to reply yes or no.

Let me recount some of my experiences. I have spent two nights in American jails, one in Washington, D.C., the other in Virginia. In both cases, of course, I was free the next day.

In the first case I was one hundred percent innocent. I had dared to be a witness against a policeman who had caused an accident while in civilian clothes. I did not know that he was a policeman, but the fact that he was was enough to land me behind bars. What I saw in that American jail was enough for me. I was told later, "Don't fight with the police in this country. You'll always be the loser." Somehow the advice had a familiar ring.

In the second case, I was guilty of the accusation of discharging a weapon in a public place. But my friends got me out of this trouble, too.

I had another experience in the American way of justice in the Southwestern city where I am presently living. I was robbed of my wallet in a department store by two criminals on probation. Later, in an exchange for cooperation with the police, the two robbers were set free without even bail or punishment. Because of these experiences and other observations, I have certain doubts about the American system of legal justice. It seems at once too harsh and too lenient. In serious cases, you have to have money or influence to win. How many of the common people have enough money or influence to prevail over the system? At the other end of the spectrum is plea-bargaining, which reduces penalties in order to make less work for police, prosecutors and judges.

For all of my problems and disappointments in the United States, I did not share the experience suffered by one of my Soviet friends, a young Armenian who fled Communism in April 1967, while on a visit to Tokyo. He had never been to the West, and he spoke no English. He was a young fellow, a simple engineer. Suddenly in the West he was greeted as a hero. There were big articles in the newspapers acclaiming him as a "Russian scientist." He was not really a scientist, but the American newspapers convinced him that he was; he started to believe his own press clippings. I once invited him home for dinner, and he insulted me and my friends because he felt he was too good for us, having been on the front page of *The New York Times*.

Not surprisingly, this fellow thought that he was going to live the rest of his life as a king. His expectations were wildly out of touch with reality. He anticipated a house, a Cadillac, an easy life handed to him on a platter. But suddenly, after the initial fanfare, he was on his own. With the first $20 that he managed to earn in the United States, he took an American girl to dinner. She did not even let him kiss her after dinner, and he was expecting to go to bed with her. He became increasingly disillusioned. He could not understand why he was now just an ordinary person.

Today this man is in prison back in the Soviet Union. After a couple of months in the United States, he ran away from his American friends and went to the Russian embassy. A few hours later Soviet Ambassador Dobrynin made a call to Secretary of State Dean Rusk informing him that, on the next evening, a Russian citizen would be leaving the United States and suggesting that it would be very nice if at John F. Kennedy International Airport the Soviets could exchange his documents. The young engineer left the United States the next night, went for a temporary period to Armenia, and then to jail in Russia.

Through no fault of their own, the American newspapers had spoiled him. I am not really blaming the United States press, because my friend obviously had his personal problems. But one must remember that in a Communist country the printed word, because it is so selective, has a tremendous effect on people. Nobody before had ever written a single sentence about this man.

But when he turned himself in at the Soviet embassy in Washington, I did not see one mention in the American press. Nobody was concerned about why he had abandoned the United States—and about how many years of his life he was going to spend in Soviet prisons after his short experiment with American freedom.

Since my arrival in the United States was accompanied by no public fanfare, and since I had a more realistic view of my new situation, I have spared myself such disillusionment. Nevertheless, my sojourn in America has had its bad moments.

For one thing, having come to America in an irregular way, I had to wait six months before I received papers attesting to my presence in the United States.

To protect yourself in situations such as mine, you usually change your name—as I did. At first the change is informal, but later you must formalize it through a court order. It is a relatively simple procedure, yet there is a period of time when you have ID cards in your new name but your name has not been changed formally. You have the unsettling feeling that someone could kill you and nobody would be able to identify your corpse. It makes for troubling reflections.

The CIA has been unhappy with me since my personal confrontation with my Polish ex-friends in Washington. The Agency considers it very serious that I did not inform them far enough in advance.

My friends in Washington are not particularly happy about my writing this book, either. But I refuse to do nothing. I am now living under an assumed name in a Southwestern city whose spirit of openness and optimism I find to be a most refreshing contrast to the closed and grim society out of which I came. I could have a most peaceful life if I so desired. But I want to leave something that will help others understand the story of my life, and that of hundreds and thousands of other human beings who were, or are, part and parcel of an inhuman system.

The idea that this book will aid my native countrymen is extremely important to me. I know that I have many friends in Poland who wish me the best. In spite of my initially confined circumstances in the United States, I am not in some kind of concentration camp or jail in America. I am free. And by the publication of this book my countrymen will know this.

I want to give a message to my friends in Poland that they should remain strong and continue to struggle. I should like to tell them that I do not regert my decision, that my desire for a free Poland is stronger than ever.

I also hope that this book will help inform Americans about the conditions that really exist in Poland. Many stories that have been written about Poland by the American press do not reflect the reality of my homeland.

Some non-Communists who have had the opportunity to visit Poland or the Soviet Union have thought that conditions under Communism are wonderful. They have gone there as tourists and discovered that—in Warsaw, for example—for five dollars you can have a magnificent dinner with drinks. They did not see poverty. They spent most of their time in Warsaw in the best hotels and restaurants. But they did not know that ninety-nine out of one hundred people in Poland never have a chance to enter such a hotel, that it is impossible unless you have dollars or other hard currency.

Furthermore, the vast majority of these dollars spent in the best hotels, restaurants and nightclubs in Warsaw are not used to improve the lives of the Polish people. They go to the Polish government to be spent on the Communist image. The Warsaw regime has expenses that must be paid in Western currency. Consider the Polish embassy staff in Washington. They have to have dollars to survive, and how can they get them? They cannot buy them for Polish *zlotys* or Russian rubles; there is no commercial bank in the Western world ready to exchange

Communist currency for dollars. This can be done only on the black market in Vienna. The embassy gets its dollars from those spent at home by visiting foreigners, or those acquired by the Polish government through trade with the West.

I would wager that any Westerner who spent a month in Poland, working and living as the people there have to work and live, would come away with a different conclusion about life in my homeland.

Even if you should read Polish, you would not discover the reality of Poland by perusing Poland's newspapers. If you were a very good Polish journalist and handsomely rewarded, what would you write? For if you were to protest, you would not be a journalist any longer and your standard of living would be reduced at once to one-tenth or one-twentieth of what it was.

I know that I have many friends left in Poland who are not afraid, in spite of government pressure, to get in touch with my family in order to help them. On the other hand, there are those who have cut off relationships with my brothers, my mother, my son. Strange as it may seem, I don't blame them for this. They felt that they had to do so for their own self-protection; most of these persons are in a dangerous enough situation as it is. And then there are strangers who have helped my relatives in a quiet way. My mother, my ex-wife and my son have received money and other assistance from individuals we do not even know, sent from as far away as Hungary.

The struggle for reform in Poland will continue, naturally, with or without me. And most of my friends understand that I was not—and never will be—a traitor to the real interests of the country.

Poland
Today

LET ME SAY A FEW WORDS ABOUT EAST-WEST relations, particularly as they affect my homeland.

I believe that there is a future to be built on the tenuous soil of East-West relations. I believe that if change is to be encouraged in Eastern Europe and the Soviet Union, the influence of the United States must be actively brought to bear.

It might be psychologically satisfying to cut off all relations with the Communists, but people cannot be kept apart forever. Moreover, we anti-Communists cannot contribute effectively to the ultimate liberation of the millions of subjugated human beings in Viet Nam or Cambodia or Poland or any other Eastern European country unless we can exert our influence, mainly on Russia.

I am therefore gratified at the signs of detente that have occurred in recent years—such as the visit by Edward Gierek, the current leader of the Polish Communist party, to President Ford; the establishing of diplomatic relations between the United States and East Germany; and the United States' moves toward normalizing relations with Cuba.

Political evolution within the Communist bloc is not impossible. In spite of the totalitarianism and barbarism that still exist in the Communist camp, there has been a subtle but unmistakable change. Conditions in Poland are better today than they were a decade ago. And the Soviet Union, for all its inhuman repression of dissidents, is not the same as during the dark days of Stalin, or during the era of international brinkmanship indulged in by the shoe-pounding Nikita Khrushchev. We should not forget that the great influences that helped bring about these changes were not those of intractability, which predominated during the period of the Iron Curtain, but those of detente, which, with some conspicuous exceptions such as the Cuban missile crisis, have largely prevailed since the early 1960s.

Most Americans whom I have met know relatively little about the situation in Communist countries. This should not be the case. Americans should know more. It is not enough to think that Communism is bad, without being aware of the hard specifics.

Young Americans are often so idealistic, yet so uninformed. To me the fact that one has the right to protest injustice in this country is still a wonder.

I have the impression that many American dissenters do not realize how fortunate they are to be able to speak out.

The people of Eastern Europe are quite capable of fighting on their own for freedom, but the chances of their winning are so limited that under present circumstances the odds are against renewed popular revolt. Nobody today is suicidal enough to attempt another uprising as in Hungary in 1956, when Radio Free Europe and the Voice of America were exhorting the Hungarians to rise up and fight but there were not enough guns and Washington did nothing and 250,000 Hungarians were killed by the Russian tanks. Nobody in Eastern Europe expects that American soldiers are going to fight and die solely for the freedom of Czechs, Poles or Hungarians; after all, it was the leaders of the West, at Yalta, who sold us to the Russians.

In sum, I believe that the West should redouble its efforts toward finding a peaceful solution to the confrontation between the Communist and anti-Communist camps, fraught as it is with the perennial threat of nuclear blackmail. These efforts must invoke first and foremost the tremendous influence of the United States.

Even though the American dollars left in Eastern Europe by tourists help finance the propagation of Communism, the tourists themselves, by their mere presence, are doing a better job than Radio Free Europe and the Voice of America put together in influencing attitudes behind the Iron Curtain.

An American tourist who spends one week in Warsaw probably does more good for Poland than a score of employees of the local United States embassy. After all, tourists can do many things that diplomats cannot—they can open the minds and the eyes of people who have never had a chance to set foot outside of their Marxist-ruled homeland.

Tourists can help cut through the officially engendered fog of distortion that exists about the West. I am still supplied with all of the most important Polish publications, and sometimes even I am shocked by the articles reprinted from American newspapers. Everything negative about the United States is translated and reprinted—articles on the suicide of a politician, the incident at Chappaquidick, a vitriolic debate in Congress, or a case of social injustice.

However, fewer and fewer Poles are accepting such articles as the whole story. Today there are many visitors from abroad to tell the truth about conditions elsewhere.

Still another development—startling in its unexpectedness—has been the selection of a Polish Catholic cardinal, Karol Wojtyla, as the new Pope of the Roman Catholic Church. This is one of the most important events of the twentieth century.

One can only imagine the confusion and concern of the Polish United Workers [Communist] Party (PZPR) as it struggles to deal with this situation. The party will have to be very careful and polite with John Paul II, for the vast majority of the Polish people are behind him and hostile to their country's political rulers. The Poles needed something to boost their morale, and now they have it—more than anyone could have dreamed.

How will the Russians react? Will they permit the Warsaw regime to dance around the Pope because he is a Pole? Or will they try to force Gierek to commit political suicide in his relations with the former archbishop of Cracow? Even the other Eastern European nations will not be immune to the effects of Wojtyla's ascension to the throne of Rome, since he is not only the first Pope from Poland but the first from Eastern Europe. And what is going to happen in Italy and France and other Western European nations with Communist movements but Catholic traditions? As the first non-Italian pontiff in 456 years, Wojtyla is going to enjoy a broad and receptive audience among all the Catholic peoples of Western Europe.

One way or the other, this unforeseen and astonishing circumstance spells only trouble for Warsaw, Moscow and the rest of the Eastern Bloc. The Pope is elected for life, and this one is young—at 58, the youngest pontiff chosen since 1846—and strong. And he knows well who the church's enemies are and how to fight them.

In the Communist countries of Eastern Europe, people are not quite as intimidated as they were in the past. The Reds still ring their national borders with guards and police dogs, and still do not let people leave voluntarily. Inside the borders, the secret police still watch everyone, directly or indirectly. But there is a new mood, a new spirit. The young people in these countries today are more independent. They go to jail; they protest, even though the fight is still hopeless.

I personally believe that a quarter-century from now, Communism will still exist. But Communist Poland will not be the same country that it is today, even as it is not the same country today that it was yesterday. This process will be costly—countless more persons are going to spend years in prison or in mental institutions.

But the day will come.

It has to come.

The fight will continue.

EPILOGUE:
1982—Martial Law And Its Aftermath

A Reflection

MORE THAN TWO YEARS HAVE PASSED SINCE THE original edition of my book, *Double Eagle,* appeared. During that time, dramatic events have occurred in Poland.

Numerous reports and commentaries are being written about the situation in Poland. I have no intention of duplicating them here, or of offering a definitive analysis of what the future may bring. However, I would like to present my own observations, based on my personal knowledge and understanding.

Because of the imposition of martial law by the Communists on December 13, 1981, and the effort to crush the Solidarity movement, this epilogue cannot only be a look back at the principal characters who figured in my original volume. Their destinies, of course, are not irrelevant, for what has happened to them has either been the inevitable result of the system in Poland or has influenced the tragic course of events there. I think for example of:

Arciszewski, the Polish diplomatic courier and brother-in-law of Deputy Prime Minister Piotr Jaroszewicz; *Czeslaw Bleja,* commercial counselor of the Polish embassy in Copenhagen; *R. Broz,* operative in Branch 1-A, Department 1, of the Polish Intelligence Service; *Brudzynski,* the Polish "friend" who recognized me aboard the LOT airliner on which I escaped from Poland; *Tadeusz Cibor,* chief of Branch 3, Department 1, dealing with Western Europe; *Cieslak,* of the Branch 1-A radio group; *Josef Cyrankiewicz,* Prime Minister during the 1956 Poznan uprising; Antoni *Czajer,* who figured in Branch 2 of

Department 1, dealing with the Americas—all have been retired, most of them prematurely.

Dyonizy Bilinski was the first secretary of the Polish embassy in Washington whom I confronted personally to protest the break-in of my former wife's apartment in Warsaw. Bilinski, at this writing, is counselor of the Polish mission to the United Nations in New York, a post he has held since 1977.

Ambassador Birecki was chief of the Polish mission to the United Nations and former Polish ambassador to France, under whom I worked in the Foreign Ministry in Warsaw. He later rose to be the second highest official in the Polish Foreign Ministry. But because Birecki is Jewish, his career went into decline during Poland's anti-Semitic campaign following the 1967 Arab-Israeli war. In spite of his outstanding intellect and diplomatic ability, Birecki and his fellow Jews in the Foreign Ministry were progressively degraded; some were reduced to working in the Ministry's archives. Finally, in 1978, Birecki applied to emigrate to Israel. He was permitted to leave, but went instead to Denmark, where he now lives in self-exile.

Edward Gierek was the former coal miner who succeeded Wladyslaw Gomulka in 1970 as leader of the Polish Communist party. In the wake of riots over prices, Gierek himself fell from power. He was deposed by Stanislaw Kania in 1980 amid accusations that Gierek was responsible for having run up Poland's tremendous foreign debt, and that his government was shot through with corruption. Following the imposition of martial law in December, 1981, Gierek was arrested—no doubt so that the Jaruzelski regime, while rounding up Solidarity's leaders, could allege that it was being even-handed with its opponents.

Wladyslaw Gomulka, the long-term head of the Polish Communist party, has just died. Aging and nearly blind, he had been very sick with cancer of the brain. In the Communist tradition of exploiting the memories of elder statesmen—even

those previously imprisoned and humiliated by the system—
the martial law regime gave Gomulka a hero's funeral.

Piotr Jaroszewicz, deputy prime minister (under both Gomulka and Gierek) and brother-in-law of the diplomatic courier
Arciszewski, was also arrested with the declaration of martial
law on December 13, 1981.

Slawek Lipowski, whose name figured in Branch 2 of Department 1, dealing with the United States, Canada, and Latin
America, is again stationed in the Polish embassy in Washington, under the title of counselor.

General Mieczyslaw Moczar, the hard-line, anti-Semitic ex-
leader of Poland's Union of Former Combatants, lost the fight
for top power to Edward Gierek in 1970. One factor in Moczar's
defeat for the leadership was that the anti-Semitic agitation he
encouraged following the 1967 Arab-Israeli war almost got out
of hand, and actually had to be repressed. Even the Russians
became concerned that they could not control Moczar. However, he was later appointed head of Poland's *Najwyszcza Izba
Kontroli* (literally, "Supreme Control Chamber"), a government watchdog agency. From this position, which he still holds,
Moczar was reportedly instrumental in destroying the Gierek
regime—even though it took ten years—by quietly amassing
damaging accusations against it. Moczar is now around 68 years
of age and may be too old to aspire to the top leadership, but
who knows? The Russian leadership is even more ancient.

Stanislaw Pichla, former Polish ambassador to Denmark,
and a classmate of mine at the Polish Intelligence Service school;
today Pichla is director of the consular department of the Polish
Foreign Ministry. His continued active service is an indication
that, in spite of the gains made by Solidarity in transforming
Poland's labor ranks, such bureaucratic redoubts of the Communist regime as the Foreign Ministry and secret service remain
essentially unchanged. Although many people have been shuf-
fled, retired, fired or have committed suicide, the power in
such bastions of officialdom is ultimately in the same hands.

Walesa and his Solidarity colleagues did not know who was important in these organizations because, except for the highest-ranking officials, the names are kept secret. Solidarity could discuss this or that factory official or boss, but I know that they were not touching the top powers of the regime.

Mieczyslaw Rakowski, the longtime chief editor of the magazine *Polityka,* the official journal of the Polish Communist party, became deputy premier under Kania and has maintained his post under Jaruzelski, under whom Rakowski has emerged as a fervent defender of the martial law regime. Rakowski is one of Poland's greatest political disappointments of the past several years. Once considered a relative liberal, Rakowski has become a servant of Moscow. He has become politically estranged from members of his own family. Rakowski's former wife, the prominent violinist Wanda Wilkomirska, is one of eight intellectuals who, in an act of high courage, signed a petition protesting Poland's martial law. Both of Rakowski's two sons have left Poland and are currently in West Germany.

Witold Sienkiewicz; as chief of the Polish Intelligence Service, UB, Sienkiewicz was once my boss. He retired from the UB around 1962 following the Great Courier Scandal and the suicide of Operative Zbigniew Dybala. After several years in retirement, Sienkiewicz—who had always been interested in sports as a hobby—became president of the Polish Boxing Federation. In this largely honorary position, he has visited the United States several times with the Polish boxing team. Imagine my astonishment and amusement when I saw Witold Sienkiewicz, Poland's former master spy, on American television during a Polish-U.S. boxing match in Indianapolis, Indiana!

Stefan Staniszewski; a member of my class in the intelligence school and a former Polish ambassador to Sweden, Staniszewski is Poland's recently appointed ambassador to Great Britain. Shortly after the declaration of martial law in Poland, it was he who announced in London that Lech Walesa would be released in "two weeks" and that martial law would soon be lifted—statements that were instantly scotched by the Warsaw regime. The incident can hardly bode well for Stani-szewski's relationships with his superiors.

Stefan Zwirski; one of my former friends in the Polish For-eign Ministry, he unknowingly provided the car and driver that facilitated my escape from Poland. Zwirski is now chief of security at the Polish embassy in Washington.

Stanislaw Szumski, radio specialist, is now stationed at the Polish consulate in Chicago, as an attaché.

Josef Winiewicz, former second-ranking official in the Pol-ish Foreign Ministry, with whom I had my last official con-versation before my escape from Poland, was retired two years after I defected to the West. He had been a close friend and supporter of Romuald Spassowski, the Polish ambassador to the United States who defected following the declaration of martial law in Poland. My defection hurt Winiewicz, and his standing, even in retirement, and he has undoubtedly been hurt further by Spassowski's highly publicized political defection.

At least seven others mentioned in the hardcover edition of *Double Eagle* have committed suicide.

Different fates, different situations, different futures—yet nearly all of the above cast of characters from the original edition of *Double Eagle* were my onetime close friends—all of them "devoted" Communists. But their destinies have been different. Some are up, some are down, some are still making careers because they are for sale. Some, rather than remain part of the system, decided to quit. Some are dead because they couldn't compromise anymore.

But the individuals involved are only pieces in the mosaic of Poland's larger drama, which I firmly believe confirms the thrust of the original edition of *Double Eagle,* which closed with the words:

"The fight will continue."

I continue to believe this. The Solidarity movement was able to accomplish more than we might have dreamed. In spite of everything that has happened since martial law was declared, those accomplishments cannot be totally negated. I firmly believe that a very strong underground movement will survive. Not necessarily in the sense of open defiance, but there will be a very strong underground political opposition. The Communist government will have great difficulty trying to eliminate this opposition.

Nevertheless, the fight will not be easy. Nor is the ultimate outcome in my homeland necessarily guaranteed. One can never ignore the overwhelming power of the modern police state—and the Communist police state in particular. Moreover, Poland still sits on the border of the Soviet Union. There is no doubt of the Russian role in, and the premeditated nature of, what has happened in Poland.

When he gained power in Poland in September, 1981, General Wojciech Jaruzelski said that Polish soldiers would never fire upon Polish workers. Therefore, everyone felt that the danger could only come from the Russians. This was a serious failure of judgment on the part of Solidarity and Western governments. They felt that as long as the Russians did not intervene, the Poles—namely Solidarity, the army and the church—would solve their differences themselves.

When Stanislaw Kania was forced to resign and Jaruzelski took over, there was no question in my mind that this was the beginning of the end. I didn't know how or when, but the implications were unmistakable. In taking this view, I was in the minority among my fellow Poles and my friends in the Western intelligence community. Polish governments, even the Communist government, had traditionally respected the Polish worker. Jaruzelski is a Russian-educated Communist, but the feeling was that he is primarily a Polish soldier and a Polish patriot.

Thus, when Kania was removed in favor of Jaruzelski, many people were not upset about the shift. They could even see advantages: all government power in one hand—General Jaruzelski; Archbishop Jozef Glemp, new primate of the Polish Catholic Church; and Lech Walesa, leader of the Solidarity labor movement, could solve all of the problems.

I believe that the decision to impose martial law had already been made in September. It is clear now that preparations for it were started as early as March of 1981. Kania and Jaruzelski were probably aware as the preparations developed, but the Russians were pulling the strings. All of the regulations spelling out martial law were printed in Russian by September. This was a 100% Russian enterprise.

Martial law was imposed at midnight on a Saturday. The timing was perfect. The details were carried out with the precision of a Swiss watch. It was superbly orchestrated. You can't organize this sort of thing overnight—it involves a complex set of problems. Every radio and television station was taken over by people in uniform. People are not routinely available in the Polish army who on five minutes' notice can become accomplished broadcasters. Every important spot in the country was taken over within a matter of minutes, including every means of public transportation and every other public service. There must have been a substantial preparatory effort on the part of many people.

The whole process of imposing martial law on the country took only six hours. At 6 A.M. Sunday, Jaruzelski delivered his first speech, and it had been prerecorded. In six hours everything was under control and every important person in the activist opposition had been interned.

The operation was a classic demonstration of the power of the Communist police state, which owes much of its effectiveness to modern technology. Not even the Czar could put uniformed cossacks on television.

Jaruzelski is a hardcore military man. Kania is not that type. On the day of Jaruzelski's takeover from Kania in September, or shortly afterward, Jaruzelski was probably told that opposition activity in Poland had to stop, that the Russians did not want to send troops to Poland nor was that move necessary. The whole operation could be done in a very efficient, well-organized manner: Polish soldiers would provide the logistics; the Polish secret police would provide the club.

The soldiers' consciences would be clear for they could tell themselves they would not shoot Polish workers, but would aim over their heads.

And because the Polish workers had no guns, the secret

police could move in and handle the situation with very few weapons.

The Polish UB has not changed an iota. It is the same, shadowy intelligence organization that it was five, ten or twenty-five years ago. Its staff is trained by the KGB, paid the best salaries, enjoys the best fringe benefits, has the best medical care. Also, it had no choice but to participate in the imposition of martial law. If Solidarity had taken over, the UB's personnel would quickly have been strung up on the lamp posts. So, the dirty job would be done.

Frankly, when Jaruzelski took over, in spite of my misgivings I was hoping that I was wrong and that the move might represent not only protection against Russian intervention but a positive development for Poland's internal situation. I felt this way knowing that Jaruzelski had to be a good Communist, but also aware of his background—he is a relatively reasonable man who understands all of the forces and factors at work in today's Poland. I realized that he could not liquidate the Communist system in Poland. But I hoped that as Moscow's confidante Jaruzelski would find the best possible accommodation, with Walesa and the Catholic Church, to solve the crisis peacefully. Wishful thinking.

However, I must say now that the whole takeover was a tremendously shrewd play on the part of the Russians. The Communist Party of the Soviet Union even created a special group under the late Politburo member Mikhail Suslov to deal with the psychological aspects of solving the Polish crisis! The question before the Kremlin's psychological task force was how to handle the situation so that there would be no reason for bloodshed. To no one's surprise, one conclusion drawn by Suslov's group was that Polish comrades needed advice on how to deal with the situation. Another was that the situation could not be handled in 24 hours.

One catalyst for swift action was a resolution passed by a workers' plenum in Gdansk calling for a public referendum on Poland's political system. It was a call for a vote of confidence or nonconfidence in the system.

In any free election in Poland, the Communist (United Workers) Party would get 10% of the votes at best. Thus the

Gdansk resolution represented the most direct challenge to the regime. Nevertheless, Solidarity committed itself to the position that, even if the Communist Party lost, Poland should continue its friendship with the Soviet Union and membership in the Warsaw pact.

At this point in the game, we can only assume that the whole plan for the implementation of martial law was pretty well complete. Also, the situation in Poland was appropriate. There were food shortages. Christmas was coming and the people were in a peaceful mood. Families were getting together. People were bracing for the winter, which is pretty tough in Poland.

So for the planners of Poland's incestuous rape, it made no sense to wait longer. Another factor was the Polish parliament, which was no longer a rubber stamp. It could not be expected to pass a law forbidding strikes. It could no longer be controlled. There could be but one solution to these many problems: martial law. For anyone who dares break this law the consequences range from two years in prison to death.

So one day in September the decision was made and Jaruzelski was told to implement it. He had been playing a game with Walesa, the Catholic church and their proposals for some time. The regime would agree to a meeting, postpone the meeting, deliberate to gain time—all the while preparing the troops for takeover—and it wasn't merely a case of preparing one hundred or so people but at least several *thousand*.

For example, they sent military teams to small towns and villages ostensibly to make sure that there was no black market in food. The real mission was to identify the local leaders of Solidarity. Suddenly all the teams were recalled to Warsaw—at the time nobody could understand why. Of course, the teams represented the initial preparation for martial law. These same teams are the people who are carrying out martial law.

It is also worth noting that even as the Warsaw government was arresting people, Soviet airplanes were landing in Poland not with soldiers but with food. Food in cans and crates. This food had obviously been readied. It had been sitting somewhere. And it reflected another psychological element that had been taken into consideration for cold-blooded exploitation;

before martial law, the Polish population was starving.

After the coup, the Russian comrades were sending food even as initial Red Cross shipments from the West were being halted at the Polish border. There were still lines at the shops, but the shops had food. It was a classic carrot-and-stick tactic: Shut up and you will get the food. People were tired. They were otherwise unable to obtain basic foodstuffs. The Communists said: Here's food; if you are not quiet we will withdraw it. There were accusations by Solidarity, difficult of course to prove, that all along there had been no basic shortage of food in Poland, that the government had been deliberately withholding it in order to make it more difficult for the people.

Predictably, the regime arrested all of the notable Polish intellectuals who were giving Solidarity moral support and advice, professors in universities and participants in faculty meetings. Not one current intellectual was left free except for those who were apologists for the Communist regime.

Today I read in a Polish army newspaper the names of 47 Communist leaders of the former Gierek government who, it is said, the Jaruzelski regime and the Russians flew to Moscow. The authorities were probably afraid to have the former officials in Poland, but they also didn't want them to be found dead at the hands of their "constituency." Furthermore, their removal can probably be thought to have had a good psychological effect on the masses, for the military regime can say that it has arrested not only Solidarity but the leaders of the old Gierek government! But while Polish Solidarity leaders are being held in awful conditions in a former concentration camp, the Communists will probably stay in a Moscow hotel for as long as necessary.

All of this doesn't necessarily mean that Jaruzelski, from the very first minute to the last, was precisely aware of the Soviets' solution. I believe that the plan was given to him after it was ready. It may have been the final act in his takeover, presented in the very final stages. In all probability the Russians told him: Either you do it or we will do it.

How could Jaruzelski do this? A *Polish* general? A *patriot?* A supposedly decent man. One should not forget that he is a

Communist. Well, Jaruzelski may have reasoned that in spite
of crushing Solidarity, imposing martial law, and carrying out
other Russian orders, he was still preserving the possibility that
a semi-Polish government would yet survive.

One might also say that Jaruzelski was trying to save Poland
from Russian intervention. After all, seven killed is a drop in
the bucket compared with what could happen if Poland should
be taken over militarily by the Russians. One can sympathize
in a way with Jaruzelski's position. Whether he is more Pole
than Communist or vice versa doesn't really matter in his situation. If he were to put Polish patriotism ahead of the Communist Party, the Soviets would wipe him out. A purely
nationalistic choice could do more harm than good. It's really
a moot question.

In a way I feel sorry for Jaruzelski. He really didn't have
any choice. I think his end is going to be very tragic—someone
will kill him or he will commit suicide. It is very easy to
condemn this man. But did he have a choice? He undertook a
tragic choice, and I'll bet that it wasn't an easy decision for
him. When he decided to implement martial law, he signed
his own death warrant.

Another tragedy is that neither Solidarity nor Western intelligence recognized what was going on. Some thought that
the lack of massive movement of Russian troops indicated that
nothing ominous was developing. Others felt that the Russians
had too many headaches elsewhere, e.g., in Afghanistan. And
nobody discovered the intensive preparations under way to use
Poles against Poles.

Wishful thinking among foreign observers led them to con-
clude that the Polish Communist party was crushed. Finished.
Such naiveté is a common problem among people unfamiliar
with the way the Communist power system works. To many
Americans, the Communists will never win in the United States
because the U.S. Communist party has only 25,000 members.
In 1945 Poland had 2,000 Communists. It's not simply the size
of the party that determines whether a government will be
Communist or not. Two thousand people in a position to shoot

anyone who objects to their rule may well establish a Communist government over many millions.

We all underestimated the political power of the Polish Communist party backed and orchestrated by the Russians.

Nobody in the Polish opposition or in Western intelligence was prepared for the imposition of martial law. I think they were foolish. Solidarity's leaders had been influenced too much by the writings of Leszek Moczulski, whose tract *Revolt Without Revolution*—popular reading in Poland in 1979—assumed that martial law would never be imposed on Poland by Poles.

There is also no question in my mind that Solidarity became a little drunk with its progress and success. Never before in all Poland's history had there been a movement that amounted to a political party with 10 million members. Ten million Poles supporting one movement: This was a real mass movement.

There is no question that when 90% of the working people are united in support of one movement, its members and its leaders may begin to feel they are unstoppable.

For all its euphoria and increasing sense of immunity from retribution, Solidarity was careful never to question Poland's friendship with the Soviet Union and Poland's membership in the Warsaw Pact. Solidarity never even questioned the Communist system even while submitting hundreds of resolutions for its improvement. It is not true that Solidarity wanted too much. The movement signed agreements with the Polish government but the government did not fulfill them or fulfilled very few.

Thus, if Solidarity's demands seemed ever increasing, it was out of frustration over the regime's not honoring its commitments. The government made promises but did not keep them. Solidarity made specific proposals about the reorganization of the country's economy and how the process of renewal should be conducted. The government said "Yes, yes," but it did nothing.

Solidarity was criticized for using strikes, but that was their only weapon. Solidarity had no power within the government, and was not represented in the parliament. They were not represented anywhere in the official hierarchy. There is no question that strikes in a situation such as Poland's are tantamount to blackmail, but there was no other solution. Solidarity had no other weapons of influence.

Lech Walesa is a terrific guy with a lot of common sense. I wouldn't need much more than five minutes to recognize him as a charismatic person, but a simple, working class man with limited education. He has a lot of good instincts, but he is not a politician. Still, he became a national hero. The workers were in favor of giving him everything to represent their aspirations. He became a symbol.

I am sad to say it, but I really don't believe that Walesa is going to survive Poland's crisis. He became such a symbol of the movement that the Soviets cannot let him continue in his role. They don't care about making a martyr out of Walesa. In Hungary Imre Nagy became a fantastic hero in just days at the head of the 1956 Hungarian revolution. But after the Russians crushed it, Nagy was arrested and, later, executed. The Communist attitude about this sort of thing is: Finish him. If he is dead he cannot talk any more. The masses will gradually forget him. Who will care in ten or fifteen years? He will be remembered only in books or statues. So?

As for the Roman Catholic Church, having a Polish pope has made its influence in Poland even more enormous. However, it is difficult to say anything about the church. With the power that it has had in Poland for centuries, the church was much stronger than Solidarity. Solidarity was in a way the church's product. But with the church's thousand years of tradition in Poland, if Walesa was making mistakes the church hierarchy should not have let him. You can accuse a poor, undereducated electrician like Walesa of not knowing how to play the game, but the church should know. It uses the masses in Poland. It pushes them too far. And when worse comes to worse, it preaches: Peace. Peace. Peace.

The Catholic church, even with a Polish pope in the Vatican, has long-range plans and programs. Who is going to win or lose? Thirty-five million Catholics in Poland made it a very good country in which to have a trial of power. The Catholic church compromised Russia all over the world. After thirty-six years of the Communists being in power in Poland, the Pope could come to Poland and be welcomed by the whole nation. Pope John Paul II undressed Communism. He showed it naked to the whole world. The embarrassment was not only to the Polish Communists but also to the Russians.

A Stalin or Brezhnev does not think of the Russian people. They think of the victory of Communism in the world. The Pope in the Vatican, whether he is Italian or Polish, also doesn't think merely of this or that country, but of how to defeat Communism worldwide. Poland was important but only as a link in the chain of strategy concerning who is to win.

Things might have been better if Cardinal Wyszynski had not died in June of 1981. Wyszynski was very shrewd. He knew how to take two steps forward and one step back. Archbishop Jozef Glemp, Wyszynski's successor as Catholic primate of Poland, came from nowhere. He may be intelligent, but he is nothing to compare with Wyszynski.

This is unfortunate because it's the Catholic Church that could influence Jaruzelski, not Walesa and not Solidarity. If the Catholic Church exercised its power, it could deal with Jaruzelski and give him support in return for a little freedom. This intervention by the Church would have benefited Walesa.

I'm afraid that martial law in Poland has been implemented so precisely by the Communists that they will crush Solidarity. There are 50,000 Solidarity activists in a nation of 35 million. Fifty thousand with no guns or other arms and no outside help while the Communists have the Russian army and the U.S.S.R. next door. But it remains to be seen whether the Communists can crush what Solidarity stands for.

Before the imposition of martial law Poland had made five steps forward; it has now dropped six steps back. The situation for a while is going to be much worse than it was before the rise of Solidarity in 1980. I'm not saying that everything that has been achieved since 1980 is going to be erased. The Polish people will need time to recover, and the movement may never again count 7 to 10 million members, but the government cannot destroy the aspirations of the nation. The Polish nation was on course. Maybe we didn't win but we came close.

What are the prospects now for passive resistance? The regime knows how to deal with that. Cut salaries. Pay in food. Give the poor producers only half their rations. Give the other half to those who produce more. Use intimidation. It takes someone very strong to stand up under this. The Communist system knows hundreds of tricks. It knows how to force people to be good citizens. When it decides to crush someone, it not only crushes him but breaks him into pieces. Nobody knows better how to use the carrot and the stick. And if that method doesn't work, the system has no compunctions against shooting the troublemaker.

Because of the Communist police state's techniques, and in spite of the demonstrations that have occurred, the prospect of a passive resistance movement in Poland is more easily conceived than carried out. There will be a lot written about Poland in the United States and Western Europe, a lot of coverage on Western radio and television for a relatively short period of time. After that, Poland will not be news any more. Heard much about Afghanistan lately?

At the same time, I don't think that everything is going to be a loss. The regime will provide some benefits because it wants to control the situation. More nonparty members will be allowed into the parliament. More power will be granted to the official, government-backed labor "movement." Some form of self-rule will be introduced into the workers' councils in the factories. On Sundays the church will have a half-hour to perform on radio. Some form of election will be implemented when the authorities so ordain. The workers will be presented two or three "candidates" for leadership of the labor movement. One will have a short nose, one will have a long nose; one will be short, one will be tall. But all will be nominated by the Communist Party. The workers will decide between the short one and the tall one. But the choice will be meaningless. In sum, there will be a number of cosmetic steps to give a veneer of semirespectability to the Warsaw regime.

This is a 50 percent proposition. Nobody can say for sure,

one way or another. I'm still 50 percent optimistic, but I also realize that the next two years or longer in Poland could be very bad. The Russians probably already have a pretty good handle on the situation. They can say: We will give the Poles some freedom or liberalization. Or they can say: We will crush them once and forever, because if we do not they are going to cause trouble. But one would have to be Brezhnev to know what the Russians have in their pocket.

I can't quite figure out how successful the government will be in its effort to break the workers of the Polish nation. No one in history has been successful. But this time the disappointment is very large; we were so close.

One lesson Poland has learned is that change cannot be accomplished too quickly or be totally revolutionary because help cannot be expected from the West. To win one must work gradually. Go too fast and be crushed.

Solidarity's leaders were basically very careful and tried not to antagonize the Communist party and Russia. But because the workers wanted so much freedom and democracy and so many human rights, the demands were too much for the Russians.

I refer again to the pamphlet by Leszek Moczulski outlining a blueprint for revolt without revolution. This pamphlet designed the whole Solidarity program from A to Z. United States news correspondents may not have understood that if Walesa was calling for passive resistance, he was simply following Moczulski's tract. It was written in preparation for Russian intervention. It says in effect: They will try to break us down. They will tell us that if we do not go to the factory they will shoot us. We will go. But they are not going to get meaningful production.

Of course progress is not going to be as easy or as open as it was during these past two years. It is not going to be in the form of open public meetings. Because they'll send trucks with water cannons arresting people, the movement will have to be more underground.

The people in Poland have learned a lesson: To abolish the Communist system in Poland is out of the question without substantial changes in Russia. What we need is a Solidarity movement in the Soviet Union.

But Russia is asleep. Sakharov and a few other intellectuals try to stir things up, but the Russian masses are asleep. They have lived under the Communist system for 64 years. A second generation of Russians has matured knowing no other system. They may complain, but they know nothing else. Also, the Soviet masses never had the traditional culture of the Poles. Today, in Poland, we know that things can be different.

Will the Russian masses ever stir? I'm rather pessimistic about this. What is so tragic about the working class in Russia is that it doesn't have any other operable set of values. The Soviet masses know the situation is bad, but they do not know that things could be different. In Poland the masses were the leaders, the intellectuals only advisors. In Russia the situation is reversed—intellectuals, such as Sakharov, try to lead a movement that doesn't exist.

In Poland we have a real people's revolutionary movement, either open or underground, at least for as long as it can exist. In Russia there are no masses to support the individual dissidents. This is the tragedy of the people in Russia, and this will be the future tragedy of the people of Poland unless something happens to change the situation in my homeland.

Reagan was right to cut aid to Poland, but why did he not apply more sanctions on Russia? The United States should close the Soviet embassy and other diplomatic missions in this country, and cut off every possible contact with the Russians.

The $28 billion that Poland owes to the West is more important in some respects than Poland itself. Of the total, approximately $2 billion is owed to the U.S. government, $2 billion to U.S. private banks, and most of the rest to West Germany, Great Britain, France and Italy. Poland owes almost everybody through an international consortium. This $28 billion of Polish debt will have an influence on what President Reagan is going to do or not do concerning the Polish situation. Or West Germany. It is very interesting that the Socialist president of France, François Mitterand, has been much more outspoken against the Communist martial law in Poland than West

Germany's Chancellor Helmut Schmidt. In any case, the $28 billion that Western nations have at stake in Poland is additional evidence that the total East-West relationship—including the economic relationship—is more important than Poland.

As for me, I am sure that I have changed. I feel more bitter and disappointed. I still maintain my own basic philosophies; I have not lost my ideals. But I am a bit disillusioned. I am confused and filled with reservations about what you can expect from the American bureaucratic establishment concerning anti-Communism. Basically, if unintentionally, this country is doing its best in many respects to help Communism.

Do you realize that this is the first time that the United States does not have any progressive movement? Students don't care. People don't want to worry about anything except not losing their jobs. Even the old materialism is not the same. A splitlevel house in the suburbs and two big cars in every garage are not only more difficult to obtain—fewer Americans find them the be-all and end-all of life. But what *do* Americans today want? I'm not sure they know.

Americans always tell you that "we always rebound from these situations." Yes, history tends to confirm this. But what will happen if American society does not rebound once? The Russians constantly track American society. We are not on the offensive. They always are. They are aggressive. And they accomplish their ends in a shifty way. We're only trying to protect, to stop, to maintain the status quo. I am not saying that we should behave as the Russians do. What we do we should do in our own way. But this country must have an historical objective, a more aggressive sense of its role in the world.

There is, however, no way that the United States can go to war to liberate Poland. Polish-Americans think that what President Reagan has done is worthwhile, good, moral support, and it is highly appreciated. They also say that the U.S. cannot do anything else except make gestures. Whatever Washington does, even though it can help alleviate the situation, is not going to solve the total problem. There are limits to what the

U.S. can do in the realm of economic sanctions. The Soviet state is so powerful that, despite its extremely poor management, it is going to survive whatever the U.S. does.

If there are limits to U.S. influence on the Russians regarding Poland, I'm sure that there will still be resistance in Poland. The Polish people are not going to give up. It may take ten years to build up another open mass movement, but Poland will never again be as it was before mid-1980. The Polish people will gain some freedom—not the freedom that they wanted, but they will gain some. The people will be bitter and disenchanted. They had high expectations and everything fell apart. But Poles are Poles, and they will not give up.

—Mr. X
September, 1982

Index

About the Authors

Mr. X now lives and works in Washington, D.C. under a new identity.

Bruce E. Henderson, a former foreign correspondent for the Associated Press and Time/Life, and later associate editor for *Time*, has co-authored four previous books.

C.C. Cyr is a Seattle-bred New Yorker who has lived and worked in the Far East and Latin America.